Broken Wafers

MARTIN KNIGHT was born in Epsom, Surrey. He is the author of many books, including working with footballers George Best, Peter Osgood, Dave Mackay and Charlie Cooke and Bay City Rollers founder member Alan Longmuir on their autobiographies. He has also written novels and several books in the true crime genre.

Broken Wafers

Martin Knight

LONDON BOOKS

LONDON BOOKS
39 Lavender Gardens
London SW11 1DJ
www.london-books.co.uk

First published by London Books 2022

Copyright © Martin Knight 2022

Cover photography: front cover Creative Commons;
back cover Martin Knight (top), Trojan Records (bottom)

All rights reserved
No part of this publication may be reproduced in any form
or by any means without the written permission of the publisher

A catalogue record for this book
is available from the British Library

ISBN 978-0-9957217-7-7

Every effort has been made to locate owners of any copyright material
used in this book. The author apologises for any omissions. Those
brought to the author's attention will be incorporated in future editions.

Printed and bound in Great Britain by
CPI Group (UK) Ltd, Croydon, CR0 4YY

Typeset by Octavo Smith Publishing Services

For Min Knight, our dear mum, and my grandchildren – Harry, Alfie, Reggie, Nyla Blue, Henry Martin – and those yet to come

CONTENTS

1. There's A Place — 9
2. Mother — 20
3. Yesterday — 28
4. She's Leaving Home — 36
5. With A Little Help From My Friends — 45
6. Good Day Sunshine — 55
7. All Those Years Ago — 66
8. Blackbird — 77
9. When We Was Fab — 87
10. How Do You Sleep? — 98
11. Wonderful Christmastime — 108
12. Ticket To Ride — 117
13. Got My Mind Set On You — 126
14. Coming Up — 133
15. A Day In The Life — 143
16. Getting Better — 154
17. Help! — 163
18. This Boy — 171
19. I Should Have Known Better — 182
20. I Don't Want To Be A Soldier — 191
21. Here Comes The Sun — 204
    Epilogue — 215
    Postscript — 217

1
THERE'S A PLACE

My surmise is that Dad was downstairs watching over my four-year-old sister and two-year-old brother trying to deflect the blood-curdling screams from my mum upstairs as she, aided by a midwife, heaved and pushed me out of her bloodied and battered body into the world. It was a difficult birth, as my mum occasionally reminded me in later life when she hoped that imparting such a fact might prick my guilt antennae and encourage me to behave a little better.

My parents named me Martin. The name was my mum's choice. Dad had wanted to call me Hillary after Sir Edmund Hillary, who a few years before had conquered Mount Everest and was a British hero, the fact he came from New Zealand dismissed then as an irrelevancy. I count myself lucky Dad did not get his own way. It could have been worse. My father was full of admiration for Sherpa Tenzing too. In the end it would not have mattered as Dad called me Garth for the first eleven years of my life. Garth, I discovered, was an early superhero strongman popular in the 1940s and 1950s as a comic strip in the *Daily Mirror*.

I was born in the bedroom in which I would spend, off and on, the next twenty-three years. It was Mum and Dad's bedroom then, as Christmas approached in 1957, but would soon become mine. Because of their fast-growing family, my parents moved to a smaller bedroom at the back of the house and filled this one with bunk-beds, chests of drawers, ottomans, shelves and children. Dad had painted images from nursery rhymes on some of the walls in readiness for the transfer. Why I was born at home when my older sister and brother, Sally and Laurence, arrived in the world at Epsom District Hospital, I do not know. There was a reason, but it has been lost. As I write, my mother is very much still with us and should be able to remind me, but a vicious stroke crept up on her in the night like a murderous footpad and mercilessly robbed her of speech and natural mobility.

For much of my tenancy the bedroom had two sets of bunk-beds against two walls, sleeping three brothers and myself in pairs. The remaining free wall we covered in posters and pictures precariously suspended by discoloured Sellotape and drawing pins. Laurence claimed one half with colour pictures, cut meticulously from *Charles Buchan's Football Monthly*, of his Spurs' footballing heroes Jimmy Greaves, Alan Gilzean and Martin Chivers. Why Laurence chose Tottenham Hotspur as his team I am unsure, but I guess he first became football aware as Bill Nicholson, Dave Mackay and Danny Blanchflower were basking in their League and FA Cup double success of the 1960–1 season. I had a massive pop-art poster of George Best surrounded by smaller images of whatever pop stars and other footballers that were my flavour of the month. A poster I was fond of in my teens was the one that came free with the Faces' *A Nod Is As Good As A Wink ... To A Blind Horse* album. It was a mosaic of tiny photographs, some of them rude, but they were so minute I don't think Mum noticed.

The fourth wall contained the window, and it was from there I first observed the outside world. The other 'big' bedroom, now occupied by Mum and Dad, looked out on to the back garden and the gardens beyond and beside. In the early years all that marked out the boundaries of our designated parcels of land on our little council estate were a couple of limp strings of wire connecting stumpy concrete posts. As time went by and privacy rose up the hierarchy of family needs, wooden creosoted fences were erected and tall hedges grown. The third and final bedroom was tiny. Perhaps you could swing a guinea pig or a hamster – of which we owned a few – but not a cat. My older sister Sally had this to herself until little sister Liz came along and bunk-beds became essential there too.

Downstairs, the main room that was situated directly below our bedroom was variously called the front room, the sitting-room and, grandly, for the benefit of others, perhaps, the lounge. In one corner stood the television from which the BBC broadcast to us. The BBC was our friend with the slightly posh voice. It was also our entertainer, our educator and our companion that we all loved. Opposite was the window on to the street; net curtains allowed me to study who walked, rode or drove in and out of the road without being seen.

Below the window was our sofa (or settee) facing the fireplace and the mantelpiece above it. The mantelpiece was adorned with ornaments – two black china elephants I remember at each end and a Swiss-chalet wind-up music box in the centre. This was a feather in the family cap; mantelpiece proof that someone in our extended family had been 'abroad' or visited 'the Continent'. Mum designated it as an ornament. It was such a rarity for anyone we knew to leave our shores (outside of wartime) that any foreign trinkets brought home were accorded celebrity status. Hanging proudly above the fireplace for much of my time was a large print of some ploughmen carrying out the harvest in an English field by artist David Shepherd. *The Last Bales* it was called and was most likely purchased from the upstairs floor at Boots the Chemists in Epsom.

Next to the lounge and with a window looking out to the back garden was the room we called the dining-room. Was it just our family that had these pretentious titles for our modest living space? We ate in the dining-room, funnily enough, sat around an extendable oak table with twisted legs. Dad alone was permitted to eat with his dinner on a tray, on his lap, in the lounge while watching the news on the television.

There was a strict eating protocol we were expected to abide by. Speaking while masticating meals was almost a capital crime and 'eat it all up' a constant refrain. If one had finished the meal it was not an option just to drift off to another room, we were expected to ask 'Please may I be excused' or even 'Please may I get down', a legacy, presumably, of when we sat in highchairs.

'Don't speak with your mouth full. Don't eat with your fingers. Don't wipe your mouth on your sleeve. Give it a chance to go down. Stop fidgeting. Slow down, the telly's not going to get up and walk off anywhere. Eat it all up. There are people in the world dying of starvation. What are you doing! You can't slurp gravy off the plate, you're not an animal. Eat all the veg. That's the best part. Full up?' These continuous commands and comments, kindly meant and widely ignored by kids in a hurry, provided the oral rhythm to mealtimes.

From the dining-room was an open entrance to the kitchen where there was a smaller drop-leaf table where we ate hurried breakfasts and teas at times when the family was not formally gathered. Mum ran a not-for-profit café here feeding us toast, fish fingers, sandwiches and orange squash before we disappeared outside on to the estate for a couple of action-packed hours before bedtime. Sometimes one of us would bring a friend home for tea. That was a ritual, and we went to their houses too. It was at one pal's house I discovered there was such a thing as sliced brown bread and creamy butter as opposed to uncut Hovis and Stork margarine.

Also in the kitchen, in the early days, was a sink and washboard where Mum laundered the clothes as well as the dishes and the utensils. I can remember her using wooden tongs to squeeze and wring everything. Her sleeves were rolled up almost to the shoulder and it was physically tiring work. Next to the washboard was a bulky white gas oven and in another corner the larder. The oven fascinated me. I had heard my parents talk about an unnamed distant relation who had committed suicide by putting his head in a gas oven. I could not figure how. You could not close the door with your head in it. What happened next? Did your head cook? Burn away? Explode? I put these urgent questions to my mum and dad, but they would not engage. Heads in ovens and piping exhaust fumes into cars appeared to be the favoured methods of taking one's life in that era. Another vivid memory of the kitchen was simmering saucepans. We were warned to keep away. Not to touch. There was always one, two or even three on hobs simmering away, and to this day I have no idea what was in them.

While Mum toiled in the kitchen the radio normally played. Before I was five I knew all the shows, and their theme tunes are embedded into my psyche: *Two-Way Family Favourites*, *Desert Island Discs*, *Junior Choice*, *Woman's Hour*, *The Clitheroe Kid*, *The Archers*, *Mrs Dale's Diary* and, later, *Open House* with Pete Murray. Pockmarked Pete, as some unkindly called him, was Mum's not-so-secret crush. All these shows came to us via the BBC again, the pirate and commercial radio stations still a few years away. Dad would tell us to 'pipe down' when the shipping forecast came on, and he seemed concerned that there were high winds at Dogger Bank. Strange, as all he had to navigate was the stairs.

In the kitchen was a door that led to the hall where there was a small cupboard under the stairs that we imaginatively called 'the cupboard under the stairs'. I spent many hours in there, hunched up among pungent-smelling plimsolls, the Hoover, brushes and brooms and tins of Cherry Blossom shoe polish hiding from nobody and shining my Pifco torch around. Rising from the hall were the white-painted, stark wooden stairs that led up to the bedrooms and bathroom. They were softened, marginally, with rough lino, stapled in the middle of the step. On the way up was an oil painting of my dad as a young man in his army greatcoat. I never thought to ask where, when and why he had that done. Mum said it was vain of Dad to have that hanging up, and it did not see the 1970s.

I gazed out my big bedroom window on to our little crescent, which formed the inner ring of a bigger crescent that was the Gibraltar council estate in Ewell, Surrey. Outsiders called it the Longmead estate after the road that the estate led out to and that joined West Ewell with Epsom and later contained Longmead School. For almost a quarter of a century I viewed the nocturnal comings and goings from that window, lying on my stomach, my chin cradled on the metal headframe of the top bunk, and in the early days, at least, wearing fetching stripy pyjamas with a string cord to keep the trousers from falling down. Curious by nature, I watched at night as the menfolk came home from the Plough, drunk as lords, their bodies tumbling into each other, but as one merged entity finding just enough balance and direction to make it to their respective family front doors. They tossed mumbled conversation at each other in a slurred, Guinness-soaked Irish brogue and drifted in and out of folk songs, soppily united in the drink and a nostalgic yearning for the Emerald Isle of their childhoods that they had had to leave as youths to find regular work.

There were a few Irish families on the estate, and some parents still spoke in a thick and, to me, unintelligible Irish accent. Those mums and dads were first-generation immigrants many drawn to Epsom by manual and domestic work in the five large mental hospitals in the borough. There was no overt prejudice towards them that I picked up on beyond Irish jokes (an Englishman, an Irishman and a Scotsman walk into a bar, blah blah blah) which were told with relish at school, sometimes by the Irish-descent boys themselves. When I reached my teens, I discovered I was myself of Irish descent. I think I stopped telling and laughing at thick-Paddy jokes about then. At least one great-great-grandfather on my dad's side had been urgently forced to migrate to England when the potato famine ravaged his land and life in the middle of the 19th century.

I squinted when the Ford Corsair pulled up down the road as teenaged Susan was being dropped off outside her parents' house. The boyfriend would switch off the engine, and I would crane my neck for a better view as he slid his arm around her shoulders and moved to kiss her, his passion being checked by the centre console. I felt, even then, his frustration as she edged sideways, opening the passenger door and deftly slipping out of the car in a single swift movement, then skipping up to her front door. There seemed to be a barely contained anger as boyfriend revved up and screeched out of the road. His hanging furry dice bouncing off the windscreen. Not getting a return on an investment of three vodka and limes and ten Rothmans could be infuriating.

I studied intently as a gang of estate youths piled out of a souped-up, brightly sprayed Ford Anglia and stood around, smoking, laughing and boasting about the night's drinking and carousing. I strained to hear their conversations, which were largely indecipherable but were peppered with audible fucks, bastards and cunts, words rarely uttered in our house. One by one they would peel off to their childhood bedrooms, where tattered colour pictures of *their* early soccer or pop-music heroes still clung to the walls, leaving just one solitary youth spitting on the floor, projecting saliva through his front teeth with a hissing noise, between taking urgent lugs of his Embassy cigarette, reluctant to retire as either the alcohol or the speed, maybe, still pumped furiously around his bloodstream.

I would muse on summer nights as the flies and moths flitted around the sallow yellow light of the lamp post outside the house. A solitary bicycle tyre hung from the top. Further down the road a plimsoll and a toy parachute had wrapped itself around a telephone line that traversed the road and was supported by wooden telegraph poles. Later we young boys would hurl our Action Men up at those lines and watch them fall to the ground, parachute unopened. Eventually a bigger boy assisted, and some poor kid's beloved birthday present was forever suspended in space.

Men, dads, emerged from the alleys between the houses, collars pulled up and caps pulled down, dutifully mounting their Raleigh bikes and setting off for their night shift to work at one of the asylums.

My parents had only been in our house a few months when I was born. Indeed, our new home, of which we were so proud, had only been built less than a year earlier. The borough of Epsom and Ewell was expanding fast as the country slowly but surely pulled away from the austere Second World War years and their grim aftermath. It was evolving from a rural market town and little-sister village to a busier commuter hub accommodating office workers who took the train up to London each day and the comfortably off who had snapped up the classy Harwood-built houses in earlier decades. People who didn't live there called it the 'stockbroker belt'. In all my years residing in the area I never knowingly encountered a stockbroker.

Mum, Dad, Laurence, Sally and I, encased in my mother's womb, had been living in rooms in a private semi-detached house, 383 Kingston Road, when the council offer came along. That house was casually devoured in one gulp when an Aldi supermarket was built next door sixty years later. My family history disappearing before my very eyes.

Gibraltar was soon filling up with families in similar situations to my parents. They gratefully and excitedly transferred from their rented accommodation, parents' houses, prefabs and caravans. Some came from an army barracks in Ewell that was providing temporary housing to young families. The breadwinners here were not from the comfortably off demographic of Epsom. Certainly, no stockbrokers among them. However, the men were certainly winning bread to lesser or greater degrees. They knew all about unemployment, as most of them would have had parents who were impacted by the Great Depression twenty-five years earlier, but this generation were generally fully employed, at least here in Epsom in Surrey.

Many of these men and women grafted in the asylums, local light industry, construction sites and a few in the horseracing stables that colonised Epsom Downs. Some of the men were picked up in the mornings by small minibuses that took them to Leatherhead, a slightly smaller town a little deeper into Surrey, where they worked at Goblin, making teasmades, or Ronson's, turning out plush gold and silver cigarette lighters that produced a deep-blue flame and smelled seductively of petrol.

Teasmades were considered the height of progressive domestic technology in the 1960s for a few fleeting years, but they fell to the whims of changing taste a decade later when consumers finally tumbled that making a cup of tea the old way was quicker, easier and more satisfying. Quality, stylish lighters went the same way when cheap imports flooded in from Hong Kong and Taiwan in the 1970s. It was a shock to the system that such a thing as a lighter could ever be disposable. It saddens me that no person born after 1980 has experienced the utter luxury of having their cigarette lit by someone firmly clicking a heavy-duty, quality silver or gold Ronson lighter illuminating two faces in doing so. Many men, though, carried a box of matches on their person rather than a lighter; Bryant and May, Ship and Swan Vestas being the most popular brands.

The mental hospitals defined Epsom. They were, by far, the biggest employers. There were five of them – St Ebba's, Long Grove, the Manor, Horton and West Park – and locally they were collectively called 'the hospital cluster'. When their construction was first mooted in the late 19th century the locals were uneasy. They didn't relish a population in their midst rivalling their own in possible numbers but consisting of 'looneys' and 'nutcases'. Lord Rosebery himself, a former prime minister and arguably Epsom's most famous (part-time) resident, led the objections. The local newspaper, the *Epsom & Ewell Herald*, headlined one story 'LUNATICS AT LARGE', and Rosebery announced at a noisy public meeting, 'I represent a constituency of the sane.' Scenes of patients being led into town, detached and shuffling nervously, only hardened reservations, and the newly opened hospitals closed in on themselves. The town accepted a sad, hidden population and the patients did not encroach on the town itself. Epsom's economy benefiting from a healthier employment market and an influx of new workers with welcome spending power helped to placate the residents and traders, no doubt.

The Manor Hospital was built 1899, followed by St Ebba's in 1902, Horton Hospital in 1903, Long Grove Hospital in 1907 and West Park Hospital, where my dad would spend a large chunk of his working life, being completed during the first war in 1916. They were built to house the 'feeble-minded' and insane people of London, although, in practice, children born out of wedlock, their poor mothers, the disabled and sufferers of the many then undiagnosed but now recognised psychiatric conditions made up a significant proportion of the patients. The common denominator uniting most of them, especially in the early days, was extreme poverty, hardship and tragedy pushing them over the edge. A large proportion arrived on a direct line from the soon-to-be-decommissioned workhouses of inner London.

They were much more than hospitals, though, their physical estates boasting churches and chapels, mini-theatres, football pitches and farms. By the time the First World War broke out, the cluster was caring for more than 5,000 souls, and they would become much busier during and after the conflict when there was a seemingly never-ending tragic stream of the shell-shocked, disorientated and battle-scarred arriving in Epsom.

Entire roads such as Lower Court Road, Hook Road and Miles Road were constructed with the coming influx of hospital workers in mind. Careers began and ended in the cluster. Staff often married, and their children would join their parents on the workforce. There were sporting rivalries: football, cricket, darts, tug of war. Big, grand fetes where mothers held their children's hands that bit tighter, just in case. We children thoughtlessly called the hospitals 'looney bins', and their inmates were referred to by us in the 1960s as 'binners'. Years later I discovered that people living in the towns near Epsom, like Leatherhead, Reigate and Dorking, used the generic name 'Eppys' for mental patients – a derivative of the name Epsom.

A resulting positive feature of Epsom people then was that we were rarely fazed by mental disability. It was all around us. By my time the closed, insular mindset had changed, and on a Saturday many of the cluster's population were encouraged out and plenty of them drifted into the town. We knew them by name. They shuffled along slowly in ill-fitting suits; eyes fixed on the floor. I learned this was an effect of Largactil, the 'liquid cosh' as it was called, that was prescribed to many patients to keep them manageable and malleable. Occasionally there were incidents. Every now and then a patient removed their clothes outside Timothy Whites or somewhere. Very occasionally they would do something violent. Mostly, though, they headed for the Dorking Gate Café next to the Magpie pub where they drank countless cups of tea and where they felt safe and secure.

When our little council estate was first mooted there was a smaller and more localised outcry than the one that had welcomed the cluster programme, I am told. Homeowners of staunchly middle-class West Ewell were not best pleased about having their peace and quiet broken by the rough and ready of the borough settling among them. Older boys on the estate told me of how when they started mixing with the children from these roads they innocently let slip that they had been warned against playing with the Gibraltar people.

Although not employing as many as the hospitals, the horseracing industry did much to inform Epsom's unique character. Men of small stature had been moving to the town from all over the UK and Ireland for over a century to pursue the dream of becoming a jockey, and many stayed working in the various yards or elsewhere when that dream slipped away. George Formby and actor William Hartnell, the first Dr Who, were both apprenticed in the town but went on to build successful careers in film and on television.

The stable lads' presence bought the average height of an Epsom male down an inch or two. The yards were operated by a clique of trainers, nearly all of whom were former jockeys, who boasted memorable names like Boggy Whelan, Staff Ingham and Scobie Breasley. Even in my time there was a deference to these trainers with the lads still calling them 'guvnor'. Those stable boys who showed an aptitude for boxing were taken up to the Café Royale in London to fight in the ring – yard against yard – while their masters feasted on lobster and champagne.

'Tips' on which of their horses was going to win or not from the lads and men in the stables were a valued currency in the pubs and clubs of Epsom, and drinks bought and fivers pressed into hands in exchange for that knowledge and inside information supplemented meagre incomes. In 1975 the lads even went on strike, although I doubt they bettered their lot.

It must have been a happy and hopeful time for most of those new residents of the Gibraltar estate in the late 1950s. The austere, uncertain, frightening and often miserable war years were fast receding from memory. Families had secured decent-looking, decent-sized, well-built houses that were not temporary. Most households were acquiring televisions. We were taking our private miniature cinema in the home for granted by the 1970s, but in the late 1950s and early 1960s it was a life-enhancing luxury marvelled at by all.

Those young couples would have looked forward to the future with growing confidence for themselves and their young children. In the year of my birth the prime minister, Harold Macmillan, declared that the British people had never had it so good, and for once it was not political hyperbole. The nuclear annihilation fears exacerbated by the Cold War were a few years in the future. The late 1950s and early 1960s was a time of recovery, cohesiveness, excitement and hope, and I think we children picked up on a growing sense of wellbeing in our parents and society generally.

A small stream ran along one edge of the estate, and it was not unknown for a kingfisher to flash past in all its colourful glory. On the other side of the newly laid Longmead Road were fields teeming with birds, plants, trees and animals. I would suggest for many of the new residents it was idyllic. I think that appreciation transferred to us children. The estate was a happy one where the families generally got along – the children playing together, the dads working alongside one another, the mums bonding outside their front doors and at the school gates, the shops and the clinic at Ewell Court where dozens of prams stood on parade. I believe we were blessed to live where we did, when we did and almost everyone I know or speak to who grew up on Gibraltar in the 1950s, 1960s and 1970s feels the same way.

Mum, however, did not *want* to live on a council estate. If truth be told she considered it a retrograde step. Although she came from a line of simple rustic Wiltshire and Kent stock, her parents had managed to become owner-occupiers of a property, and she expected to do the same. Each generation is very uncomfortable about the thought of moving backwards economically. My dad, on the other hand, was raised in relative poverty in Battersea and was thrilled about having a shed, two gardens (back and front) and an inside toilet. Plus, this house was not shared with three other families. To him a three-bedroomed dwelling, even if it was ultimately owned by the council, was a result.

They did a deal, my mum and dad. Mum did not have a lot of cards to play with this bump (me) in her tummy and two toddlers, but she agreed to move on to the estate on the condition that they saved money like mad and moved into their own mortgaged home at the first possible opportunity. They were still there forty years later.

2
MOTHER

Mum was born in Surbiton in 1931. Later Surbiton would become famous as the fictional home of Richard Briers and Felicity Kendall in the 1970s TV sitcom *The Good Life*. The writer selected it, I imagine, as the archetypical commuter town in which the mid-20th-century middle class aspired to live. Indeed, Britain's most frustrated middle-class television commuter of the 1970s, Reggie Perrin, passed through Surbiton on his torturous daily journey to Waterloo station. 'Giraffe on the line at Chessington,' he would proclaim. In my time Surbiton was merely a place you passed through on the 406 bus on the way to Kingston, and the only time we kids ever got off there was to swim and lark about in the famous Surbiton Lagoon. In those days there were open-air lidos all around London and the suburbs. Bearing in mind our mostly inclement weather, this was a testament to the British refusal to let small details get in the way of nice ideas.

Mum's dad, Donald Brown, who we children called Gaga (which felt awkward as we reached our teens but were reluctant to abandon because we loved him so much), was an uncomplicated country boy born in Staplehurst, Kent, in 1906. His father, my great-grandfather, Arthur Brown, was the village postman and was by all accounts a fierce, occasionally violent man who had lost his hand in the war and in its place wielded a fearsome hook. He was said to be 'cruel' to his wife. This fact was sanitised and made suitably vague for the benefit of us children but meant that he knocked her about. A family story I liked to hear again and again was how, when Don grew up, he drove his car down to Staplehurst, and while his father was in the pub boozed up and waving his hook around in the snug rescued his mother. They took her away to live with one of her daughters, and she never saw her husband again. Such drama.

Don became a bricklayer and a master-builder and managed to buy his house from Wimpy when he was constructing an estate of semi-detached houses around River Way, Ewell. He was running the job and was offered very attractive terms to buy, and that's how Mum came to be in Ewell. Captain Hook was born in a hamlet called Boughton Malherbe in Kent, and from there the Browns stretched back centuries. When I was in my teens one of Don's aunts wrote a letter to me recounting her late-19th-century memories to aid me with a family-tree project I had undertaken at school. She thrilled my young self by recalling her ancient grandmother who was born at the end of the 18th century and who she maintained was a bona fide witch. A good one, though, she said.

Mum's mum was Catherine Lavinia Staines, born in 1901 in Shepherd's Bush, but she was not a Londoner as such. Her father travelled with his job as a water engineer and happened to be there when Kitty, as we knew her, came along. The family were later living in Goudhurst, Kent, and it was there, at a fete, that she met Don. One of the family secrets that emerged in the internet age, when revelatory historical dates came tumbling out of the sky like unwelcome rain, was that not only was she a bit of a cradle snatcher (five years older than Don) but she was five months pregnant when she married him. She would have been mortified if she knew we knew.

Kitty's family on the maternal side came from a farming village in Wiltshire called All Cannings, on the route of the Kennet and Avon Canal between London and Bristol. When, in my middle age, I embarked on my family-tree history once more – this time digitally powered – I was able to trace the line back to the 14th century. Generation after generation was born, married and died in that country village, right up to Kitty's mother, who married into a family called Staines from Essex. The dominant All Cannings family name was Maslen, and as an adult it was a strange experience to wander around the little churchyard and literally walk over the bones of my relations who had lived there for four or five centuries buried six feet (hopefully) beneath me.

Kitty sometimes mentioned, with her ample bust heaving with pride, how her grandfather had been the governor of Devizes Prison. Even as a boy I found this incongruous. Here was a rural family that for generations had ploughed the fields or scrubbed, polished and cooked as servants and maids, and one of their number became a prison governor and it didn't even get him out the village. Then one day I eagerly tapped into the census records online and there he was, Daniel Maslen. He worked at Devizes Prison, for sure. But he was the caretaker. Fortunately, Kitty went to her grave believing in her over-achieving grandfather, but my mum was a little crestfallen, and amused, when I told her.

Kitty genuinely *did* have an illustrious relative and he really could have been a fabrication of a vivid imagination. Bill Judd was one of Kitty's uncles having married one of the Maslen girls, the daughter of the prison governor/caretaker. He was a tabloid and *Boy's Own* magazine superstar. A turn-of-the-20th-century Bear Grylls. He initially worked as a bargeman transporting cement up and down the River Thames. Somewhere along the line he got it in his head to become a big-game hunter, as you do. No doubt he had read about their bravery and heroic exploits against fierce African creatures and thought, I'll have some of that.

Old Bill made his way to Kenya and in time established himself as one of the country's leading big-game hunters, taking the royal family, the Rothschilds and other such notables on safari and making trophies of countless innocent lions, tigers and rhinoceroses, no doubt. He met what some will argue was a karmic end in 1927 when he was gored and trampled lifeless by a bull elephant he and his son were stalking. The moment of imminent death has been captured in a well-known print of an oil painting that is often for sale on the internet. The *Daily Mirror* ran the story on its front page with a detailed account of the trampling from his son, Young Bill, who eventually felled the animal with several blasts from his rifle.

My nan was immensely proud of Bill Judd, and when he came up in conversation old yellowed press cuttings were produced from an ancient toffee tin. I guess I was proud too. In the early 20th century he was considered a buccaneering, courageous hero. A man who risked his life in the name of exotic adventure, fame and guineas aplenty. If Bill existed in the early 21st century his photograph would be plastered all over social media and people would consider him fair game himself to be trolled, hunted and hounded. His death would undoubtedly have been met with widespread satisfaction and jubilation in some quarters. A great deal changes in a century.

My family research also uncovered another interesting relative on Mum's side from the tiny Wiltshire village of All Cannings. He was convicted in the early 19th century, as a sixteen-year-old boy, of smashing up agricultural machinery. This was when farm labourers were fearing that the new-fangled mechanical ploughs and other agricultural plant were about to put them out of work. They were often right. History has recorded these protestors as Luddites. The court records show that the dozen or so men charged alongside my ancestor were all sentenced to hang, and there is no reason to believe they were not. My relative, thankfully, was sent off to the penal colony of Australia instead because of his tender years. The story has a happy ending because he returned to the village as a man having done his time and married, raised a family and died there, and if you so wish you can go and stomp over his remains in the churchyard too.

When I first knew Kitty and Don, they were a wonderfully matched, happy late-middle-aged couple. He was a quiet, gentle man who spoke with a soothing country burr and had a kindly face and manner, his skin leathered by his bucolic life. I really adored him. One of my first but faded memories is sitting on his lap as he drove a dumper truck around his beloved smallholding in Small Dole in Sussex. By the time I fully remember my maternal grandparents they were prematurely retired in Mile Oak, near Portslade, in a charming little bungalow the garden of which backed on to the beautiful, rolling South Downs. The vista past the telly and through the french windows was truly stunning.

I say prematurely retired because Don had contracted emphysema and was forced to sell the smallholding – his life's dream. The disease made him breathless, and each year he could do less and less. It was literally squeezing the life out of him. I never understood the logic, therefore, of them buying their bungalow on the top of a bloody great hill in Graham Avenue, Portslade. Within a few years of being there Don could not walk down the hill to buy a paper. Well, he could, but he would have not been able to get back up again.

Kitty was his opposite. Sweetly garrulous, she was a scream. There was a touch of the Hyacinth Bucket about her. She dressed very elegantly with pearl ear-rings and necklaces, rings on her fingers and had a healthy obsession with royalty. She was born in the year Queen Victoria died, and Kitty attached some significant relevance to this, but her heroine and role model was the Queen Mother. In her spinster days she had briefly been in service at the home of a cousin of her long-time monarch and felt because of this she had a special connection to all things royal. She was not untypical of many women of her vintage on that score.

As she got older she would tell us yarns about how she had been stopped on the High Street by complete strangers who had complimented her on her coat, her dress, her hair. Of course, this never happened in company. When she went shopping she imagined herself as the Queen Mother deigning to mix with her subjects when she was merely going into town to fetch the Omo, Ajax and Vim.

In a way she henpecked Don, but he didn't need any haranguing to carry out household chores. He was a master carpenter, and if Kitty needed a shelf, she would have a shelf. The garden and greenhouse were immaculately cared for, as was the tiny pond with little goldfish in. I can remember walking out of the gate at the end of the garden and seeing miles and miles of green fields and spectacular rolling hills. I had never seen so much open land. As I opened that gate with a 'don't wander off too far' behind me I felt like Lucy going through the wardrobe and arriving in Narnia.

Kitty would regale Don with a forensic recall of conversations she had had with Mrs Whoever down at the Boundary Road shops:

'... and Mrs Gage said to me, "Kitty, I don't know how you manage, I really don't. You're marvellous," and I said to her, "Don't be silly, I do what I have to do." Did I tell you her sister won £1,000 on the Premium Bonds? Don, are you listening ...?'

'Yes, Kit. Her sister won £1,000 on the Premium Bonds.'

'That's right, £1,000 on the Premium Bonds. Anyway, they said no publicity because they didn't want their other sister appearing out of the woodwork. The troublesome one. Do you remember, Don? I told you about their sister. Oh my, terrible drinker, she is, by all accounts. Starts a new bottle of sherry every morning ...'

It was not in Don's nature to tell his wife to shut up. He had learned to interject his 'Yes, Kits' and nods at the right junctures and just about keep a handle on what she was saying even while checking his pools coupon when the football results were being read out on *Grandstand* and rolling a cigarette with the other free hand. It was no mean feat. I cannot think of Gaga without also thinking of kindly Frank Bough perched on the corner of a desk as the teleprinter chattered behind him.

My mum always said her parents would have been well off if her dad had been a better businessman. When he had his own building firm, she claimed, he often did work for nothing or very cheap because he felt sorry for people. He was also very poor at chasing money, feeling it was rude to ask or that if someone was not paying there must be a good reason, and perhaps they had fallen on hard times. Don saw the best in people.

Stories about him were often told around the table at Christmas during those special days when we were all together before the Grim Reaper started plucking us away one by one. The stories were told by Kitty as if her husband was not sitting at the table with her. Don would sit and smile and lift his eyes gently upward in a 'here we go' gesture. The following is one of my favourites.

Don and Kit were asleep in bed one morning, and they were rudely awoken by an urgent rapping on the door. It was 4 a.m. and still dark. Don dragged himself out of bed, walked downstairs and opened the door to find nobody there and no one in sight. The next morning it happened again. This time Don ran to the window, and he spotted the back of a man running up the road. He and Kitty were angry and perplexed. What was going on? So Don placed a poker next to the front door and set his alarm clock for 3.30 a.m. the next day. Sure enough, as he waited by the front door, he heard steps pattering up the drive. Don flung the door open and brandishing the poker grabbed the man by the shirt.

'What are you playing at, matey?'

The man was terrified. 'What's up?'

'What do you mean, what's up? You've been banging on my door the last three mornings at this ungodly hour. Aren't you a bit old for playing knock-down ginger?'

'It's Arthur's wake-up call. He asked me to give him a knock on the way through to the dairy.'

'Arthur?'

'Arthur Rogers. He's the new milko down at our dairy. He said knock him up, so he'd get ready in time. This is 17 River Way?'

It turned out Arthur lived at number 70. Don and the knocking man had a good chuckle over it in the end, but Kitty always told the story as if it was an incident that was caused by her husband's innate incompetence and stupidity.

Another favourite tale was how Don had employed a rough-and-ready labourer on his building site when they were working on a development deep in the Sussex countryside. The man drove a powerful motorbike and one day he gave Don a lift home from the job. As they wound down the country lanes he pulled up outside a large house.

'I've just got to pop in here, Don. Won't be two ticks.'

Don watched as his labourer walked up the long drive carrying his tool bag wondering what business he had there. After what seemed an interminable time the labourer returned dumped his bag into Don's arms and kicked the bike into action and sped off. As Don sat pillion he timorously glanced into the very heavy hold-all. It was full of silver candlesticks and ornaments.

'See,' Kitty would say. 'How thick is he? Accessory to a robbery. The shame he could have brought on to the family. He could be in prison now for cat burglary.'

Don's innocent, endearing kindness may have been inherited from his maternal grandfather, John Growns from Headcorn, Kent. John had been the village butcher and bell ringer whose business had similarly suffered from extending tick to people who couldn't or wouldn't clear their debt. His stock with his wife fell even further when he was caught and admonished for throwing cigarettes and small cuts of meat wrapped in newspaper over the walls of Maidstone Prison for hungry inmates during those difficult times.

Mum and her older brother Ken (who Kitty inexplicably called Knob, which was a term of affection rather than an insult) worshipped the ground their father walked on, and their love was sharpened by his absence during the Second World War when he served in the RAF as a tail-end Charlie. Even fifty years later when Mum told me how her dad returned from the war one day, unannounced, and walked up the garden path, putting his kitbag down and opening his arms wide as she and Ken rushed to embrace him it moved her (and me) to tears.

The Second World War had been a defining time for my mum, and she sometimes mentioned that in retrospectives, films and documentaries about the war how disappointed she was that so little attention is paid to those who remained at home. They lived in constant fear of bombing, attack, invasion, internment and even genocide. Despite all the rhetoric during and after the conflict there were no guarantees that the war would be won. The very real prospect of Nazi occupation must have been terrifying. Fortunately, there was then a united media and establishment that was firmly behind the country during the crisis that broadcast and published hope and bolstered resolve.

Mum was evacuated to Cornwall and, although there is a genuine romanticism and nostalgia attached to the evacuation programme, for her it was a miserable and frightening time. For the first time, literally days before her stroke, Mum told me of her unhappy experiences. It was like she was clearing the decks. She was placed with a family where the father was a tyrannical type ruling his clan like a Victorian schoolmaster. Mum was immediately unhappy. One evening the father decided to take her and no other children to the cinema. Mum was expected to show gratitude, and she probably did but was extremely uncomfortable. During the film the man's hand arrived on Mum's knee and began to run up her leg. She rebuffed him, but I don't know how the incident ended. Mum could have been sparing me more unpalatable detail.

Back at the rural cottage Mum wrote to Kitty, careful not to mention any incident but pleading to come home and stressing how unhappy she was. Inevitably the old pervert intercepted the letter and read it. Over breakfast he called her out in front of everyone, accusing her of being an 'ungrateful little madam' and said *he* would be writing to her mother to have her removed. He was probably hoping for a replacement that would succumb to his charms more easily.

Barring this experience and the separation from her father, my mum has fond memories of the war too. The black-out was exciting for teenage girls, as was rushing to air-raid shelters and even adapting to new foods as rationing took hold. All the stifling rules and strictures of childhood were upended. She assures me that the wartime spirit we hear so much about was very real, not an imaginary national emotion created for propaganda purposes. At a time of horrifying uncertainty and fear, ordinary people pulled together to help one another. Mum remembers relatives in Australia, émigrés from the Kent village of Headcorn, who she had never met, sending over food parcels. Neighbours rallied around those who had the misfortune of being bombed out of their homes. Cakes, sympathy and support were delivered to those who had lost a son or husband in action. While the international powers seemed intent on destroying the world, Mum saw the very best of human kindness and strength of character, and she never forgot it.

3
YESTERDAY

Dad's forbears were scarred by endemic London poverty that had cascaded down the generations; his paternal forefathers predominantly coming from Battersea, Lambeth and Southwark, the maternal line from Ireland. His father, grandfather and great-grandfather all derived modest and hard-fought livings from the Thames as lightermen and watermen, sawyers and dockers. The family-history detail on this side is littered with workhouses, suicide, unemployment, imprisonment, lunatic asylums and disease.

One of Dad's uncles, Charlie, jumped off a London bridge to his death. He took this drastic course of action following the collapse of his small grocery business and deep despair at not being able to provide for his family adequately in the 1930s economic depression. My father's own father was a casualty of the First World War. Henry Knight Sr made it home from France but died in Millbank Hospital in 1919 overlooking the river that had sustained him. Dad's Aunt Maggs and his cousin Julie were killed in the 1940 Luftwaffe bombing blitz of Battersea. It was an uneasy sensation for me to see one great-grandfather's status listed in an old census as a 'lunatic' and another as an 'imbecile'. It was a grinding existence. There were no celebrities and few celebrations on this side of the family.

Harry Knight, my dad, was born in 1920 at Lurline Gardens, Battersea, London. He never met his father, who returned from the First World War with just enough energy to impregnate my grandma before succumbing to the effects of whatever trauma he endured in France. We still have his sweet embroidered postcards sent from across the Channel. So formally composed – *My Dear Nell, I do hope you are well* – as if he was away on a lightermen's convention in Ramsgate yet all around him humanity itself was being blown to smithereens.

Harry, my dad, was born on St Patrick's Day, and in recognition of the patron saint of Ireland his mum gave him the second name Patrick. Dad always said he was relieved he was not born on Pancake Day. He was a sharp, eager-to-learn, intelligent boy and won a scholarship that got him into the Salesian College in Wandsworth, but his wanderlust prevented him from developing his formal education beyond the age of fifteen.

Dad never really volunteered too much information, but in the years between the ages of fifteen and nineteen (when the Second World War broke out) he managed to run away from home several times, walk around England, stow away on a ship, join the merchant navy, enlist in the army, desert from the army, spend time in the glasshouse and end up living in a monastery while on the trot from the military police.

His youthful rebelliousness partly stemmed from not having a father around. Grandma often told the tale of how she fetched a passing beat policeman (remember them?) into their basement rooms in Lurline Gardens to scare her truculent son into getting out of bed and going to school. My dad's relationship with his mum was one of respect and love for one another, but I have no memory of them ever hugging, kissing or demonstrating physical affection. Nell was struggling most of her life to feed and house them both, and my impression was she was battle-hardened and weary. She wasn't one for cuddling, wittering and petting.

For my dad, though, the arrival of a stepfather was the catalyst for his wanderlust and restlessness. That and the avid consumption of boys' magazines. *The Boy's Own Paper* and *The Magnet* comic have a lot to answer for. Nell married local man Jim Tregent in 1933 when she was fifty-five. She made no bones about the union being a marriage of convenience, as Jim was a printer on the *London Evening News* and had a secure post and earned good money, especially in that austere decade. There are no echoes of David Copperfield and his wicked stepfather Mr Murdstone here; Dad maintained Jim was a decent and nice man who provided well for my grandmother. But he was a latecomer, a cuckoo in the nest, and Dad was gone for good within a couple of years of Jim moving into the family home.

Harry ran away to sea at just fifteen, and after his death I spoke to his younger cousin who had accompanied him on this seminal trip to Southampton, Frankie Mitchell. Frank, then deep into his tenth decade, said my dad would instruct him to chat up the shopkeepers on the way down to the port town while he stuffed bread and fruit up his jumper. This was not the quiet, law-abiding dad that revealed himself to us kids. He managed to stow away on a ship and got as far as Ireland before being caught and made to work his passage back. His young cousin didn't even make it on board. Frank Mitchell developed into an excellent runner, possibly helped by being chased by angry shopkeepers, and in later years was a coach to several Olympic athletes.

At sixteen Dad joined the army, lying about his age. The discipline and order did not agree with him, and he soon deserted. At one time he was banged up in military prison in Aldershot and then deserted again. He lived until he was nineteen as a 'wanted man'. He even went to the trouble of forging new identity papers in the name of an Irishman. We found these in his belongings when he died. Cousin Frank recalled a covert meeting with him during this period and said, bizarrely, my dad spoke with a thick Irish accent throughout the evening in a Deptford pub.

In 1939, according to my dad, he was excused his deserter status because the army needed all the fighting men they could lay their hands on for wartime service. He claims almost all absconded soldiers were similarly pardoned. He enlisted with the Royal Army Medical Corps and was sent to Norway early on. Once he showed me some paperwork listing prisoners who were being treated in a battlefield hospital. Dad said his job included sending belongings home to the relatives of the men who died. On his list was the name Magnus Magnusson.

'Dad, you looked after the bloke who does *Mastermind* on TV!' I was disappointed when he told me that Magnus was much younger than him and Magnus Magnusson is as common a name in some Nordic regions as John Smith is in England.

Dad was never very forthcoming about his army career or maybe I didn't show enough interest, but I do know he served in Italy, Greece, Mesopotamia (Iraq) and, I think, Egypt. Somehow he picked up, or studied, various languages, and he became fluent enough to teach English to French, Italian, Portuguese, Spanish and German workers who were living and working in the Epsom cluster in later life. One day many, many years later, Mum, Dad, myself and my wife and young family were sitting in a hotel in Bahrain where I was working when Dad began conversing with a young hotel manager in Arabic. We were all astounded, including Mum.

'I didn't know you could speak Arabic,' said Mum, puzzled.

'I can get by,' he said, modestly.

'How did you learn that?' I asked.

'I was in Mesopotamia during the war. If you're in someone's country it's a bit rude not to learn their language,' he reasoned.

Dad was very close to his cousin Charlie, who was five years his junior. Charlie blamed himself for the death of his mother and sister in that fatal air raid over Battersea on 11 November 1940. Charlie was fifteen and did not like retreating to the air-raid shelters and persuaded the family not to go down when the sirens sounded. Their home at 184 Wandsworth Road took a direct hit. Charlie's mother Margaret, whose husband, Charlie Sr, had jumped off the bridge only four years earlier, was killed along with his nineteen-year-old sister Julia. Charlie and his sister Mary were badly burned and injured. When we were children Charlie and his wife Jill would often visit, and his severe twitching and stutter served as a constant reminder to my dad of the tragedy and destruction the family had suffered and to we children brought home the life-changing reality of that often-mythologised conflict.

I know Dad spent VE day in Italy. My mum and dad's close friends Sheila and Dominic visited the house one day in the 1990s. Dominic was Italian and liked to ask my dad about his wartime experiences in his home country.

''Arry, can you remember where you spent VE day?'

'Yes, of course,' said Dad. 'I got very drunk and spent the night with a prostitute.'

My mum spat her tea into her saucer. Sheila burst out laughing. Dominic leaned sharply forward his chair gripping the arms. Dad was *never* indiscreet. His expression didn't change. He seemed baffled his statement had provoked such a reaction. We did not know it then, but we had all just embarked on the long, sad road of Dad's Alzheimer's.

When he returned home from Greece, where he was sent in a peace-keeping role immediately after the war, he flirted with communism. He may even have joined the Communist Party. He claimed a lot of returning soldiers did. I have seen some correspondence between him and his cousin Margo, survivor of the Battersea bombing raid of 1940. In it they both bemoan the huge loss of life in the war and the futility of it all, noting that the working classes were bearing the brunt of the devastation yet again and how the ruling classes would emerge, as usual, relatively unscathed.

My Uncle Terry told me how he went to see the film *All Quiet On The Western Front* in the early 1930s. He was just a boy, but it was a strong memory for him. There was a hard-hitting anti-war message, and many of the audience were First World War veterans who at the end stood and applauded in a sombre fashion. As they filed out the cinema these battle-scarred ex-soldiers were shaking heads and muttering 'never again'. Just a few years later they and young Terry himself would find themselves embroiled in another world war.

Harry's cousin Terry was barely mentioned during my childhood, but Dad knew him well because Terry's father Dan spent most of his time at their house before the war as he was permanently unemployed and at a loose end, and he often bought young Terry with him. When Harry went off to war he gifted Terry his prized bicycle.

Terry was equally disillusioned after the war, but he chose a different path from flirting with communism on his return. With his group of friends, which included his Sheepcote Lane neighbours George and Freddie Foreman and future train robbers Tommy Wisbey and Buster Edwards, he rejected the inevitability of precarious and low-paid employment and pursued a life of crime. Consequently, Terry spent time in prison and that would be one of the reasons his name rarely came up around the dining-room table during the 1960s.

I learned in adult life that Terry was, among other things, part of an industrial shoplifting gang that plundered the West End department stores stuffing silk scarves and other lightweight but valuable items into specially adapted long overcoats. Later Terry and his pals used to drive out to the southern English market towns on a Sunday in a van, dressed in tan-coloured overall coats and flat caps to give them the look of removal men. They would pull up outside a menswear shop, and Terry would open it up with a skeleton key. Cool as cucumbers the men would then empty the shop of the best suits and overcoats.

In the 1960s, when I was innocently watching Valerie Singleton showing us how to make things from Fairy Liquid bottles on *Blue Peter*, Terry was cruising around London with George and Freddie, driving the latter over to east London to see his friends, the Kray brothers. George Foreman, Terry's closest friend from babies, was shot in the groin area by a jealous husband, and Freddie swore revenge. Ginger Marks was allegedly a casualty of that dispute. Terry told me that while he was a villain and a thief he was never into violence, and as the 1960s underworld became increasingly gun-happy he pulled away. Going the other way, however, was never a regret for Terry. He saw it as a necessity. He even expressed to me frustration and disappointment in his own father, Dan.

'We were starving much of the time, Martin,' he explained. 'Not enough to eat. Not enough heat in winter. I could see the despair in my mum daily. OK, so my dad couldn't find work. Well, if I had kids and they were not eating or they had no proper clothes to go to school in, well, you would go out on the nick if you had to. Wouldn't you? My dad never did that, and I could never understand that. Still don't.'

Terry's reasoning and recollections were fascinating, but even in his tenth decade he was careful not to say too much. He told me that when he was in Brixton Prison Dr Bodkin Adams came in on remand while awaiting trial. Adams was an ostensibly respectable Eastbourne GP who stood accused of murdering many of his female patients after they had gifted him money in their wills. The case was manna from heaven to the *News of the World*. Terry said that he shared a shower unit with Adams, and his body was completely hairless. Like a big, fat adult baby. It was an image that Terry never forgot. Adams, by the way, escaped the hangman and lived to a ripe old age. It would have been sweet serendipity, Terry observed once, if Adams's doctor in his final weeks had been Harold Shipman.

Deciding there was not much for him in Battersea after the war, Dad decided to start a life in Epsom, a town he was familiar with and fond of through visiting the Derby horserace meeting most years. Epsom and the Derby held a mystical, nostalgic allure for most working-class Londoners in those days. It was a day off and a day out. A day where fortunes could be won and pittances lost. As a boy Dad and his mates walked and rode there from Battersea. Dad also visited Ewell regularly as a boy because the Salesian College playing fields were situated next to the railway station. He told me he had always aspired to live in Epsom and Ewell one day, and he got his wish.

Some time around 1948 he landed a job as a librarian at Epsom Public Library. What thought processes took my dad from soldier to librarian I cannot say, but his love of books, authors, poets, culture and literature was a key part of his life. As a boy he spent his pennies going to watch

Shakespeare plays in preference, often, to visiting the cinema and watching Flash Gordon or Laurel and Hardy. He read voraciously, from Billy Bunter through to the classics. He cherished a book called *Jacob Faithful* by Captain Marryat, which chimed with him because it was about the adventures of a lighterman on the Thames – the family profession he may well have continued had his father not perished. It was a good job he did not follow that path, as the transport of goods by river diminished rapidly after the motor engine took hold. *Jacob Faithful* must have made a great impact on Dad as he was recommending it to me when he was in his seventies, and I remember him being thrilled to visit Captain Marryat's gravestone in Norfolk in that same period.

Another work that influenced him was a book called *Boy* by James Hanley. Whether Dad liked the book because it reminded him of his short time as a boy at sea himself or whether it was the book that spurred him to stow away, I don't know. As an adult I researched and read the book and was shocked to learn it was banned when it was published because of scenes of brutality and male rape. Strange my dad would recommend that one to me when I was a mere lad.

He also owned a set of encyclopaedias called *Pictorial Knowledge*, published by Newnes, hefty red volumes that served as his world wide web and, later, ours. They survived the bombing of Nell's Eland Road wartime home and, according to Nell lore, they were left intact but steaming among the rubble on return from the shelter and an air raid that destroyed that family home. Later, when we kids consumed them too, there was barely a page in the entire set I was not familiar with, and this was before starting school. They depicted a world where British tentacles spread to every corner, nook and cranny of the globe. The encyclopaedias were written by contributors assured in Britain's imperial superiority and passionate about the force of good this country had spread around the world. As a very young boy the books with their myriad black-and-white photographic plates made me grateful I was not picking tea in Ceylon, bent double with heavy baskets on my back and head, and was in a warm, comfortable and loving environment with the only work in front of me a Sunday paper round.

Dad had not been in the library too long when his eyes alighted on two young girls, friends who were working as library assistants. Eileen was chirpy and outgoing, and Minnie was shy and quiet. Minnie was my mum, and she had recently left Danetree Road School in Ewell with her matriculation certificate. She mainly worked in Ewell Court Library, part of the Epsom family of libraries, which was literally around the corner from her house.

When she first left school Mum had a job as a dental assistant, which she did not particularly enjoy. She also worked in a children's home in Kingston, a post that she loved. In caring for children, she knew she had found her purpose in life, although the inevitable and incessant upheaval in the youngsters' lives weighed heavily on her. She could not help but become attached to her charges, and then they were gone. Hopefully carried away to caring, loving foster or adoptive parents or, better still, back to their own families now better placed to care for their child. However, she knew in her heart that very often this would not be the case, and she was waving off a child to further unhappiness, instability or even worse. She was particularly sad for the black children in her care, for when the prospective white foster parents came to 'view' the children they normally did not engage with them at all. Mum vowed that were she ever in a position to do anything about that she would.

By now, in 1950, all this was behind her. She was a young woman finding her feet in the world. Giggling, laughing and exploring life with her friend and soulmate Eileen. She relished her job in the library, meeting the public every day and helping the children. The chief librarian, Mr Dent, was a fusty old sod who liked to be treated with due respect. They almost had to curtsey when he arrived in the room.

'Good morning, Mr Dent.'

'Silly old fool,' Eileen would whisper under her breath.

Meanwhile, Min would be looking over at Mr Knight.

'Take your eyes off him, Min. He's eleven years older than you. Strange, he's a bachelor too, at his age. Something not quite right there.'

Mum blushed. Within two years shy young Min and elderly worldly wise Mr Knight would be married.

4
SHE'S LEAVING HOME

My recollection of my pre-school years is slight. I do have a clear memory of our GP, Dr Trevan, coming to the house to see me about my ears – I had perforated eardrums – which were a genuine and sometimes pretend ailment throughout my schooldays. Dr Trevan was a kindly, angular man with sandy-coloured hair and lightly freckled who always wore a suit and tie and arrived, when summoned, in his car. He carried a shiny-but-worn black leather bag which contained the tools of his trade and, perhaps, his sandwiches. There were very few motor cars on the estate in the late 1950s and early 1960s, and those that did appear were more likely to belong to a visitor than a resident. Dr Trevan would peer into my ear with a little torch and sometimes dig out some hardened wax with a cotton bud. To take my mind off what he was doing he hung his stethoscope around my neck.

It seems like a distant dream now that a doctor would come out to see you, especially for minor and unsubstantiated ailments. Now you must go and see them and then every possible hurdle is put in your way to prevent even that objective being achieved. Today you are ordered to spend only a few minutes with your doctor if you do penetrate the receptionist's wall of steel, and you are instructed that only one complaint can be dealt with at each visit. Woe betide you if you are suffering with cancer, diabetes and a stutter. One day a government will realise that stealing the time people once enjoyed with their general practitioners is a false economy of gargantuan proportions.

'You'll have to stop being ill soon, young man,' Dr Trevan said as I swung around on one of the two metal poles in the back garden that supported the washing line.

'You'll be starting school any day now. You're not allowed to be ill then,' he laughed.

My mum stood with a plastic basket full of washing cradled in her arms and pegs in her mouth nodding agreement. He was gently joking, but I remember feeling fear and apprehension. My older siblings Sally and Laurence were already at school, and I loved having my mum all to myself for most of the day. I didn't want to lose that, and I sort of knew instinctively that a world bulging with rules and regulations and fewer cuddles awaited.

There are very few other pre-school memories that I retain. Some I have most likely reconstructed around surviving photographs. Mum playing records on our gramophone with me and dancing is a genuine recollection. This was the pre-Beatles explosion, and we owned very few discs, as we called them. 'Wooden Heart' by Elvis Presley was one that Mum must have bought, because I know my dad would not have. I can remember Elvis slipping into German lingo for a bit of it. Mum would hold my little hands, and we would dance around the living-room. Another was a rousing number called 'A Scottish Soldier' by Andy Stewart. Don't know what made them acquire that as we had no Scottish ancestry I was aware of. I think, though, it would have been Dad's choice. Later it was 'A Little Loving' by the Fourmost that we played repeatedly. Mum would pick me up and throw me in the air in time to the song and I would squeal with delight.

I *do* remember where I was when President Kennedy was shot. I was watching Harry Worth on the TV. Mum and Dad were in the kitchen standing next to one another, one washing the dishes and passing them to the other to dry and replace in the cupboard and drawers. Harry (Worth, not my dad) was a bumbling, besuited comedian in a trilby hat replete with feather who I had taken a great liking to even at that young age. I was permitted to 'stay up' to watch him. The programme was interrupted with a newsflash. I swear the newsflashes in those days were heralded with images of bolts of lightning. I knew also by the tone of the announcer's voice that this was something serious and ran into the kitchen to fetch Mum and Dad. The way they lowered themselves into their chairs, Mum wiping soap suds on her apron and Dad still with a tea towel in his hands, alarmed me. I could see the shock and fear on their faces, and that instilled worry in me.

The Second World War had not been over twenty years. The Cuban missile crisis had just happened, and we know now a third world war was narrowly averted. My parents must have been scared around this time having this growing young family, and the spectre of a return to war – this time more likely to be nuclear than the conventional one they had just endured – must have haunted their night-time thoughts. I guess they saw the assassination of JFK as a real threat to the world order. I discovered later in life that my dad felt this fear more acutely than he let on at the time.

Another early memory I retain was a year and a bit later when Sir Winston Churchill died. We went into school, and Mrs Watson, who was our year teacher in the Pink Room, had written across the blackboard in big white chalk letters 'WINSTON CHURCHILL DIED'. We all had to copy this into our 'news books', a small exercise book in which we were encouraged to write down the various goings on in our lives. I loved filling in my news book at school and would sometimes spill over into pure fiction. Trips to the seaside in Dad's non-existent car were commonplace. I was especially chuffed when the teacher would stick a coloured star on my work to indicate their approval. The occasional award of three stars encouraged my powers of exaggeration no end.

Mrs Watson, who had also taught my mum, carefully explained to us what Churchill did and what an important figure he was. Her gratitude to Winston made a big impression on me. She was fighting back tears. That appreciation and reverence for our leaders was commonplace then. We were taught to laud our British heroes, and I never dreamed there would be generations after me who would not know who these people were and what they did: Captain Scott, Lord Nelson, Clive of India, Florence Nightingale, the Duke of Wellington, Robin Hood, Grace Darling, Monty, David Livingstone and many others. I never heard a word against Churchill until I was a longtime adult. Back home his funeral was later relayed on television, and I remember the iconic moment when the cranes bowed as his coffin passed them in a boat on the Thames.

The Second World War was a constant presence in our lives during the 1960s. I was going to automatically use the word spectre, but that was not the case. Despite the huge loss of life, the terror and the misery suffered, my parents and most other adults appeared, on the surface at least, to regard it with nostalgic affection. It was more Gracie Fields, Vera Lynn, Tommy Handley and *Dad's Army* than Adolf Hitler, Neville Chamberlain, starvation and the Gestapo. Then I considered it to be ancient history, but it was fresh. It sends shivers down my spine now when I consider that men, women and children were still being exterminated in death camps just twelve years before I was born.

There was a civil-defence training area on the other side of the railway from the estate where we played. Another reminder of the war we had just missed and to the pessimists another indication that a third world war may not be far away. We called it 'the army dump' because it was next door to the real waste dump. It consisted of especially constructed houses and buildings that were built half-bombed to recreate the terrain of an urban battlefield. Territorial Army troops trained there, but we snuck in through holes in fences and had the most terrific games. The crumbling houses were realistic to the point of having wallpaper hung and pictures mounted and numbers on the front doors. How nobody was killed among the rubble and structures was a miracle. The flagship structure was a scaffold tower several storeys high, and I can remember an older boy – Michael Doyle – hanging from the top-floor bars by one muscular arm.

I enjoyed the neighbouring waste dump almost as much. I would walk over mountains of festering, steaming household rubbish, sometimes my little body sinking waist deep like I was wading through grain in a silo. In those days not much of value was discarded, but I would normally come away with something, be it some handlebars for a future bike or a doll missing an eye. Seagulls squawked around me, and putrid fumes rose from the debris, and every now and then I would pass and nod to another little boy similarly searching for plunder.

As children our perception of the war was fashioned more than anything else by the Sunday-afternoon films that, incredibly, were barely ten years old then when we were first lapping them up. We knew them by heart: *Albert R.N.*, *The Colditz Story*, *I Was Monty's Double*, *The Cruel Sea*, *Reach For The Sky* and the comic contributions from Will Hay, Gracie Fields and George Formby. The British were always portrayed as honourable, straight-backed, pipe-smoking brave men with no fear of Jerry and who always prevailed. RAF pilots normally sported handlebar moustaches and names like Fortescue-Smythe, yet oddly they were not figures of fun (then). We got to know all the actors: Kenneth More, Jack Hawkins, Michael Wilding, Virginia McKenna, John Gregson, John Mills, Sylvia Syms and

Sam Kydd, their quintessentially British faces always welcome in our living-rooms.

The third world war, which had not yet happened, remained a menacing presence throughout the 1960s. There was a 'training' film we were subjected to in our junior school that depicted what might happen should a nuclear war kick off. It was fucking terrifying and upset a generation of kids. It wasn't until the next decade that society started to treat the threat of atomic bombs as a possibility rather than a probability.

When I said I was alone with my mum before starting school, that was not quite accurate. Baby sister Liz had joined us, and I was much perturbed by this arrival, reacting almost violently to the child I feared was usurping me in my mother's affections. Apparently, I approached her pram and punched her, which is awful, and, to my eternal shame, I treated her badly for a long time.

A couple of years later my mum was persuaded by social services to take in a boy toddler with Jamaican parentage called Vivian, and shortly after that a little two-year-old girl, Fiona, whose roots were in Tobago. Mum was fulfilling her promise to herself to foster the black and brown children who were so often overlooked by prospective parents at the children's home.

Viv and Fiona were intended to be short-term foster care placings, but Viv stayed with the family until he was in his twenties. Some years later, in 1969, Stephen, a little boy from Barbadian parents, joined us. He was three years old, and he too stayed until adulthood. These were my brothers and sisters, and we melded together as a multicoloured, multiracial, multihappy family. The word multicultural had not been invented then. I didn't even describe my siblings as black because they weren't. I talked about my brown brothers and sisters. I can remember being told by Mum, after a few years, that we had to start using the word 'coloured', as black or brown was no longer acceptable. Winnie Wilson, our social worker, had probably guided her. Black, brown, coloured was never an issue. Not for any of us, at least. They were simply our brothers and sisters.

It was a bold undertaking by my parents and a far more difficult thing for Viv, Fiona and later Stephen than I ever appreciated at the time. They were practically the only dark-skinned people in the area. However, I do not recall witnessing much racism, personally, in those early days that came from a place of hate or viciousness. But, as for casual unthinking racism, that was ingrained and everywhere, but it is only with 21st-century eyes that I now see it.

Astonishingly, adults and children would stop us in the street and politely ask if they could 'feel their hair' and even more astonishingly my parents allowed it. The stranger would then smile benevolently at, say, Viv and run their fingers through his wiry black crown and invite their friend, brother, sister, husband, butler to do the same. This was only fourteen miles outside of London, but in 1963 it could have been in rural Cornwall where we understood people still lived in clay huts in Anglo-Saxon villages.

Many people had never seen a black face in the flesh and rarely on the television. There were only two channels, and on BBC1 there was *The Black And White Minstrel Show* (I remember being disbelieving when my mum told me that the men singing with black faces, white-painted lips and straw boaters were white; even at that young age I wondered whether it wouldn't have been a lot easier just to get black people to do it), while on ITV Kenny Lynch regularly popped up. He was a pop-star-turned-comic's-stooge and a multitalented all-rounder supporting Jimmy Tarbuck, Eric Sykes and the like. That was literally it. So, Viv, Fiona and Stephen must have felt quite different and awkward at times.

Very young children, though, have limited perception of racial difference, and I think and hope my siblings' infancy, at least, was happy. If we were playing football on the green next to the house somebody (probably me) would say to Viv or Stephen, 'You can be Pele.' It was an innocent, even affectionate remark. Today that child would be frogmarched off to a sterile office to undergo intense unconscious-racial-bias training.

The casual unthinking racism (or 'racialism', as it was commonly termed then) I referred to earlier extended to our own family. My grandmother from Battersea certainly needed re-educating. Viv loved to travel up to Clapham Junction on the train with Dad to see Nell, who by then was living in a small flat off Lavender Hill. Looking back on it maybe he enjoyed seeing faces like his own. We would sit on Grandma's small, hard settee while Dad passed over the large bottle of Guinness he always fetched her from the off-licence.

'Do they want somefing to eat?' she would say to Dad nodding at us.

'I don't know, Mum, ask them,' replied my dad. He was always very direct with his mother.

'Do you want some cake?'

We shook our heads, having learned not to accept Grandma's fruit cake as, Dad warned us, it could be years old.

'What about 'im?' she pointed to Viv.

'What about him,' Dad replied.

'Do 'e want a banana?'

Dad sighed and shook his head.

Grandma should have known better, as Battersea and Clapham already had large Jamaican populations by then. But, in her defence, Nell was knocking eighty and had long withdrawn into her flat and was not generally mixing outside. She was an old Victorian, with Victorian views, Victorian values and even Victorian clothes. Possibly Victorian cake. The only contact most Victorians would have had with black people would have been as missionaries or defending colonial outposts against angry, displaced tribes and indigenous populations. Viv, bless him, never took the old lady the wrong way and grew very fond of her.

I do remember one incident that upset us in those early years. Mum came in from shopping, Viv in tow. He followed her everywhere like a loyal puppy. She slumped into her armchair and was crying, wiping her eyes with the handkerchief that lived in her lower sleeve. It is very disconcerting to see a parent cry, and I was very distressed, but she would not say what was the matter, and at seven or eight years old I would not have understood. Viv cuddled into her, his big cow eyes staring up, worried that he might have done something wrong. She reassured him and me, folding us both into her arms. Years later she told me that a man – a stranger – had passed her at the top shops and hissed hatefully in her ear, 'Nigger lover'.

Ignorant casual racism aside, I don't go along with the view that the people of Britain were all malevolenty racist as is increasingly suggested now. At least not from where I was sitting. Our role models and heroes included Pele, Eusebio, Muhammad Ali, Sammy Davis Jr, Jimi Hendrix, Marvin Gaye, Diana Ross, the Four Tops and the Supremes. A bit later still, in the 1970s, there was Bruce Lee and Shaft and on the football terraces almost every London club boasted a famous black or brown terrace leader. If there had been an intrinsic hatred or dismissal of people of different colours, these examples of childhood adulation would never have happened.

Fiona had been with us for three or four years when Winnie Wilson, our social worker, brought us the most devastating news. An uncle and aunt of my little sister from the island of Tobago had decided they would take her in and, because of the direct familial link, this meant neither Winnie nor my parents could do anything about it. She was fostered, not adopted, and that's how it worked. It was an awful time, and although I was only six years of age the crushing sadness of those weeks when we knew parting and the actual leaving day was imminent is seared into me.

I know the date was late 1963 to early 1964 because Winnie bought us a record to remember Fiona by. She said it should conjure up images of the tropical island that Fiona would be living happily on. The song was 'Maria Elena' by Los Indios Tabajaras and it was in the pop charts during that period. For many years my mum, sister Sally and I could not play it without it prompting raw grief and pumping tears.

The parting was gruesome. Mum and Dad had been open with us about what was happening. I remember being aware that the night before she was being collected was to be her last with us. Mum had asked us to be brave and there were all sorts of reassurances of visits in the future, but even we tiny children knew this wasn't true. Getting to Wimbledon was a feat, let alone Trinidad and Tobago. Fiona was only four, and if my memory is right she was bemused and excited by all the fuss rather than distraught. The next day we waited for Miss Wilson to come in her Mini-Minor to drive Fiona to Southampton where she was being passed on to a chaperone who was to take her on the long sea voyage to the Caribbean. I feel for Fiona. No child should have to deal with the emotional upheaval she had already experienced in her four short years on this earth.

Mum was crying as she changed Fiona into her best clothes, and the rest of Fiona's belongings were packed into a small light-blue suitcase. There were also shocking tears in my dad's eyes, and now as I recall these long-buried details and emotions there are tears in mine. Although Fiona's stay had only been two to three years it was most of her life and half of mine. My younger sister was being removed for ever. Winnie came to the door, and we all hugged and kissed Fiona goodbye, walking her down the garden path to the car.

There is a scene in the film *Let Him Have It* about the notorious Craig and Bentley police murder of the 1950s. Poor Derek Bentley's mum and dad stand in their sitting-room clutching each other looking at the clock knowing that on the hour the executioner will be putting the noose around their dear innocent son's neck. When I first watched that as an adult the feelings of the day Fiona left us came flooding back.

She sat in the front passenger seat, her eyes wide open, clutching her favourite doll as she waved us goodbye. Mum went with her. She was a lovely and loving kid. Eager to please. Never would I ride on her back around the lounge again. She had long arms and legs and was physically strong. Stronger than me. We stood there – a family distraught – as the Mini drove slowly off the estate. We walked inside in silence, slumped on the settee and clung to one other and cuddled and cried. A family battered and united in loss.

Three or four hours later there was a knock at the door. Still stunned and red-eyed Dad got up to answer it.

'Look who's here,' he said as he opened the lounge door.

Mum was there, Fiona in her arms, fast asleep, head slumped on her shoulder. We jumped up and danced around them, believing momentarily there had been a reprieve. Had the family in Tobago changed their minds? Had the boat sunk?

Winnie Wilson explained that when they arrived in Southampton she learned that the voyage had been delayed by a day and she did not know what to do. So, joyous as we were to see our sister, we cruelly had to go through the whole emotional wrench again the next day after spending our second 'last night' together.

Mum told us that this time they were caught in traffic and only just made the boat. She described running down the corridors in high heels to find the cabin and the chaperone. The final parting between foster mother and daughter was brutally rushed, but perhaps that was for the best. Mum was badly affected by the whole experience, and I think it could have been the cause of some depressive episodes she suffered in later years. She told Miss Wilson that she would not be taking any foster children in again. It was a vow she was not able to keep.

5
WITH A LITTLE HELP FROM MY FRIENDS

Mum shopped at the top of our estate on the Chessington Road. We called this busy thoroughfare the 'main road' and were taught – often with the aid of a helpful squirrel called Tufty – the importance of looking left and right and waiting for a space in the traffic before crossing. This didn't prevent my friend Eddie getting knocked over by a car. Fortunately, he was unhurt. There were two shopping parades within walking distance, and we called one the 'bottom shops' and the other 'the top shops'. I wonder now if people who lived up the other end of West Ewell switched the names around.

I accompanied Mum on these daily visits, holding her hand or carrying the empty shopping bag. She would put on a bit of make-up before we left. She had a little pink case that opened into a small mirror and some powder that she puffed on to her cheeks. Sometimes Mum would add a touch of pale-pink lipstick. Inevitably she would pull me towards her and take her hankie, lick it and dab my face where bits of bread and congealed Marmite had attached themselves to the corners of my mouth and chin. I hated that.

The shopkeepers invariably wore a tan overall or jacket with a sharpened pencil in their breast pocket to distinguish themselves from their customers. Their shops never opened on a Sunday and closed regimentally on a Wednesday afternoon. Indeed, an obsession, it seemed to me, of shopkeepers was to hover around the door at 1 p.m. on a Wednesday itching with eagerness to flip the OPEN sign hanging on the door to CLOSED. To me, even then, this seemed a strange ethos. If I were a shop owner I would want to keep my premises open as long as I could to shift as much stock as possible.

It wasn't until the Asians booted out of Uganda by Idi Amin in the early 1970s arrived on our shores that these attitudes started to change significantly. The British corner-shop mentality was swept aside, and eventually shops opened all hours, including Sunday. The public warmly welcomed a genuine convenience store, and that shopkeeper in his brown jacket was soon banished to history and Ronnie Barker's imagination.

Mum would buy some meat from the butcher, get a few 'bits' from the grocer, Mr Welham, a loaf of bread from Lyons the baker, perhaps some sweets for me from Mr Parker at Bedford's and a ball of wool or two from Susan's, the knitting shop next door. Susan was a glamorous lady with a mane of black hair. Her husband wore a tweed jacket and a cravat, smoked a pipe and had hair that curled up on his collar. In an era of short haircuts for mature men he stood out.

My mother knitted a lot, the sound of clashing needles one of the perennial background rhythms of the house, along with the whistling kettle and the hum and tremble of the immersion heater. She knitted us identical jumpers, which we were thrilled with because they were lovely and warm but became embarrassed to wear as we grew bigger and older. The synchronised clothing thing made people laugh at us, or so we older children felt. There was a period when we three senior siblings could have stepped off the pages of an Enid Blyton *Famous Five* book. Other clothes were darned at the elbows and patched at the knees and passed down as one child outgrew them. This was not unusual on the estate and not a cause for embarrassment, as we knew no different.

Mum would knit furiously, glancing sideways at a pattern book perched on the arm of the chair. I would be cross-legged on the floor in front of her, eyes fixed on the television. The programme on was *Watch With Mother*, and that's exactly what I did. It featured a slot called 'Picture Book', and I liked the bit where the presenter showed us a tray full of objects and then brought it back with some objects missing and we had to guess what had gone. There was also *The Woodentops, Andy Pandy* and *Bill and Ben*. They were all puppets with the strings operating them clearly visible. My favourite daytime show, though, was *Tales Of The Riverbank* featuring Hammy Hamster and Rodney Rat, which used real animals in a studio environment. Johnny Morris, who we would later enjoy in *Animal Magic*, provided the voices.

For one birthday I got a hamster in recognition of my fondness of *Tales Of The Riverbank* and, of course, I called it Hammy. Hammy seemed to live for years, but I guess it was only months. I am surprised he lasted that long bearing in mind the energy he expended on his never-ending wheel and my compulsion to remove and replace him from his cage zillions of times a day. I was almost hysterical when I found him dead on his floor one morning. He was stiff and on his back. Little stumpy legs in the air. Dad picked him up and placed him in a saucepan filled with cotton wool and straw. He then heated the pan up on the grill. Miraculously, Hammy stirred. He opened his eyes, lifted his little head a tad and then sunk back and died again. That really happened. Mum and Dad said he had come back to life to say goodbye to me, and that made me feel so much better. We buried him at the top of the garden in a biscuit tin, and Dad made a small wooden cross with Hammy painted on it. He recited 'Dust to dust' and all that. The memorial stood there for years. Or was it months?

I was also gifted a yellow budgerigar one Christmas, who I christened Jimmy Greaves. I became well disciplined in emptying his husks and filling up his food trough and water daily. Weekly I would have to clean out his floor, as the bird shit accumulated. I'd treat him to millet and cuttlefish regularly. Like Hammy I was confronted with him dead, stiff and legs in the air one morning, and this time Dad was unwilling to warm his dead body back up in a saucepan.

I know I felt betrayed rather than excited or fearful when it came to starting school. There was no pre-school nor playgroups for us in those days to ease you into this life-changing moment. One minute you were the apple of your mother's eye and she of yours, with your lives and arms entwined around each other, and then you were thrust into a new world of strange, formal adults who *didn't* smother you with kisses and hugs, and for the first time you encountered queues, plimsolls, strange food, uniform clothing, hard chairs, prayers, hymns and scores of other kids competing for attention.

Ewell Grove Infants' School was a charming, red-bricked, long-windowed, high-ceilinged, late-Victorian building with pointed roofs giving it a church-like look and feel. There was a sloping playground at the front and at the back an apple orchard. To me the footprint seemed enormous, the ceilings and beams so high, the corridors long and cold, but when I pass it now it looks so small. The apple orchard where we lost ourselves hiding among the trees and shrubs is now a small parcel of land not much bigger than a suburban garden. The whole area has shrunk as I have grown but also because the playground and orchard has been filled with outbuildings and extensions as pupil numbers have increased in line with the general population.

I clung to my mum and screamed and kicked as she tried to disentangle my arms from her neck and then waist and then legs. She must have been upset too as a teacher came and took my hand and tugged me away from the school gate. She probably told my mum to scarper in the nicest possible way. I was not the only one. Other hysterical kids and their tearful mothers were playing out the same emotional trauma. I could not comprehend that my mum would leave me in a strange place with strange people. I was genuinely terrified, upset and disappointed in her. That first realisation in my life that other forces and other people could over-rule my parents was a shocking one.

The teacher put a label around my neck that, helpfully, read 'MARTIN KNIGHT' and led me to a classroom called the Blue Room. We were shown to single rows of desks and chairs. I was also allocated my own peg, which thrilled me. It was the first piece of furniture I owned. It was metal, black and shiny, and on it I hung my little coat in which Mum had written my name on the label inside. At the back of the classroom was a sandpit and there was also a couple of small cradles in case some of the children could not be snapped out of the habit of afternoon sleeps. The lady teacher checked us all in and then encouraged us to go and play in the sandpit. Here we started to talk and interact with one another. Playtime and then lunch soon followed and, finally, at 3.15 p.m. we were told to lift our chairs and put them on the desk and repeat after the teacher the following prayer:

> *Hands together, softly so,*
> *Little eyes shut tight;*
> *Father, just before we go,*
> *Hear our prayer tonight.*

Before we ate, we were taught to stand, push our hands together pointing upwards and say grace:

> *For what we are about to receive,*
> *May the Lord make us truly thankful.*

This was altered by older boys to:

> *For what we are about to leave,*
> *May the pigs be truly thankful.*

We babies thought this highly rebellious. God, Jesus, the Bible, good, bad, evil, thankfulness, forgiveness, charity and all manner of religion-related concepts whooshed into my life for the first time like a righteous tsunami.

Mum was at the gate with all the other mums as we poured out of the Blue Room into the playground at the end of the day, and I ran into her arms. She must have had a rotten few hours, I'm sure. I think the next day the parting was still difficult but easier. After about a week I was looking forward to school. It was fun.

I had made friends. These were the first people of my own age I had contact with outside of the family. I first met Tony, Bill and Eddie on a drain. During the breaks some of us charged around the playground, and if we became overexcited or naughty, we were ordered by the patrolling dinner ladies, whistles on string hung around their necks and teacups in hand, to stand on a drain for the duration. The offences that could result in this punishment included running into people, throwing things and lifting girls' skirts. There was a lot of the latter going on. It was done under the guise of a game called kiss chase. The upper floor of the school was used by the junior girls only, aged eight to eleven. They wore red cardigans, black skirts and, as we soon discovered, navy-blue knickers. There was something very exciting about creeping up behind them and lifting the dress, pointing at the knickers and running away. The older girls giggled, screamed and slapped, but a good time was had by all.

There was a playtime in the morning and another at lunch, which lasted only an hour but seemed to us to be never-ending. We would retrieve marbles from among the fluff and congealed confectionery in the pockets of our shorts and roll them down the slope. The bigger marbles were called alleys. I do not remember how you won or lost the game, but I think that if you hit the other boy's marble you claimed it.

In the autumn we picked up conkers fallen from the horse chestnut trees that lined the Grove next to the school and drilled holes in them, threading through dirty old laces from pungent plimsolls. Then we would do battle. A winning conker was one that smashed the other until it broke. A conker that was victorious was called a oner, a twoer and so on as it claimed more victories. At home we soaked them in vinegar, as legend had it that it made the prized conkers tougher. Mum would tell us to go easy on the Sarson's – it costs money, you know.

Calling each other names was normal. We zoomed in on a surname and tried to find something within to goad the person. I was flattered, not insulted, when a group of girls surrounded me and chanted:

> *Martin Knight had a fright*
> *In the middle of the night*
> *Saw a ghost eating toast*
> *Halfway up a lamp post*

To think (wrongly) that a bunch of older girls had gone to all that trouble to write a ditty about me did wonders for my fledgling self-esteem.

Another game entailed flinging our arms around each other's shoulders and wandering around the playground in a chain chanting, *Who wants to play war in 1964?* Those who did would attach themselves to the growing line. By the point enough numbers had been gathered in one long link it was normally time to go inside. If a game were started there was always an argument, because nobody would agree to be a German and therefore it was impossible to muster two sides. No such problem with Cowboys and Indians. There was no shortage of boys who would be an Indian. In fact, it was much more fun to charge around the playground making a war cry noise while banging your open mouth with palm for effect or jumping on another boy's back and felling them to the ground than making a gun from pointed fingers and shouting 'Bang, Bang'. Amazing that it would be another half a century before it dawned on me fully that the goodies were actually the dispossessed Red Indians and the baddies the invading cowboys.

Quieter boys preferred non-contact games, gently clutching the back of each other's shirts and chugging around the playground as trains, making steam noises and whistles, stopping here and there to pick up and discharge passengers. The girls enthusiastically played hopscotch on a properly painted grid on the ground, unlike the poorly chalked versions on the estate. They had songs and rhymes they too recited as their friends hopped and scotched. Other girls played cat's cradle, where they did weird unfathomable manoeuvres with their hands and balls of string.

The aforesaid drains were not adjacent, but you inevitably peered across the playground to see who else was in playtime prison. We drain occupiers soon located one another, recognising a commonality. Bill Owen was a massive kid. He looked eleven at six years old, and throughout his life his size defined him, often being blamed or singled out for things he didn't do. It was inevitable if Bill gently pushed one of his classmates they would go flying. He was only behaving the same as the rest of us, but the results were often more impactful. He lived in the village in a bungalow tucked away in a private road. He was an only child with parents who seemed older than most of ours.

Tony and Eddie, I quickly discovered, lived on my estate as near neighbours in Gibraltar Crescent. Eddie was a taller, quiet boy with a permanent grin on his face, forever amused by the antics of those around him. Tony was mischief from the start. A boy in search of adventure and thrills. I was immediately attracted to him. Tony, Eddie and I were soon walking to and from school together each day, no longer needing the reassuring clasp of a parent's hand.

The transformation from cosseted toddler to independent little boy was dramatic and rapid. I was six when I started walking to school unparented, although there were probably thirty boys and girls from the estate wandering the same route in knots and pairs each morning and afternoon. I would cut through the car park and meet Tony and Eddie as they came around the block. On the way we crossed the railway over the newly built footbridge. My brother and sister not long before had been crossing the railway line on an unmanned level crossing without gates. Incredible, looking back. On the journey we climbed up on garden walls, clambered up trees, stamped on stag beetles, kicked hard, white dog shit down the road and played it and feet-off-ground. The daily journey to and from school became an adventure in itself.

One day we decided to play truant. Whose idea this was, I cannot remember. Mine or Tony's. How we even had the concept of truancy at the age of six or seven is baffling. We decided we would spend the day in the secret, alluring, filthy space underneath the grandstand of Epsom and Ewell Football Club. Eddie, who always had far more common sense than Tony and I combined, decided it was not for him and continued on his way to school. Graham, who lived a few doors from me and who I was now escorting to school since he was barely more than a toddler, came with us.

Epsom and Ewell Football Club stood halfway down West Street. It was a lower-league team with a ramshackle ground with holes punched through its perimeter fence that we would, later, use to watch games without paying. There was a club house, a standing area for about a dozen diehards with a corrugated roof – a poor imitation of the Chelsea Shed – and down one side a seated so-called stand. A tiny, stern old lady dressed in a mac and a beret patrolled the entrance to the grandstand, taking a couple of pennies from you should you wish to avail yourself of the alleged extra luxury. The rows between the seats were open, and you could look down beneath the stand. It was a dark area and had never been cleaned, an unpleasant soup of Smith's crisps bags, Corona bottles, Woodbine cigarette packets, chocolate-bar wrappers and, unfortunately, a smattering of human waste.

The time whizzed by as we three children trudged among the debris picking up matchboxes, discovering old football programmes and even cigarette cards depicting players from before our time tossed down by uninterested adults. After a while we became bored.

'What do you reckon the time is?' I asked.

'Must be home time.'

None of us had such things as a Timex wristwatch (yet) nor a sense of time. We dawdled home not questioning why there were no other kids on the normally busy route back.

When we arrived at our houses to our surprised mothers all hell was let loose. It was 11 a.m.! We had been away from home barely two hours. Graham's mum was on the doorstep practically suggesting we had kidnapped her son on account of me and Tony being older. Tony's mum came around, and it was jointly decided to march us to school and tell the headmistress what we had done. There were dire warnings about waiting until our fathers got home. We really could not see what all the fuss was about.

Miss Smith, the headmistress, sat behind her desk looking sternly at us over half-moon glasses. She was by then coming to the end of her career. Her hair was stiffened by spray and stayed in the same position even when her head moved, she wore a blazer-like jacket decorated with a prominent brooch and a touch of make-up. She had a hard, pointed face but kindness lurked beneath. We stood on the springy, soft carpet across from her desk. It was a new sensation for me, our floors at home being covered with a mosaic of lino, rugs and hessian mats. Graham was excused the inquisition. He had been led. Easily. Looking back, he was probably thoroughly confused by the whole incident.

'In all my years I have never come across such outrageous behaviour. What in the Good Lord's name made you want to play truant?'

Silence. We did not know where to put our little hands.

'Stop fidgeting the two of you. Come on, I need to know. Are you unhappy at school?'

'No, Miss Smith. I like school.'

'No, Miss Smith. So do I.'

'Well, I don't know what to think. I really do not. If you were older I would send you to Mr Bell in the boys' school next door. You do understand if you did this at junior school you would be caned?'

'Yes, Miss Smith.'

'Yes, Miss Smith.'

'Well, you will have to be punished. I need to decide on a suitable measure. Come and see me first thing in the morning after assembly. Off you go. Back to your classroom.'

That suitable measure became clear the next day. Two desks and chairs were placed outside in the apple orchard behind the school, and we were to sit there for the whole day. We were only allowed out of our seats to go to the toilet and to eat at lunchtime. The thinking, I presume, was to shame us, but it had the opposite effect. We were always in awe of the junior girls, and we could see them looking out the windows at us. Some were laughing and waving. At play time they swarmed around our desks, offering us apples, sandwiches and sweets. These little infant boys who had bunked off fascinated and delighted them. Our peers were not allowed in the orchard; they were confined to the front playground watched over by vigilant dinner ladies. There were two drains to fill. It was just us and these girls in red cardigans who seemed so grown-up, although none was more than eleven. They were only just touching puberty and we were miles from it, but there was something that stirred that day for Tony and I. Tony, particularly. He may have taken two things away from the whole experience: crime pays and girls like a naughty boy.

6
GOOD DAY SUNSHINE

Besides school, my life revolved around the house, the few yards outside of the house and eventually the park. The general rule from when I was of infant-school age was that I was allowed outside but should not venture beyond the view from either the sitting-room or the landing windows. For a year or so I really believed my mum was sitting at the window monitoring me.

Below the landing window, attached to the side of the house, was a small green. There had been a 'NO BALL GAMES' sign once, but that was long gone. The council then planted a tree in the middle of the green to deter footballers, but for a while we played around it (and it was more skilful than some of us) until the friendly estate vandal pulled it out. It was then a pitch to double up as the Oval or Wembley. Dad painted a cricket wicket on our shed wall to aid our cricket games, which would not have endeared him to some of our neighbours but pleased others because he had drawn noisy kids away from their houses. Cricket consisted of one boy batting, another bowling with a grey tennis ball (green ones were an innovation that was still a decade away) and the other fielding while funnelling the lumpy dregs of a Sherbet Fountain down his gullet. Much of the game was taken up by arguments over whether the bowler was deploying daisy cutters or not (underarm rolling of the ball along the ground) and cries of LBW (leg before wicket). I found the game both at the top level and the level played outside my house profoundly boring. My preference was football.

'Michael, Michael, come on in, your tea's ready.'

Michael spun around. He wears a white, mud-stained school shirt, grey shorts with a snake belt, rolled-down socks and bumper boots.

'Mum,' he pleaded, 'it's 13-12. I'm gonna equalise. Wait a minute.'

'I'll give you 13-12 round your bloody 'ead, you bleedin' little tyke ...'

Interruptions such as these were typical of football games played on 'the green'. The green when I look at it now is not quite the size of a tennis court, but to us it was vast. I would have debuted on the green as early as six or seven years old. My brother Laurence would have placed me in defence. I obeyed a simple 'stay there' and became the final hurdle for a nine-year-old budding Johnny Haynes to navigate after dodging some dog shit, some passing pedestrians and an opponent of his own size before hitting the ball as hard as he could over a frightened goalie who had turned his back, tensed himself and squeezed his eyes shut.

'That was over the bar,' hollered Steve, who was in goal because he was useless on the field. He had just surfaced from underneath Mr Wilson's Austin Cambridge, ball under arm, hair now streaked with Castrol oil. How he reached his conclusion is unclear. There was no bar. A shot was over or under the notional bar depending on where the respective target man and goalie were currently placed in the estate pecking order. The goal stood, Steve capitulating as Johnny Haynes called him a cheating bastard and approached him with menace.

The incessant games of football on our green didn't please everyone, Mum and Dad among them. The ball would be kicked over the big wall into our garden four or five times a session. If Laurence or I were playing it was not a problem because we simply nipped in the back gate and retrieved it, but if other boys were playing without us, they felt obliged to knock and ask, 'Can we have our ball back, Mrs Knight?' Mrs Knight would get mightily frustrated with all of us if it was a wet day and the muddy ball hit the sheets and garments that were pegged up on the clothes line. I used to stop momentarily when fetching the ball and walk into those billowing sheets and inhale their cleanness.

Talking of the big wall, it was about seven feet high and marked the perimeter of the green and our back garden. I considered it a great feat of daring and achievement to stand up straight and walk the length of it. I imagined I was Charles Blondin, the tightrope walker, and crowds were watching my daring from behind their net curtains. They were really thinking that the idiot child was up there showing off again. Serves him right if he falls off. My exhibitions of bravery and balance came to an abrupt halt one day when Peter Bromley from across the road took aim with his air rifle and shot at me, causing me to fall.

By the age of seven or eight I was wandering around Marsh Avenue and Gibraltar Crescent joining in other football games being played on their own green patches. They were our away matches. Riding my bike opened things up more, and it was hard not to cross the main road and venture further afield. Parents didn't mind too much where we were when we got a bit older as long we were in for tea. There was this one-hour period between 4 p.m. and 5 p.m. on school days when we all played out before going in for tea and the beginning of children's' television. *Blue Peter* on a Monday and Thursday, *Crackerjack* at five to five on a Friday, *The Adventures Of Twizzle*, *Sarah And Hoppity* and *Torchy The Battery Boy* as well. The imports from America and Australia were of higher quality. Shows like *The Terrible Ten*, *Skippy* and *The Magic Boomerang* from Australia and *Bewitched*, *Dennis The Menace* and *Flipper* from the States were among my favourites. We were spoiled for choice. *Flipper* was superb. I envied the two brothers who lived quayside with their water-ranger father and had access to bikes, soda and motorboats. Flipper was a clever dolphin who was able to communicate with humans by nodding or shaking his head and even throwing it back and laughing. He or she had an astonishing ability to nose out criminals and help the father and boys to apprehend them.

The fun was normally over by 5.45 p.m. when the *News* came on. Boring men in boring suits and ties talking about boring men in boring suits and ties. Sandwiches at Number 10. Picket lines. New motorways. The Breathalyser. Harold Wilson. Ted Heath. Barbara Castle. In one ear and out the other. Mum and Dad shushed us should we dare chatter while it was on.

Skills were honed on the greens and some boys (not me) became very adept players even before they reached junior school. As we got older the green became too small for our growing bodies and strength and we would decamp to Baker's Field or the Gibraltar Rec and play with the big boys. Literally.

Here a mixed bag of estate boys and other local lads from the tree-lined roads surrounding the park would gather. Twenty to thirty enthusiasts lined up, and the two captains (usually either the two eldest boys, possibly as old as eleven or twelve, or the two best players) would pick their team, one at a time. This was designed to ensure an even match. One of life's early shames for a young boy was to be that person who is picked last. That was never me, but sometimes I was close enough to feel the blood running to my cheeks.

Other times we 'dipped' to decide players or other things like who was going to go in goal. One of the crowd would point at each person in turn, including himself, and say 'Dip, dip, dog shit, you are not it' or this more convoluted one that began:

> As I was walking down Inky Pinky Lane,
> I saw two Inky Pinky children,
> They told me this, they told me that,
> They told me the colours of the Union Jack,
> Red, white, blue,
> Cat's got the flu,
> Dog's up the chimney,
> So out goes you.

There were no toddlers allowed now in these huge games, and the ages ranged from eight to fifteen and some good football was played. For the first time a sense of positioning was introduced, as was the curious concept of passing the ball.

By now we had all picked professional teams to follow and could stay up late on a Saturday to watch *Match Of The Day*. Always one boy mimicked David Coleman's football commentary when he got the ball to enhance his experience – 'Mills picks it up, beats one, beats two ... Foul! Quite remarkable.'

Another boy used to shout, 'Dougan is a wanker. Dougan is a wanker.' This he must have picked up from forensic listening to *MOTD*'s background crowd chants. He had no idea who Dougan was or who he played for and even less of an idea about masturbation but had been hypnotised by the mantra.

The big boys were awesome to us youngsters. There were players among them who would have been picked up by football clubs had they had been spotted. 'Babe' Mardle, a few years older than me, was the Gibraltar wizard of the dribble. Later his nickname changed to Buzzard. He was our junior truancy partner's older brother. Alan Newton was fully expected to become a professional. My brother Laurence was handy on the field and in goal.

Some of the others were just solid and strong. We dared not tackle them, even if we could catch them, but we youngsters did have Carl. A year or two younger than me, he was blessed with brilliant ball control. Like our very own Georgie Georgie Georgie Best. Much as they tried, the big boys could not get the ball off him. He was a delight to watch. Thrilling. Frustrated by him making a monkey of them, the older lads resorted to shoulder-barging him and even kicking him up in the air. By now, some of these youths were aspiring Shed Boys and, no doubt, had learned the dark arts employed by a certain Mr Ron 'Chopper' Harris in a blue shirt.

The games had no halves, no referees, no time limits. After an hour or two the first boy would announce he had to be in for tea and wander off. Slowly the numbers dwindled. Some shuffling of players took place to keep the team numbers even. If necessary the keeper was declared rush goalie, meaning he had permission to come forward and join in the main scrum. Eventually, though, facts had to be faced. There were only six boys left and the sun was beginning to descend behind the council yard, and the game would be declared over or the cry of 'next goal wins' would herald one last crazy burst of energy.

Another game played on the green or in the park that I have not seen any child play since my childhood was splits. It entailed a penknife or sometimes, worryingly, a bigger sheath knife. Boys stood opposite each other, a few feet apart, legs slightly spread. The knife was then hurled with force into the turf near the opponent's foot. For the life of me I cannot remember how the game was won but the thrill, undoubtedly, was the possible impaling of a foot or slicing off of a toe.

There was a plethora of other games we played on the estate, in Baker's Field, in the playground or down the park: rotten eggs, what's the time Mr Wolf?, feet-off-ground, knock-down ginger, piggyback fighting and British bulldog to name a few. The latter was an extraordinarily rough affair. Two sets of boys (mainly) charging from opposite ends of the playground to get past the other team. Nothing was out of bounds in preventing your opponent passing. I was reminded of the game in adulthood when watching the film *Braveheart*. People got hurt, and eventually our school banned it.

Competing with football for our leisure hours were the other delights offered by the Gibraltar Recreation Ground. A railway line ran alongside the back of the estate, and if we went into Tony's back garden, climbed the fence, crossed the line and scrambled over the other fence we'd be in the Rec in seconds, but generally we didn't. The railway line was out of bounds and, adventurous and danger-courting as we were, we rarely played around it, even on the sidings. This was despite older boys helpfully telling us that if we jumped on the live rail with both feet and were touching nothing else, we would not be electrocuted. Instead, we cut through the estate garages as dads tinkered contentedly beneath Ford Consuls and crossed the railway bridge into West Street where tiny old Victorian farm-labourers' cottages dotted the short walk to the imperious gates of Gibraltar Recreation Ground.

The Rec had it all. Once through those large iron gates you could lose a day with ease, and if we were 'down the Rec' or 'over the Rec' our parents would never fret, as on summer weekend afternoons it was teeming with life. The head keeper's house stood authoritatively next to the gates, and the keeper himself would often be in the garden on his leather-padded knees tending his flower beds. He looked up at us as we came in and gave a friendly nod that welcomed and warned at the same time. Hello and behave yourself was the message his eyes transmitted. His wife would be in the back garden too, attaching washing to her clothes line, and she would smile if there was not a peg clenched between her teeth. Besides locking and unlocking the gates I never really worked out what the head keeper did. Men from the council came and mowed the grass; Parkie, as we called him – a junior keeper – dished out the putting clubs and took the money for the tennis courts and various ladies served refreshments. I made a mental note that when the time came and I had to choose a job, head keeping was not a bad option. You did bugger all and got a home thrown in.

Stretching out in front of the head keeper's house were a couple of football pitches rearranged for a few weeks in the summer to accommodate cricket. To the left stood a pavilion that had seen better days. The description 'pavilion' accorded this structure more gravitas than it deserved, as really it was little more than a large shed with a locked room behind which the gardeners kept their tools, mowers and oil drums. During my Rec-going days the pavilion disappeared altogether – the victim of an act of suburban vandalism. Two local boys managed to break in one day and ignite the petrol drums. An almighty explosion followed that had the older residents of the estate rushing to their curtains fearing a recurrence of the

Blitz. When we set off for school the following morning adults were outside marvelling up at a wheelbarrow that had literally been blown sky high in the explosion and landed on the roof of a house. The youths suffered severe burns and were packed off to houses of correction, and I didn't see either of them again for several years.

Walking around from where the pavilion once stood was the place we called simply 'refreshments'. Here, through serving hatches, ladies with white hair and neat white cardigans served teas, ice creams and scones to the small audience watching the cricket and sometimes, huffily, to us. The menfolk sat on collapsible canvas chairs and sipped their teas from cups and saucers and lazily clapped what was happening or not happening in front of them, throaty grunts of approval rippling between them.

Knowing where we were not welcome, we would normally pass 'refreshments' and linger for a while at the public toilets where the strong smell of urine and bleach and the unpredictability of what you might find inside always fascinated us. Sometimes Wayne and Wendy, a young courting couple from the estate, were inside. We sneaked in and looked under the door getting hugely excited that one or other's jeans were dropped around the ankles and imagining what they might be doing. Sometimes Wayne would chase us as he became more and more exasperated at not only trying to take this girl's virginity standing up (she was taller than him) but having giggling children attempting to witness the event.

The cubicles when we ventured inside gave us a preview of a new, seedy world as we read and tried to make sense of the messages scrawled all over the walls: 'JOHN DAVIS IS A QUEER', 'RING 9566 FOR A TOSS', 'PARKIE LOVES KIDS', 'LINDA BENNETT IS A PIG AND SUCKS DICKS'. At seven or eight years of age these bizarre declarations meant very little, although we instinctively knew that these public conveniences had more to do with dirty and rude stuff than going to the toilet. Even if you did not understand all the words, the crude diagrams got the message across far more effectively.

Hints of this odd thing called sex were seeping into my consciousness from other areas too. An older boy down the Rec recited a rhyme to me which remains in my mind today, so it must have made an impact:

This is number one and the story has begun
Roll her over in the clover
This is number two and her hand is on my shoe
Roll her over in the clover
This is number three and her hand is on my knee
This is number four and we are laying on the floor
This is number five and I think we're still alive
This is number six and we are really in a fix
This is number seven and she says she's gone to heaven
This is number eight and the doctor is at the gate
This is number nine and the twins are doing fine
This is number ten and she wants it done again

There was another rhyme I picked up to the tune of 'Bye Bye Blackbird' which featured dynamite and juries and which is best forgotten, but both served as cryptic introductions to an element of life that would encroach more and more.

Behind the toilet block was the manicured lawn of the bowling green where more elderly people in white V-necked pullovers, white trousers and shoes as black and shiny as the big bowling balls shuffled around silently. It struck me that they were just playing marbles like we did at school but with bigger balls. Men and women together but barely speaking, the silence being broken only by the echoey knock of balls gently clashing at the other end of the green.

Here too was Parkie's office, and he would sit in front of it watching the bowling and occasionally taking coppers for the putters. Parkie was much older than the head keeper and wore a heavy tweed dog-tooth-patterned jacket in all weathers. His thick tortoiseshell glasses did not quite hide the serious damage to one eye. It was all white with just a hint of eyeball in the extreme right corner. At home we watched a programme called *Mad Movies*, presented by Bob Monkhouse, and one of the old silent screen stars featured was a man called Ben Turpin, and other than Parkie he was the only other person we ever saw with eyes like that.

He was quite friendly, sometimes glad of the company, and would roll cigarettes from his tobacco tin as he talked to us. His fingers were stained yellow with nicotine and gnarled, and he smelled strongly of Old Holborn;

it was an odour we all knew because many of our fathers smelled the same. Once when asked how his eye got like that he claimed to have been kicked by a horse while working on a farm and that the eyeball had shot into his head.

'Will it come back?' one of us asked.

'Not now, son, not now.'

To the side of Parkie's office was another gate, and this was the gate that effectively separated the adults' section from the children's area. On the other side of the gate stood a square brick column with a small button tap on the top. This was glamorously referred to as the water fountain, and on hot days dehydrated boys and girls would take turns to clamp their lips around the tap and gurgle down common-or-garden tap water as if it was an elixir. If there was enough pressure in the tap, we would block the flow with a finger and then lift it slightly to gloriously shower the person behind. Another ruse was to fill our cheeks with water and see how long we could hold it in there before emptying the fetid contents over each other several minutes later.

Passing the tennis courts, we'd head down to the small area in the very corner of the Rec that we called 'the swings', but was a bit more than just swings and from the age of five the main attraction. As you walked into the swings you were met by the roundabout which some called 'the witch's hat'. It was like a wooden cone balanced on a central steel pole and the cone was made from metal bars and had planks of wood for sitting on. These were really designed for small toddlers to sit on, clasping the bars as their parents gently spun them around, but I rarely saw it used in this fashion.

The swings had long been taken over by kids like us, and parents with toddlers rarely ventured in. The big boys would spin the witch's hat around at frightening speeds and then clamber on and, with their weight on either side, would manage to crash it in and out from the central pole at the same time. The roundabout would make ominous clanking and banging noises, and urban myth had it that sometimes it flew off its pole, injuring all those on it.

Next up was the American swing. Essentially it was a large seesaw, and again innocently intended for a couple of infants each end pushing themselves off the ground with little feet, but it had become the most daring ride in the playground. Andy Bailing and Roger Street would stroll in wearing their sleeveless jean jackets and studs, both twelve or thirteen years old, and stand either end and in a synchronised fluid movement of bending knees and pushing forward until the swing was almost upright both sides. Sometimes they would let you stand in front of them hanging on for dear life as you hurtled towards the concrete and skimming it at the last millisecond as the swing sliced through the air. Again, there was the day when it tipped right over, and people fell off and smashed heads, but nobody knew when this day actually was or anybody who was on it at the time. Gibraltar Rec was a bubbling cauldron of suburban myth.

The slide was the highest structure in the playground, but because there was no movement and danger of it breaking it held few attractions, and only once when Franco the Spanish boy from our school fell from the top and was taken to hospital did we see any injury potential. It was also said that Tommy S had a habit of urinating down it, so we steered clear. (Tommy later achieved peak notoriety when he was allegedly responsible for burning down Trickeys, a toy warehouse on the Chessington Road. He was another one we never saw again.)

There were two sets of actual swings – the kiddie swings and the grown-up swings, although I never saw a grown-up on them. The kiddie swings had little safety bars to hold you in and were hard to fit into anyway once you passed six or seven years old and were only good for hurtling them through the air as hard as you could in an attempt to wrap them around the top bar for Parkie to unravel later. The grown-up swings were a simple contraption of two chains attached to a top bar and a green wooden seat. All the rides had been green once, but the years and the sun had cracked the paint and the kids were forever flaking it off until the wood or silver metal underneath became the dominant colour again. The game with the swings was to sit on them and, with the same learned body movement employed on the American swing, get yourself flying high and then jump and sail through the air. Markers were put down where you landed to see who had launched themselves the furthest. There was no point in joining in unless you could achieve some height on your swing as you let go of the chains and flew through the air because if you fell short you landed clumsily on concrete and would be nursing grazes and cuts all the way home.

The Rec remains to this day. Seems so much smaller now. Each ride has been replaced by something softer and safer. Chipping landings bedded down all around. The slide less than a quarter of the size of the old one. My ghost is there, along with all the other boys and girls who piled in and played together a little dangerously but happily and innocently. Little children with doting mothers are in there now – as they were meant to have been all along. They are enjoying it and know no different, but there is a rapidly diminishing pocket of men and women now in their fifties, sixties, seventies and eighties who remember the breathtaking thrill, danger and excitement of a summer's day 'down the Rec'.

7
ALL THOSE YEARS AGO

Our next door but one neighbours were a hearing-and-speech-impaired family, the Tuttes. Then, without any malice and with unwitting clumsiness, they were known by everyone, including officialdom, as deaf and *dumb*. It is almost unthinkable now that vulnerable people were labelled and classified so casually and unthinkingly then: spastics, cripples and mongols, for example, were terms that have been rightly chased out from our everyday vocabulary. One label that I thought, even as a child, was cruel was 'illegitimate'. This was an official and oft-used description for a child who was not born to wedded parents. Dictionary definition: *not authorised by the law; not in accordance with accepted standards or rules.* Imagine being saddled with that for life! Plenty were. It could have been worse for the Tuttes – only a couple of decades earlier they may have found themselves incarcerated in one of the Epsom asylums.

The mother, father and daughter were all profoundly deaf and unable to speak, but their son John was not similarly afflicted. He was a bright boy with acute hearing and a highly developed vocabulary who was sent away to boarding school. I imagine social services had something to do with that and were striving to give him a better chance of personal development than he would have had he been permanently ensconced in the family home. I remember him telling us once that he slept next to his baby sister because if she awoke and cried, his parents would not hear and he alone was able to alert them. John spent much of his summer and Easter holidays in our house. He and my brother Laurence became good friends, and John flourished in our lively and knowledge-curious family unit.

Mum, to her eternal credit, learned sign language and was able to be a true friend to Mrs Tutte, especially. She came most days with letters from the council and social services for Mum to explain and advise on. Mrs Tutte was forever grateful, and they remained friends until Mrs Tutte died, half a century after they arrived on the estate. I would watch those two ladies in awe as they stood in the kitchen signing away furiously to one another and engaging each other's eyes so kindly. My mum had enough on her plate with between three and seven children at various times, so what she did was a great thing.

There was a programme at the time on the television called *Vision On*, fronted by Tony Hart, that was specifically aimed at the hearing-impaired. This was an early, commendable and non-politically correct effort by the BBC to cater for minorities and the socially disadvantaged. The programme became mainstream, and artist Tony Hart a kids' favourite.

The next-door-but-one neighbours travelling in the other direction were the Hayes family, and the mother, who we were encouraged to call Auntie Pauline, was Mum's other close friend on the estate. Pauline was glamorous with jet-black hair and carefully applied make-up. I thought she was very elegant and pretty. She was also good fun, and my memory is of her and Mum sitting at the kitchen table, sharing an ashtray as they gently puffed on their Guards cigarettes plucked from a smart white-and-red packet. Pauline would invariably be throwing back her head laughing. She was married to Bill, who often smoked a pipe. He worked at the Decca record factory and got first dibs when a new record was pressed. Or so we were told. Their children were all older than me, but my older siblings became good friends with them.

Another neighbour – a girl a couple of years older than me – died when we were kids. I didn't know her very well; she didn't play out much, but that was probably because she was ill. It was very sad and the first time I heard the word cancer whispered. It was a rarer disease then and one that people didn't like to admit existed. Society believed that by not talking about it we could keep it at bay.

I knew Jean who lived across the road much better. She was a bubbly, self-assured, good-looking girl who, at fifteen, already had older male admirers turning up on the estate on scooters keen to be her suitor. My lasting memory is of her upside down with her legs against the wall as young girls were inclined to do then. Her younger brother played football with us on the green most days. Poor Jean cycled to the top shops one day up the Chessington Road. On the way back somehow she collided with a lorry and was killed. It was awful. Everyone felt terrible about her life cut so short and for her devastated family. On the estate then it was the practice for somebody to call door to door and collect for a wreath for the bereaved family, and when the funeral cortège arrived people stood outside their houses. Men removed their hats, the women put down their shopping, the kids got off their bikes. It was a respectful community.

A boy from around the block died in our school playground. He was accidentally struck by a bat during a game of cricket. The poor kid was four or five years ahead of me and I was not yet at the school, but the shadow of the tragic event hung around even in my time. A couple of residents at least took their own lives, and later on a man was shot dead in his home by a family member. Premature death was something we learned about quite young.

Warmth was not something we took for granted. Our heating came principally from paraffin heaters and electric fires. Many neighbours still had coal fires. Dad would walk up to the shops and fill his tin from a vending machine. The paraffin heaters were placed strategically around the house to generate maximum heat, and from a very early age we kids were taught not to touch them. That did not stop me curling up very close to hog the warmth and watch the blue flame flicker behind the tiny central window. Only in the sitting-room was there an electric fire. This was premium heat. It was used only in deep winter because of the expense. If it was severely cold, as in 1962, we even put both bars on. The red bars glowing seemed to envelop our hearts as we kids sat in front of it, protected by a fire guard, our souls bathing in the warmth and our minds soothed by the genial television.

Upstairs there were no such luxuries. No hanging around in winter. You jumped into your beds and nestled deep down below layers of coarse blankets and flower-design bedspreads. If it was seriously chilly Mum would give us all a hot-water bottle. I liked to use it as a pillow and seeing how long my cheek could withstand the heat. In the morning there were often icicles and condensation on the inside of the windows. We kept our socks on in bed. Slippers were a necessity to avoid the cold lino and tiled floors on the way to the bathroom. In that unforgettable cold winter of 1962 all the blankets had been used, and we laid our duffel coats on top of our beds for extra warmth. In the morning it was often so cold that we would dress under the covers from the clothes mum had laid out on the end of the bed.

Baths were not daily. Sunday was a bath night and, later, Tuesday and Thursday. Often my dad ran the baths, testing the temperature with his elbow. Me, Sally and Laurence bathed together when very young. The rest of the week we washed at the sink with a flannel, standing on a stool. There was a grown-up obsession in those days about washing behind one's ears and under the arms. I cannot say I ever saw kids with a significant accumulation of dirt behind their ears – even the poorest ones – so I don't know what all that was about. We boys all wore vests. I rarely see them now. Dads would work on their cars or motorbikes outside in their more macho string vests, wiping oily hands on the Trend-washed white cotton as they delved under the bonnet deep into the steel jungle of a car engine.

Mum and Dad did not have a bank account; neither, I suspect, did hardly anybody else on the estate. Dad would bring his wages home at the end of the week and the cash was divided up across a set of carefully labelled St Julien tobacco tins kept in the middle kitchen drawer. A pound note was folded up and placed into the tin marked 'Food', half a crown went into the tin marked 'Electricity', a florin into 'Television rental', a shilling into 'Birthdays' and so on. Is now the time to confess to opening those tins and stealing the odd florin?

Dad did other part-time work to supplement his West Park Hospital income. He was a gardener at the weekends for a couple of old widows who lived locally, one or two evenings a week he taught English to students and newcomers from overseas working in the mental homes and as late as 1971 he was the Census man. Money was not too tight to mention. I knew it was a constant worry and pressure for my parents in my early childhood.

When I was about six Dad went away to Cambridge for a whole week. He revealed he went on a course to train to be a spy. It was the height of the Cold War, and MI6 were recruiting openly. Dad applied, and maybe on account of his languages was invited to attend the course. He failed, or at least he said he did, and when pressed on this episode when we were teenagers claimed he had signed the Official Secrets Act and could reveal no more. It was a curious interlude which my mum could never throw any light on. A tea towel with pictures of Cambridge tourist scenes that Dad brought back hung about the house for many years after. Who knows what that really was all about?

The milkman arrived early in the morning. The stop-start electric-motor music of his float was as familiar a sound to me as the dawn chorus of the local house sparrows, starlings and blackbirds. He wore a white coat and black peaked cap, and his leather money bag was slung over his shoulder. On the passenger seat lay his book with its sturdy leather cover and stuffed with notes and scraps of paper, like a bloated Filofax, which he thumbed and flopped open to record who had paid up and, often, who hadn't. Par for the course, all the milkmen I remember whistled. When I was a bit older I helped our milkman for a very brief period. He was a young man called Vic. He paid more than I got for a paper round, but it was hard work running up and down garden paths, bending down picking up empties, deftly carrying ten or more bottles at a time, making full use of each digit. I had never seen so much money as went into the money bag. Thick wads of green pound notes and brown ten bobs as well as a treasure trove of change. Not understanding how dairies worked I assumed then that all this money was Vic's. To me he was a millionaire on wheels.

Families only bought the amount of milk they thought they needed for each day. That is why it was a common occurrence to ask a neighbour for the loan of a pint or half a pint when demand had exceeded supply. The reason housewives only bought the limited amount was that it didn't keep, especially in summer, because most of us did not yet own a refrigerator. I was in the habit of stepping into the larder (others called it the pantry), closing the door behind me and swigging the milk from the bottle. I did this once when it was curdled. It made me retch, and I have never drunk milk neat since.

The larder was deep and dark and somehow the coldest part of the house. You could feel the drop in temperature as soon as you opened the door. Here the cereal packets were neatly lined up – Corn Flakes, Rice Krispies, Frosties, Weetabix, Sugar Puffs and Shredded Wheat; the jars – Marmite, Robertson's marmalade and jam, chocolate spread, Gale's honey and peanut butter; the bread – Sunblest and Mother's Pride; the squashes

– Tree Top Orange, Quosh Lemon and Ribena; the biscuits – bourbon, iced coloured biscuits, Garibaldi, Jammie Dodgers and custard creams. Sometimes, digestives. Lining the higher shelves were the tins – Ovaltine, John West salmon, Farrow's peas, Smedley's, powdered milk, Bird's Custard and assorted products from Heinz.

The baker arrived in his van to deliver our bread. He probably came thrice weekly, unlike the milkman. Sometimes Mum would buy crusty rolls, which to us were the height of luxury, a real treat and change from the normal diet. I remember the first time Mum came home with finger rolls – we all thought we were heading towards the aristocracy. Dad would often toast bread for us, cutting the slices into shapes like castles or cars. The toast was cooked on a tray with a handle on top of the oven and it was somebody's job to 'watch it' and turn it over at the appropriate time to get both sides done. Such effort. When the pop-up toaster arrived we all lost something. I'm not sure what, but we lost it.

The coal flat-bed truck would arrive laden with sacks of the black stuff, and with plenty of banter the coalmen would alight from the cab humping the sacks of coal on to their backs and running their load up the garden paths and into the back gates and bunkers of their customers. They were quite a sight the coalmen. Many wore black berets and leather sleeveless jerkins showing off their rippling muscles. With their coal-brushed faces they resembled the French Resistance from the Second World War. They could also have been a dance troupe from a Hollywood musical with their almost synchronised whistling and athleticism. I studied them in awe.

Peter Kay tells, arguably, the best council-estate joke. He said when he was a kid his mum and dad told him that if the ice cream man was playing his tunes that meant he had run out of ice cream. Peter's crack will resonate with anyone who lived on an estate during the second half of the 20th century. In the summer the ice cream vans came every day, sometimes twice or more. Our parents could not afford for us to have ice creams every day, especially if there were five or more kids. It was out of the question. We were lucky to be treated once a week. The rest of the time we begged. The smallest and cheekiest one (often me) would be chosen to approach the van's serving hatch, put my little hands on the counter, my face just visible, and plead, 'Any broken wafers, mister?'

Mister was Peach Bar, or Peachey as we called him, who was an avuncular, balding Italian man with a round face and beaming smile who would then pass out a clear plastic bag of broken wafers originally intended for ice cream bricks, and we scuttled off to the green and shared them out. I suspect he may have broken the wafers up himself in preparation. We were an investment who one day not too far in the future would have a paper round and pocket money to spend.

His ice cream was rudimentary – a hardish scoop lumped into a cornet and dipped in hundreds and thousands or with a squirt of raspberry sauce. If you had more money, you'd get half a flake poked in, and it was called, exotically, a 99. Lollies were cheaper and lasted longer, so more sensible children opted for these. I remember Zoom, Fab, Mivvi, Rockets and the ones that changed colour as you sucked them also leaving colours on your tongue. Sometimes, normally on a Sunday, Mum would come out and buy a block of ice cream off Peachy for our puddings. It would be a luxurious, three-colour confection – vanilla, pink and chocolate. Where did she keep it? We had no refrigerator. We must have eaten it there and then.

There was boy a year older than me called Mick. He lived down the other end of the estate, and Peachy would park outside the Bromleys' house, which he judged was the epicentre. Mick must have heard the bells as Peachy entered the estate and hopped on his bike. Each day he rode up Marsh Avenue with his cow-horn handlebars and playing cards pegged to his wheel spokes for extra noise. The thing was he rode no handed, his hands stuffed into his jacket pockets not gripping the handlebars and managed to sweep up to the serving window without having to steady himself. He could order his 99 with raspberry sauce and crushed nuts and return down to his house, cornet in one hand and the other in his jacket pocket. I tried to emulate Mick in private but never could and still cannot. I mastered riding in a straight line no-handed eventually, but turning corners and picking up speed was a bridge too far.

Peachy was not the only ice cream man. The trade was fiercely competitive. At various times we had Tonibell, Mister Softee and Mr Whippy, but none built the same relationship with us as did Peachy. Perhaps the broken wafers engendered a deep loyalty. However, when Giovanni came on the scene those loyalties were sorely tested.

Giovanni had a sleeker and newer van than Peachy. He played different, more sophisticated tunes, like 'Greensleeves'. But, above all, he served the most delicious soft, creamy ice cream. It was exquisite, like nothing we had ever tasted. It knocked Peachy's lumpy fare into a tin hat. Giovanni gave bigger portions too at the same price. It was a fight for market share. Ice cream wars. Even then I would look over and see Peachy parked up, peering through his hatch as queues formed across the road at Giovanni's van, and felt for him. Peachy was on the way out. Then one day there was no Giovanni, and Peachy was back smiling and laughing dishing out the cones and the lollies.

'What happened to Giovanni, Peachy?'

'We won't be seeing him round here any more,' replied an emboldened Peach Bar. I am not suggesting that anything improper happened, that Giovanni's body and van will be found one day in the foundations of Bishopsmead School, which was being constructed at the time, but I like to fantasise that Peachy had some Mafiosi connections back home and a word was had, such was my feverish imagination.

Besides the milkman, ice cream man and the coalman, various other tradesmen and workers came on to the estate. The rag-and-bone man with his trusty old horse was good value. He jolted his old nag along ringing his bell and calling out something unintelligible. We kids ran out to feed carrots to the horse. Even if we had no rags or bones for the old boy, he was getting his horse nourished for free.

The besuited rent man knocked monthly to collect the cash, which he put into a leather bag slung across his shoulder. A neighbour knocked for money for the clothes we had purchased from the mail-order catalogue business she managed. New catalogue arrivals – Burlington's, Kay's and Grattan – caused great excitement as we rushed to see what new toys (and later clothes) were on offer to buy on the never-never. Talking of the never-never there was the man and his daughter from the Cox Lane estate who knocked in the evenings selling the Vernons pools coupons. We knew we were never, never going to win a fortune but still 'played'.

Door-to-door salesmen (never women) were commonplace. They flogged anything from vacuum-cleaner bags to encyclopaedias. Wanted to sharpen our knives and garden tools. Derby week offered up Gypsy women selling heather. Jehovah's Witnesses were regular, persistent and tiresome callers. Sometimes when we were alone Laurence was too polite to shut the door on them, and I would creep up unseen and kick the door shut mid-conversation to my brother's horror.

People trying to convert us or sell religion was a common theme when I was a child. One team, looking back on it, struck me as curious. They came into the estate on a Sunday in three or four cars and asked us as we played if we would like to attend Sunday school. We ignored them at first as we had been told not to talk to strangers and especially never get into anybody's car. But when these men and women said there would be food there, attitudes changed. What sort of food? Cakes, biscuits and sandwiches. We went inside and asked our parents, and after a cursory brief conversation with these 'Sunday-school teachers' we jumped in the cars off to Ewell Village and a place called Staneway Chapel. It was all completely innocent, and I can only guess they were trying to show us ragamuffins *the way*. I would never say we went hungry in my house, but there was no grazing, no fridge to raid, no eating between meals and we could always do with more. We probably consumed far fewer calories than children do today, but we knew no different. The offer of free food was a compelling one.

So, at Staneway we were obliged to listen to a Bible reading, sing a hymn or two and invariably endure a talk from a missionary. (There were missionaries everywhere then – in our schools, on the television, on the radio. Can't find one for love or money today.) And then we piled into the back room and stuffed fruit cake and iced buns into our mouths. We got as much in as we could in case others ate it all. I can remember the shocked faces among the teachers and missionaries as we struggled to reply to their gentle questioning, our mouths being so full. They were worried we might choke. The next team of people who came on to our estate to convert us some years later were workers not preachers, and they were from the Gas Board bearing the gift of natural gas.

The paranoia about getting in cars had been heightened by the Moors Murders case in 1966. Myra Hindley and Ian Brady were on the TV nightly, and although I understood they had murdered children, the full depth of the wicked torture and sexual motive had been successfully kept from me. Parents across the land were horrified that as a couple they lured these poor children into a car and took them off to their terrible fate. For the first time my generation had to get our heads around the fact there were adults out there, strangers too, who wished to do us harm. I remember being scared by that realisation.

'Do not get into anybody's car, you understand? Not even if you know them,' pleaded my mum, gripping my little forearm and looking into my eyes to get her message across.

Always one to challenge parental logic, I asked, 'Even if I know them?'

'Yes, even if you know them.'

'What about if it's Uncle George?' I countered.

'Especially if it's Uncle George,' Dad shouted from the kitchen.

Later a child herself murdered two toddlers up north. Her name was Mary Bell, and her cherubic features and fringe were a constant on our TV screens for a period. I can remember the sheer shock and horror that a young child, and a girl at that, would gratuitously murder two little boys of around three years old. These high-profile murders affected my generation, I believe. To me they certainly introduced the cruelty humans were capable of and the dangers out there and put some pretty hefty dents in my childhood innocence. Years later I watched the same impact that the Madeline McCann and Jamie Bulger cases had on my young children.

The intrusion of bad things into our idyllic childhoods continued in that same year of 1966 when we watched on television the Aberfan disaster unfold. I was off school. Pretending to be sick, I guess. I was in the lounge watching TV, and Mum would have been dusting or polishing, gliding quietly from room to room. Reports came in of a tip sliding down a mountain in a Welsh mining village and smothering and suffocating a school. It took a while for everyone to take in the enormity of what had happened and that more than a hundred children and their teachers had perished. The register was being taken as the slide hit. We were glued to the screen and to the unbearable pain etched on the faces of families who had gathered around the little school hoping their little boy or girl would be saved. Adults were scrambling in the mud, digging furiously with their hands. When I looked behind me Mum was sitting there sobbing into her handkerchief. She pulled me towards her and hugged me hard. I was the same age as many of the children who had just had their young lives tragically and brutally cut short.

These sad events were few and far between, and the news was largely boring and frivolous, even happy. Goldie the eagle that escaped from

London Zoo captivated the nation for several days around this time. News bulletins kept us posted on all the poodles he did not eat until he was recaptured. Pickles, the dog who found the Jules Rimet Trophy, became a national hero, and Guy the Gorilla's amorous adventures a national bus-queue talking-point. It was predominantly a time of innocence.

Frank West, the greengrocer, personified that generally upbeat mood. He visited the estate weekly in his yellow van that opened at the sides and when it did a flash of colourful fruit and veg was revealed. He sang, whistled and danced in and out of the houses, engaging the ladies while his two daughters rushed to and fro laden with cauliflowers, bananas and carrots. I can remember him tap dancing in our kitchen and rolling his leather trilby down his arm and catching it. He was a good-looking, tall man who demanded attention. He loved a chinwag, a joke and a yarn, and we kids looked forward to his visits. His wife was a small, demure lady who seemed to shrink in her husband's shadow. Besides the two industrious daughters – Trudy and Tracey – there was also a quiet young man who formed part of the team. That young man told me nearly half a century later he remembers me sitting on the garden wall but purposely left the delivery into my house to others. I knew he was speaking the truth because he described a cowboy outfit I was wedded to and wore long after I should have grown out of it. He said he never spoke to me. He did not want to rock any boats or cause a fuss.

8
BLACKBIRD

Mum and Dad's shared love of books and appetite for knowledge was passed on to us children from a very early age. Long before, as five-year-olds, we were introduced to the school curriculum and the *Janet And John* series. Dad often sunk us into his lap and read from *Look And Learn* and *Treasure*. These two magazines were very different from the comics we devoured. Sally and Laurence were fixated on *Look and Learn*, eager to absorb more knowledge presented in glorious colour while I, being that bit younger, lingered on the lighter, more cartoony *Treasure* although later I too would be soaking up the back copies of *Look And Learn*, now collated in red-and-gold plastic volumes for posterity.

However, almost straight after I learned to read I had become addicted to comics. The funniest thing about them for me was that they were not very funny. I never laughed while reading one and I never saw anyone else clutching their sides either. But this did not detract from my enjoyment of them. They were a gateway into a special world, a world where adults did *not* rule and, in fact, were lampooned, humiliated and browbeaten. We were not alert to it then, but *The Dandy* and its slightly younger stable mate *The Beano* were also heavily into domestic violence and highly xenophobic, racist, sexist, fattist and practically everything else —ic and —ist to boot. Delicious!

No wonder we are now a confused and uncertain population. Generations of boys and girls were encouraged to laugh and poke fun at obese people (Greedy Pigg, Hungry Horace, Fatty from 'The Bash Street Kids'), special-needs children (Smiffy from 'The Bash Street Kids' and Thick Head from 'Big Head And Thick Head'), child-beaters (Mr Minx, Minnie's dad; Mr Dodger, Roger the's father; and, very memorably, Mr Menace, father of Dennis the) all handy with a slipper. Boys who aspired to achieve academically (Walter, hated foe of Dennis the Menace) were ridiculed. There were also deformed boys (Plug from 'The Bash Street Kids'), robbing Arabs ('Ali Ha And The 40 Thieves'), the dodgy aristocracy (Lord Snooty), Indians (Little Plum) and people of colour (Sparky), generally all there to laugh at.

Black people were often depicted as savages, standing next to smoking cooking pots where they were waiting to immerse their next white-human meal. Invariably they had bones piercing their noses. These comics helped form our view of the world and were ably assisted by television, teachers, older children and adults. It always surprises me that societal, political and so-called thought leaders were themselves surprised at the resistance encountered when they endeavoured to move the British masses on to a more inclusive and 'tolerant' plain. What could anyone expect? Intolerance is a lazy word currently used as a catch-all for that mindset, but it is not true. The British tolerated difference, we just didn't think too much about it.

Currently there is a movement to recognise and erase 'white privilege' and 'systemic racism', and working-class white males of mature years are routinely fingered as the biggest offenders. The notion that the working classes of the 20th and 21st centuries had any real input into the system and values they grew up under and enjoyed much privilege is laughable. Those ideas, attitudes and systems were evolved and put in place by the middle- and upper-class establishment, the very class that wag those manicured accusing fingers today.

Middle-class boys were more likely to be the readers of such comics as *The Hotspur, The Victor* and *Valiant*, with patriotic heroes such as Captain Hurricane, who was known to single-handedly bash up a platoon of 'Nips'. One cover of *Valiant* I remember had Captain Hurricane holding a terrified German solider overhead about to launch him and a bubble coming out of his mouth saying, 'Off you go, Fritz', or some such thing. These three comics were grounded in the Second World War and Britain's military superiority. There was also *Eagle*, featuring space hero Dan Dare. The only place I ever saw *Eagle* was in the dentist's waiting-room (alongside *The Illustrated London News* and *Country Life*), but I never met a single boy that took it. Perhaps by my time *Eagle* had had its day. All of the aforementioned comics were encouraged to celebrate Britain's military history, her empire and her innate greatness and goodness. These readers too were expected to reject and denounce all patriotic and jingoistic emotions and beliefs in middle and later life without question. My mum, who was only twenty-five years ahead of me, recalls that at her school they had a day off every 24 May to celebrate Empire Day. If that was even suggested now there would be uproar. How quickly and furiously the world turns.

I can remember the excited anticipation I felt when *The Dandy* was pushed through our letterbox every Tuesday, tucked inside the *Daily Mail* or *The Times* and alongside my sister's *Bunty* and my brother's *Valiant*. I scanned it eagerly before I went to school and then again in a more leisurely way when I came home. Finally, I would file it away on my chronological pile under the bed in my room.

The running order of *The Dandy* pages stays with me: Korky the Cat, Desperate Dan, Greedy Pigg, Brassneck, Black Bob (don't panic, it was about a sheepdog), Corporal Clot, Winker Watson, My Hometown, Big Head And Thick Head. I briefly switched to a new comic called *Buster* which I thought was even more irreverent, especially when they gave away a gift called Bang! or Thunder Bang! with its first issue. It was a piece of card that if you flicked it hard it let out a disproportionate clap, like a firework exploding. It was simple but ingenious, unashamedly intended for creeping up on elderly people or those with heart conditions and scaring them out of their skins and inducing heart attacks. *Buster*'s early promise was not sustained, and I felt like I'd made a silly mistake, like abandoning the Beatles for the Troggs. I was soon back with *The Dandy*.

The casual *Tom And Jerry* violence was delightful. Korky squashing mice with a hammer, parents being soaked and hit by metal buckets perched on top of doors and with throbbing bumps leaping out of their foreheads, teachers sitting on fireworks or being blown up in chemistry labs. The masters (always masters – no mistresses) had a particularly torrid time. They all wore mortar boards (which perhaps says more about the background of the storywriters than the readers) and wielded canes but were invariably outwitted by the pupils. This was the key to the comics' success. The 1960s and early 1970s was still an age of deference towards adults from children. Generally kids were seen and not heard. No answering back. No talking in class. Bedtime. Tea time. Be in by dark. Switch the light off. *The Dandy* and the others took you out of all that into a rebellious, impudent and mad world that dissipated the stiffness, the order and the regimen of a child's 1960s existence.

Unsubtle changes made to the characters in more recent years sounded the death knell for comics as the publishers bowed to the rise of political correctness and associated virtue signalling. The comics are no longer with us. Not in paper form, at least. No longer would children be hit with slippers and canes; Dennis the Menace's dog Gnasher was domesticated against a backdrop of the Dangerous Dogs Act. No more cow pie for Desperate Dan as he became a vegetarian. Probably a vegan by now. Many characters were dropped altogether. Minnie the Minx was accused of stereotyping lesbians in her beret and short trousers, Keyhole Kate of voyeurism, the kids in Bash Street of not being diverse enough. Dennis the Menace himself had a makeover to soften his features and apparently make him more palatable to the sensibilities of 21st-century young people. Once this transformation took place comics lost their *raison d'être*. Their point. It was over.

For me it was over by 1968. I was in my newsagent's waiting to fill my bag with newspapers for my paper round. Mr Parker says, have you seen this new mag? It was the first edition of *Goal!* with a luxurious colour picture of George Best smiling sweetly on the cover and a promise of a voyeuristic peep at Bobby Charlton's diary inside. It was weekly and cheaper than *Charles Buchan's Football Monthly*, the only competing title on the market at the time. I treasured it and caressed it. Digested every word. Cut the glossy colour pictures out and Sellotaped them to my bedroom wall. Comics were never same after that day.

There was a piece of land close to our house we all called 'over the back'. Technically it wasn't at the back of us – more to the side – but it was at the back of the houses on Marsh Avenue, so my guess would be that someone from that road first coined the name and everybody else used it. The 'back' was a wild, untended, untamed parcel of land that bordered Longmead Road, Hollymoor Lane, Baker's Field, Longmead School, the St Ebba's Bridle Path and the so-called 'new estate' of Harvester Road and beyond. A tree-lined path snaked its way across the middle, and the rest was given over to long grass and scrubland with no particularly pretty features. It was mainly used by the estate children and the odd dog walker (some very odd indeed), yet it was a haven of unexpected wildlife pleasures and treats. Here we learned that dock leaves were the natural antidote to stings from nettles and were also a perfect substitute for toilet paper should you be caught short. We were normally having so much fun it would be unthinkable to run home to go to the toilet.

Before Longmead School was built the area had been a sewage farm, and an old farmhouse stood in the middle. I have only very vague memories of this. I am still not quite sure how a sewage farm works. What exactly is farmed and how? Whatever, wildlife galore was attracted to these aged repositories of local excrement, and, despite the encroaching urbanisation, this offcut of rural Epsom was an oasis of nature that doggedly clung on long after it should have done. Pheasants abounded, croaking all over and scaring us as we scared them when unknowing Tuf shoes came crashing down on their nests of eggs in the summer. In the early days we spotted grey partridges too. Kestrels and sparrowhawks nested in the tall trees by Baker's Field, and on the spot where Ajit's shop now stands skylarks laid their eggs on the ground and would spiral upwards when you came near and land further away trying to trick you away from their nests. The range of birds was extraordinary. In addition to the expected roll call of garden and urban species, I marked down in my pocket-sized *The Observer's Book Of British Birds* sightings of yellowhammers, reed buntings, linnets, tawny, little and barn owls, coal tits, lapwings, nuthatches, tree creepers and warblers all.

Frederick Warne & Co., who published *The Observer's Book Of British Birds*, also helpfully gifted us *The Observer's Book Of British Birds' Eggs*, making the volumes sufficiently slim so that they could be taken on egg-thieving expeditions and up tall trees. Many of the boys collected eggs; it had recently been made illegal, but a rural pastime passed down the generations was not easily erased. We went to extraordinary lengths to improve our collections and outdo each other. My friend Paul and I found a great tit's nest deep in a hole in a tree over the back and we could not fit our hands in to remove an egg, so I nipped home to fetch the long spoon my dad kept specifically to scrape out the coffee from the large jar of Maxwell House. With a little bit of bending I managed to insert it in the hole and scoop out an egg. I am sure I replaced the spoon in the kitchen drawer without straightening or washing it. Another time, in an underhand effort to improve my standing among the egg-collecting fraternity, I once went to Epsom to purchase gulls' eggs from a poultry shop opposite the Magpie pub.

One time Paul discovered a bullfinch's nest in a hedge in the alley next to Ewell Castle School with the mother sitting defiantly on it. Her breast swelled out in alarm while a red-breasted male flitted and tweeted urgently nearby. Paul gently lifted the mother off and I took an egg. Her bravery completely humbled us. Paul said he could feel her little heart pumping as she sat in his hand refusing to desert her young. I think that little episode was a big step towards us packing the 'hobby' in.

Blowing an egg was an art. When you came home with your haul you went into the garden and pierced the egg each end with a needle from the sewing box. Somehow you delicately held the egg between forefinger and thumb without crushing it and blew the yolk and white on to the floor. Sometimes the egg was addled, which meant the embryo was formed, and you chucked it away as it would soon rot and smell. Frequently, especially with tiny eggs like those of the wren or the blue tit, they disintegrated easily. The surviving eggs were added to the collection. The more serious among us had display cabinets made by their dads and were carefully labelled. I, and most others, had them rolling around in hay in light-blue shoeboxes and stuffed under the bed next to the piles of *The Dandy* and *The Beano*.

We did not really consider the ethical side of what we were doing. There was an unwritten rule that you never took the last egg in a nest. In fact, you wrestled with the guilt of not taking one and leaving just one because there was a belief that a mother deserts if only one egg was left. However, if an egg was sufficiently rare I think we overlooked the rules. One such case was a yellow wagtail. It was a much more uncommon species then than the pied or grey wagtails. Paul and I spotted a pair nesting in a small hole next to a decorative balcony on the wall behind the Horse Pond in the centre of Ewell Village. Paul waded out as the cars passed on Spring Street. He carefully pushed his fingers into the hole after waiting for the mother to fly off in search of food.

'There's only two,' he shouted over to me. I was keeping watch.

'Take one,' I hissed, decisively.

In the churchyard in Ewell stood an ancient ivy-entwined tower. It was all that remained of the original St Mary's Church and was a good 600 years old. The story was that peregrine falcons nested at the top. I probably made that up. That was enough to encourage myself and others to scale it, though. It was highly dangerous and surrounded by iron railings, but it was secluded and shielded by trees, and we were able to climb the fence and then enter by a glassless side window. A stone staircase worn down by many thousands of ascents over the centuries wound up the side of the tower. At intervals were wooden floors eaten away by rot, and the pigeons quite happily laid their eggs on the surfaces. Some boys ventured out on to the rotten floors to pick up an egg. Madness. At the top was a creaking old weathervane and some panoramic views; Tolworth Tower could be seen clearly in the distance in one direction and Epsom Grandstand in the other. What fascinated me were the carvings in the flint and brick. Boys' names from as far back as two centuries earlier. I would love to see them again now and look them up online. They would most likely have been boys from our school. If our parents had known we were up the top of a prohibited tower that had been closed for safety reasons some 150 years earlier, they would have had seizures.

My fascination with birds moved on from eggs to the birds themselves. I would occasionally find fledgling blackbirds and thrushes and bring them home, convincing myself I was rescuing them from feline predators. They were rarely still alive in the morning. The boy across the road, Colin Holder, had a pet jackdaw. I was very jealous. The bird would perch on his head and shoulder, and I swear it talked. I have since asked friends who remember Colin and the jackdaw, and they are split on this; some remember it talking, others say not. It was not uncommon for boys to keep wild birds in those days. Bill had a house sparrow that seemed perfectly happy in a budgie cage for several years.

One day I came across some boys throwing stones at an injured carrion crow on the way home from school. Seizing my chance, I picked up the bird and took it home. It was enormous with a fearsome-looking beak. Mum was dubious about keeping it and said, 'Put it in the shed until your father gets home.' Dad liked the bird at first. And it grew on Mum. It used to swagger around the back garden, coming up and tapping on the kitchen door when it required food. Which was often. It would sit on the wall and watch us play football on the green and even follow me down the road, hopping along behind me. The highlight was placing it on the cow-horn handlebars of my bike as I proudly cruised the local roads – a ten-year-old Hell's Angel with an evil crow in tow. In my head I thought I had it for months, but the reality was probably a few weeks. The RSPCA turned up one day. Said there had been a complaint about the crow attacking a local cat and took my great feathered friend away, unceremoniously bundling him into a sack. I spent the next few months plotting revenge on the various cat-owning neighbours I believed may have made that call. Now I wonder if it was my parents. They had been saying for a while that I could not keep it for ever and saw me growing more and more attached. Dad's change of opinion had something to do with his shed. Every surface was encrusted in white birdshit, and it stank to high heaven. Its favourite roost was on the Escalado horseracing-game box which normally came out at Christmas but was now white, sodden and unusable.

Later, in 1969, I went to see a film called *Kes* and read the original book, *A Kestrel For A Knave* by Barry Hines. Up to that point no film had had a bigger impact on me. It told the story of a poor northern boy from a broken family who didn't quite fit in at school and who found happiness and solace keeping and training a young bird of prey, Kes. Fate would have it that Paul found a young kestrel that had fallen from its nest in the big trees lining Baker's Field and had brought it to me knowing his parents would not let him keep it.

Despite the crow experience, my Kes became resident in the shed. To be fair, his excrement was localised and far less pungent than the crow's. It was soon time for our annual holiday to Hastings, so Mum said I had to let it go or find someone to look after it. I thought of Gary Sullivan. He lived down Belfield Road, and his dad kept wild birds in an aviary. He had linnets, goldfinches and bullfinches. Gary obliged. When we got home I raced around to his place on my bike to reunite with my dear falcon.

'Sorry, mate, he died,' Gary announced casually.

'You what?'

'Got up one morning, came down to the aviary, and there he was on the floor. Dead.'

I was shattered. I suspected Gary forgot to feed it or even went with his dad to Club Row where wild birds were still bought and sold and flogged it. After that film there was a thriving black market in young kestrels.

I remember a dead fox causing a stir. Dad took me over to see it. This would have been in the early 1960s, and a fox was a rare visitor from the real countryside. When we got there a crowd of parents and kids were standing around looking down at the freshly dead animal with its rusty red fur and bushy brush. I am pretty sure my dad had never seen one either. A decade later I remember similar excitement when as a commuter we passengers would regularly see a family of foxes playing and tumbling down the railway bank between Wimbledon and Clapham Junction. The sight prompted people to stand up to catch a glimpse of them from the window, such was the novelty. Yet another decade on, and they were everywhere. Nowadays they are more common in towns than wandering dogs and cats and as rare as hen's teeth in the shrinking countryside.

The real wildlife over the back, though, was supplied by the boys and girls themselves. A rope swing was the chief attraction because it traversed dangerously over a stinking, rancid swamp that one would fall into should you lose your grip or mistime your run or when the thick twine finally snapped from overuse. You were left covered in the most objectionable smelly black slime, a remnant from the sewage-farm days, and walked bow-legged and dripping back home for a change of clothes. Nevertheless, we were soon back queuing for our next jump into the danger zone.

The 'ropey', as we called it, became a social meeting place. Older boys and girls sat around smoking, flirting, laughing, playing and shouting. It was exciting, as boys and girls from the council houses on the other side (did they call it 'over the front'?) of the fields also turned up, and we cased one another out. Although the distance between our houses was less than half a mile we were entirely different tribes. If someone was flush with money, they were sent up the 'offy' to buy crisps, Maltesers and Top Deck shandy for all.

Sometimes the older boys took delight in setting the field ablaze. It was a tinder box in the summer, and a single Swan Vesta flicked into the undergrowth would have grown into a field fire by the time you had crossed the Longmead Road and were safely back indoors innocently watching *Dixon Of Dock Green*. I can remember viewing the crackling blazes from my landing window to a background of approaching fire-engine bells and worrying and fretting about those terrified skylarks and pheasants.

One older boy was notorious for it. They called him a firebug. I would watch him from my landing window run back to his house knowing that through the gap in the houses I would soon see the seductive glow of fire.

One day I took a box of Bryant & May matches out of the kitchen drawer and went to a far parcel of the back adjacent to the Bridle Path. I figured that a fire would not cross the path and would be contained. I walked around the dry grass until I was sure there were no dog walkers, flashers or other kids in sight. I struck the match and dropped it and walked away, my stomach somersaulting as my pace quickened. I could hear crackling but did not look back. I didn't hear any fire engines once back indoors, but the next day went back to the scene of the crime to see a black stain the size of a football pitch. I felt quite depressed, shocked and guilty at the thought of the wildlife I may have killed or, at best, caused to flee and desert nests. I never did it again nor had that strange, visceral urge.

9
WHEN WE WAS FAB

Life on the estate was a constant adventure. My boundaries had expanded, and I would go around to Tony's, Eddie's, Paul's and other people's houses and gardens and they to mine. Most of our homes were identical, and we felt comfortable with the geography of one another's living spaces.

We went through a phase of collecting cigarette packets. This was a public service compared to bird-nesting. Not only were we safely occupied but we were picking up litter – a 1960s obsession and the subject of countless notices and public-information films on the television. There was a popular but short-lived Keep Britain Tidy campaign that caught the public imagination.

Once you had collected all the common packs – Woodbine, Kensitas, Senior Service, Guards, Benson & Hedges, Player's, Capstan, Cadets, Weights, Gold Leaf et al. – it got harder, and the thrill was finding the rarities. I remember alighting on my first Everest packet down near the railway bridge. These were menthol flavoured and far less common than Consulate, the leading menthol brand whose slogan was 'cool as a mountain stream'. There was another menthol brand called Solent, depicting a boat sailing through the Needles on the packet.

One day Babe, who, although a few years older than me, was not much bigger, showed me his collection – it was phenomenal. I sat hypnotised in his bedroom, flattered that an older boy had time for me. He had a flop of brown hair that hung over one brow, which he intermittently righted by a flick of the head. I was soon copying his alluring twitch even though I sported the compulsory short back and sides. He showed me packets I had never seen or heard of: Chesterfield, Nelson, Salem. Exotic brands. Old brands, now long discontinued.

'You have to travel, mate, to get them.'

He took me down to Ewell West station, and I followed him on to a train. I am sure no tickets were purchased. The station was a quaint one. A rickety footbridge linked the up and down platforms, and there was a waiting-room with a gas fire and wooden table. A bit like Buggleskelly in the Will Hay film *Oh, Mr Porter!*, it was manned by the same three characters for what seemed like donkey's years: Vic, Taffy and Tom. Vic was a tall, angular man with swept-back black hair and a thin pencil moustache. A decade later Ron Mael from the band Sparks put me in mind of him. He was a lovely man who always had a smile, and when we were youths, having known us most of our lives, would overlook asking us for tickets he knew we didn't have. If nobody was around he would give you a wink and nod you through. Tom was a Captain Mainwaring lookalike and was the opposite to Vic, a stickler for the rules and payments for travel, but fundamentally a nice old boy. Finally, Taffy, who may have been Welsh, straddled the two. A quiet, thoughtful man. He would want to see your ticket, but if you just ran through the gate couldn't be arsed to give chase. There was a stationmaster who lived on site, but we never saw him, a bit like Captain Mainwaring's wife in *Dad's Army*.

That day with Babe I think we got off at Wimbledon where he took me to 'posh' streets, and sure enough I was picking up a different class of cigarette packet off the ground. It was not the first time I had been on a train, as we often went up on a Sunday to Clapham Junction to visit Grandma, but it was the first time I had been on a train without an adult. Babe may have been eleven or twelve, but I was no more than seven or eight. I didn't tell Mum and Dad because I'd have been in big trouble. We were meant to ask before leaving the estate, let alone going up the railway line. So I failed to mention it, and when Mum asked what I'd been up to I said I'd just been playing football. I crossed a line that day. Wilfully doing something I was not allowed to and lying about it afterwards. Getting away with it was great.

The Beatles were torching the globe. Such was their fame and worldwide adoration the excitement about them permeated down to me, only just six years old when 'She Loves You' had everyone Yeah, Yeah, Yeahing. There were Beatles haircuts, Beatles jackets, Beatles toy guitars and Beatles bubble gum. Christmas of 1963 was dominated by them. Laurence had 'I Want To Hold Your Hand' as a Christmas present, Sally had 'She Loves You' and the EP *Twist And Shout* with the boys pictured on the sleeve jumping on a wall was for sharing. I remember the tracks we played endlessly – 'A Taste Of Honey', 'There's A Place', 'Do You Want To Know A Secret'. The discs stacked up on the centre pin of the record player waiting for the stylus to knock them on to the revolving rubber turntable before the stylus lowered itself and joined the spinning disc at just the right point. The technology excited me, and I was as bewitched at watching the smooth mechanics as I was by the music.

The following summer Sally was joining a gang of older estate kids outside who were off to the Odeon in Epsom to see the film *A Hard Day's Night*. This six-year-old did not want to be left out, and Sally trying to shoo me inside was not working. Eventually Bobby Reed, who was even older than Sally, perhaps twelve or thirteen, went to my mum and asked if I could go with them, and she said yes. Bobby was what Mum called a sensible, responsible boy. Had Babe been making the same request the answer would have been different. It was not my first ever cinema visit; that had been *A Stitch In Time* with Norman Wisdom about a year before. Mum had taken Laurence and me, and we, like the whole audience, threw ourselves around with laughter at hapless Norman. I was itching to go again, and Mum and Dad took me to see *Mary Poppins*. I was enchanted with the whole experience.

A love for the Beatles was born that Christmas of 1963 and cemented over the next few years of explosive Beatlemania. It was like a national virus had taken hold, and it joyfully infected everyone, not just me and my family. The hangover from the war was finally lifting, food rationing had stopped, men had jobs and there was a bit more money around. I think it was quite a hopeful time as the world shifted from monochrome to colour. Clothing was becoming more adventurous; young people were asserting themselves. People spoke of the generation gap, but by and large society, at my end of it, struck me as being at ease with itself. I consumed everything the Beatles released. Film, TV, magazines and music. I was not able to buy records yet, but my parents got them for us. I remember watching the Beatles at Shea Stadium on television as well as *Two Of A Kind*, which starred Morecambe and Wise, and the *Pops And Lenny* show.

Talking of the generation gap, we had our very own clash of the generations play out on our estate. Jimmy Ansell was a boy about seven years older than me. Intoxicated and emboldened by the much-discussed teenage revolution, he decided to grow his hair long. Not Beatles just-over-the-collar long but Roger McGuinn of the Byrds over-the-shoulders long. His dad told him to get his hair cut – 'Getcha 'air cut' being one of the many much-mimicked catchphrases uttered by Alf Garnett to his son-in-law Mike in TV's *Till Death Us Do Part* – and Jim refused. The stand-off deepened to the point that Eddie, the old man, threw Jim out of the house. Jim got himself a tent and erected it over the back, living on handouts supplied by mates and the sympathetic parents of mates. Eddie was a stubborn old sod. A little man with furry eyebrows and unkempt hair giving me the impression of an angry owl, a pigeon chest thrust forward and an often truculent demeanour with a growling voice to go with it. It was an estate debating point as to who would give way first. Occasionally I'd see Jim wandering around, his face swollen from insect bites. Eventually they compromised. Jim cut his hair a bit and Eddie let him home but, to me, the brinkmanship seemed to go on for weeks.

I never thought I would need anything else musically beyond the Fab Four until one day I was basking in the sun in Eddie's front garden around the block. His two older sisters, Jenny and Jackie, were playing records in their bedroom with the windows flung wide open as Eddie, Tony and myself lay on the lawn in their front garden chewing blades of grass and blowing them between our thumbs to make farting noises. 'Well, I told you once and I told you twice / But you never listen to my advice ... Well this could be the last time / This could be the last time ...' – the thumping beat and Mick Jagger's sneering, contemptuous voice came blasting out the window; ultimatums dropping in my lap. Then 'Get Off Of My Cloud' followed. I went to the girls' bedroom and looked at the records, as you did in those days, moving the disc with the blue Decca centrepiece lovingly around in my hand careful not to get my fingerprints on the surface. I got the sisters to play the B-sides, one of which was 'Play With Fire'. 'The Last Time', 'Play With Fire', 'Get Off Of My Cloud': these were threats and warnings. The edginess compared to the safe and cuddly 'She Loves You', 'I Feel Fine', 'I Want To Hold Your Hand' was stark. The Stones were not interested in purchasing tickets to ride and they did not feel fine at all; instead, they had the right hump and wanted to boot you up the arse and clean off of their clouds.

From that day the Stones replaced the Beatles as number one in my pop-musical affections. I saw them on *Top Of The Pops* and *Ready Steady Go!* soon after, and Mick, Keith, Brian, Bill and Charlie yanked me in. I was attracted to their rebelliousness and the danger that seemed to lurk just below the surface. Suddenly, they made the Beatles look tame in their matching jackets, ties and mop tops.

I took to imitating Jagger whenever the chance presented itself. I could push my lips and bottom out and gyrate and shake my head in a way I thought captured my new hero. I shook imaginary maracas. The adults seemed to like it. I heard that the band's management worked out of Ewell Village, and I spent hours stalking the large house I was told said manager lived at. My source was Peter Camp from across the road, who was three years older than me. He also went to Glyn Grammar School, so it must have been true. My mum told me to stop hanging around down there and said the Rolling Stones would not be visiting Ewell Village. Not wanting to be seen to be on a lost cause, I lied to my mum and claimed I had seen them leave the house and followed them to Ewell West station where they boarded a train to London.

'All five of them?' she asked.

'Yes.'

'Did you speak to them?'

'I just said hello.'

'You'd think they'd have a chauffeur.'

By the age of ten I was a music nut, buying one or two trade magazines every week. I became a student of teenage culture and had not even reached thirteen myself. It is surprising how quickly a boy can migrate from *The Beano* to *Melody Maker*. One summer I am engrossed in 'The Bash Street Kids' and the next I am reading Chris Welch in-depth interviewing the likes of Donovan and the Yardbirds. *Melody Maker* carried the pop chart, but even I could see that the paper was almost begrudgingly covering the new artists, thinking or hoping that upstarts like the Monkees or the Tremeloes were a passing fad. It yearned to get back to covering authentic jazz musicians and obscure blues artists from the swamps of America.

I moved on to buying the *New Musical Express*, or the *NME* as it preferred to be known. This was more me. At least they admitted when the time came that groups like Slade and the Rubettes existed – even if they didn't like them very much. *NME* did not take itself so seriously (then), and it was packed with news about the English pop and rock scene. Yes, I knew the lingo and was well versed in scenes and grooves, man.

There was another quaint little paper called *Record Mirror*, which came out on a Thursday. I sometimes bought this as well, only because it carried some colour pictures and the others did not. Good for taping to the bedroom wall. It was an anomaly that this fast-moving, dynamic and lucrative music industry was for so long poorly served by a dinosaur music press. If you wanted decent coverage of the artists that the rest looked down their noses at you had to buy a girls' magazine, and the main ones were *Fab 208*, *Jackie* and *Rave*, all glossy colour issues packed with pictures of Peter Frampton, Stevie Marriott, Sandie Shaw and the like. The serious music press patronisingly called this audience segment 'teenybopper', and the music was often sneeringly dismissed as 'bubble gum', even though these artists probably provided three-quarters of the industry revenue.

Music was second only, arguably, to clothes in defining who and what you were. Walking home with a newly purchased *Highway 61 Revisited* or *The Seekers Sing Their Big Hits* album under your arm said as much about you as your clothes, hair or anything else. It got to a stage when schoolchildren who bought, for example, Lieutenant Pigeon's 'Mouldy Old Dough' (and there must have been plenty because it was number one for a few weeks) were forced to deny owning such a record.

It was at Epsom and Ewell football club, the scene of Truancygate, that I met my first pop stars in the flesh. We spent a good deal of time here watching football. The first team played at home one Saturday and the reserves the next. Epsom and Ewell played in blue and were planted in the lower regions of something called the Isthmian League. Or was it the Athenian? However, only when the Showbiz 11 turned up was there anyone on the pitch remotely famous. It was a common joke that the match programme issued by the club and the puff in the local newspaper would bear little resemblance to who actually turned up on the day among the 'stars from the world of show business' – the term 'celebrities' hadn't really been coined then. Jess Conrad always obliged, as billed, but nobody knew what he was famous for. Not even sure Jess did. The others had links to fame even more tenuous. Retired footballers who had played two senior games for Crystal Palace, someone who was briefly a Pirate (backing Johnny Kidd) and actors whose appearances in *Z-Cars* had passed us by. Once, however, Ronnie Corbett played and performed well. It was before his *Two Ronnies* period, but he was already well known on the television. I remember him climbing into the ramshackle stand to accept a trophy from the aviator Sheila Scott, looking quite incongruous and uncomfortable, elegantly dressed in a wide-brimmed hat, brooches and flowing silk scarves and sitting on a long bench plastered with lumps of ancient chewing gum like barnacles among the scruffy kids, empty fag packets and spilled Bovril.

I believe that it was at this match Tony and I met Ray and Dave Davies of the Kinks. They were flying high, arguably in the top five bands of the period along with the Beatles, the Stones, the Hollies and the Who. They were not playing for the Showbiz 11, having arrived late, although they were meant to have been. They stood in the clubhouse, drinking beer and signing autographs. Dave wore a silk scarf tied tightly around his neck. It was pre-'Lola' but post-'Sunny Afternoon'. I chatted to them about pop music, and they were mildly amused that a boy so young and so small was so knowledgeable about the 'scene'. I knew who was touring, who had a new album coming up and could name most of the top-thirty singles – the 'hit parade' as it was then known. Tony asked for a swig of their beer, which made them laugh, and they gave us a sip each looking around to make sure no other adults were watching. One of the brothers gave us a 'lug' of his fag when pressed. It was my first taste of beer, and I remember thinking how rank it tasted compared to R. White's lemonade or Tizer.

'Where's the scout hut?' asked Dave. He explained they couldn't get another drink because the licensing hours forbade it and that he had been told that beers were being made available for the showbiz stars at the scout hut.

'Just around the corner,' I said. 'We'll take you there.'

So, there we were, Tony and I, leading two Kinks down West Street to a hidden asbestos-riddled scout hut behind some old farm-labourers' cottages. We went inside with them until being told to leave. As we were shooed away Dave Davies pulled a half-crown from his hipsters and ruffled our hair as he folded my hand around it. When I got indoors and casually told Mum I had just been having a beer with the Kinks she gave me that look, the look she gave me when I had told her I had just seen the Rolling Stones in Ewell Village. Boys and wolves spring to mind.

'That's nice. Did they have their guitars with them?'

Around this time, in 1965 or 1966, I developed a short-lived but nevertheless intense obsession with James Bond. I pestered Dad to take me to the cinema to see *Thunderball* with Sean Connery. At seven years old I must have been one of the youngest members of the audience. I liked it so much that I begged Dad to stay put, and we watched it through a second time, including the supporting feature, which I remember vividly was a film starring Herman's Hermits called *Hold On!* The success of films featuring the Beatles and Cliff Richard had encouraged others to commit to celluloid. The Dave Clark Five had made *Catch Us If You Can*, but I never thought Herman was in that league. However, I lapped it up.

Part of the attraction of *Thunderball* was a bounty of beautiful women in bikinis lapping along in floodlit pools. I was beginning to become obsessed with them too but had not yet joined any dots. Somehow, I got to see *Arabesque* with the beautiful Sophia Loren. A scene with a pink towel captivated me. Her beauty gave me butterflies. That strange churning feeling had not yet descended below my waist, however. I think my dad may have taken me to see *Arabesque* also. Now I understand why and how he endured two helpings of *Thunderball*.

On the Chessington Road, in Burgess's toy shop window, there was a pyramid of boxed toys – a Corgi model of 007's Aston Martin – and on top, out of its box, the car was displayed in all its glory. The price was 9s 11d, and up to then I had never wanted something so bad. I would stand and stare and go home and dream about it. I pestered Mum and Dad, but they genuinely could not afford to buy it for me. Besides, as they often said, if they bought me one, they would have to buy the other five kids a gift of equal value. It was at such times that I got quite cross about not being an only child. I was told to wait until my birthday. I could not. I saved my pocket money, ran errands and searched the ground for coins. Eventually I walked into Burgess's and made the purchase. I was not disappointed. The car was sleek and had guns that shot out of the headlights, but the *pièce de résistance* was the ejector seat that on activation shot James or his companion out the open roof and halfway across the sitting-room. Mums across Britain were forever having to empty their Hoover bags to retrieve these figures when they were reported lost.

From the car I moved on to a James Bond gun, which came with a much-valued silencer – strange, as the gun made no noise. I can remember running around Epsom Common. I had the gun in my hand, and at the approach of an unsuspecting dog walker would emerge from behind a tree, crook my arm, position the gun on it and point it at them before scurrying off into the undergrowth. Today that would be enough to send the helicopter up and the child psychiatrists in.

I had probably finished with James Bond by the time of my birthday, never to revisit him again. I have not watched a Bond film since at the cinema or on TV. He was replaced in my affections and fantasies by Action Man. I cannot think of any other toy that swept the country so comprehensively up until then. Yes, there had been Meccano and Scalextric, but the phenomenon of Action Man was ... phenomenal. They were dolls for boys, but to ensure that there was no threat to developing masculinity these dolls were soldiers, complete with iron jaw and battle scar. It had to be crystal clear this was nothing like owning a Sindy, Tressy or Tiny Tears doll. The beauty of the Action Men was that they arrived in basic army-issue fatigues, and you could buy various uniforms and accessories to build a wardrobe. When you purchased those accoutrements you were awarded stars, and when you collected twenty-one stars you could then claim a free Action Man, which, naturally, needed dressing. Rinse and repeat. It was marketing brilliance.

My parents were again pushed to help me complete the wardrobe. I liked the German uniform best, so much smarter – with the high collar and a flash of red in the epaulettes – than the British one. Even the Russian uniform was better than ours. I succeeded in getting the money together to buy the deep-sea-diving outfit, which was the priciest kit out, and it shared my bath time for a good few weeks. Tony and I had this strange habit of taking our treasured toys over the back and placing them high up in trees and leaving them to fend for themselves overnight. We were excited to go over in the morning and find them still there. Where did we think they would go? They were dolls.

When my Action Man craze came to end, I decided to mark the end of an era dramatically. I reckon it was Guy Fawkes Night 1968. Dad had built the bonfire in the garden as usual, and we were working our way through boxes of Brock's and Standard fireworks. I remember the television advert now imploring us to 'Light Up The Sky With Standard Fireworks!' Mum was poking potatoes in the fire. I poked my first Action Man in too. Mum looked at me, horrified.

'What on earth are you doing?'

'I can't let him waste away. Left in a box in the loft or something. He has to die young.'

And I watched as the fire heated my cheeks and quickly melted my favourite ever toy. Mum stood to the side of me shaking her head.

Bonfire Night was a big event for kids. On the estate we would start building a massive bonfire in a field behind Gibraltar Crescent weeks before, and on the night a big crowd would assemble. No safety officers or adults in sight as we chucked bangers into the fire and aimed other fireworks at each other. Rockets were launched into the sky from steamy empty milk bottles. Bangers were sometimes poked through the letterboxes of people we did not like, but a more common use was to embed them in dog shit and blow the poo all over the show. In those days nobody picked up dog shit, so it could be argued we were performing a service in breaking up the waste matter.

Before 5 November we would milk as much money as we could from a ritual known as 'penny for the guy'. The idea was to make a life-size model of Guy Fawkes from old straw and clothes, pin a sign to it and wait. We became lazy and would not make the guy. Instead, as the smallest, I would wear a Guy Fawkes mask, old coat, dirty wellies and plonk myself into a wheelbarrow, legs and arms hanging out akimbo as Tony and others wheeled me down to Ewell West station. Already pennies were becoming devalued, and kind or inebriated commuters would bung us threepenny bits and tanners. Sceptical travellers would sometimes look closely at me and ask if I really was a guy, to which I would reply, 'Yes.'

Urban myths abounded, and one that did the rounds was that a boy such as me in London (always London) was posing as a guy and a man jokingly ran a garden fork through him thinking he really was made of straw. This worried me a little, and I used it as a negotiating point to claim a bigger share of the kitty as I was taking all the risk. This ploy was firmly rejected by my pals.

Mum did not approve of us guying. 'Isn't it a bit early for penny for the guy?'

'It's 10 October, Mum.'

'It's no better than begging.'

'What's wrong with begging? I need money.'

'Well, people might think we don't feed you.'

'I've got a mask on, Mum. They don't know who I am.'

At which point she gave up.

10
HOW DO YOU SLEEP?

St Mary's Church of England Boys' School – known variously as West Street School, Ewell Boys' School, Eggs, Bacon and Sausages or simply EBS – was directly next door to our infants' school. A wire-mesh fence separated the two playgrounds. It was a fence we would often approach, like infant David Attenboroughs, to watch the big boys in their natural habitat. They seemed so old and so BIG, charging around the playground chasing a ball. Sometimes we would see them fighting, rolling around the ground, punching each other. It seemed a different, rougher world, and I was very apprehensive about joining it.

First up, though, was a trip to Hodges, the department store in Ewell Village. 'Department store' was overegging it – the whole village could have fitted inside the likes of Swan and Edgar or Gamages – but the shop was long and *did* have two floors, albeit with a single step separating them. They did good business in uniforms for all the local schools. Money was always a restricting factor, and pullovers, shorts and shirts may have been passed down from my brother, but a new blazer and cap had to be invested in. That first day at West Street I arrived in a black, knee-length raincoat lashed around the waist with a belt, a black-and-red blazer and cap, short grey trousers secured with a snake belt, long socks and black lace-up, round-toed polished black shoes. I felt like a new soldier going on parade.

Laurence was already at the school, and I had met and knew some of the friends he had two years above, plus the bulk of the boys from my class next door had moved up with me, so the passage was not as traumatic as it might have been. I was disappointed to see, that inaugural day as we gathered in the playground, that many of the boys were not wearing the full uniform, and that included Tony and Eddie. Over the coming weeks I slowly but steadily migrated towards the casual clothes they wore, much to my mum's annoyance, having just broken into four tobacco tins to dress me.

That first day everybody was sussing each other out. I noted how, when asked where I came from and replied 'the Gibraltar estate', teachers registered a mild change in facial expression. I could not understand why. It was the best place to live.

The school was steeped in history. Its most famous old boy was the playwright John Osborne, although I didn't know that then. He was not celebrated in the school in any way, even though these were his peak professional years. Osborne was one of a group of emerging writers in the 1950s categorised as 'the Angry Young Men' and whose most famous work was the play *Look Back In Anger*. In his 1981 autobiography, *A Better Class of Person*, Osborne certainly does look back in anger at his time at Ewell Boys' School. He remembers the place as being in 'perpetual shade and holding out the promise of harshness and pain'. He recalls a culture of humiliation and bullying. The following extract, especially, stuck in my mind. Talking of his fellow pupils, Osborne observes:

> The boys in the village were a hostile bunch, probably the remainder of what was once Ewell. Their encampment was bounded by the new by-pass on one side and the growing collection of council houses in West Ewell on the other. The Gibraltar rec. was their reservation.

Later he suggests Gibraltar Rec was not safe to go to alone or at night, and this was nearly twenty years before my estate was built. There were barely any council houses in the entire borough during John Osborne's childhood, so I conclude the hostile presence he felt was largely in his head.

Just as I arrived at EBS it had celebrated its centenary, making it almost half a century older than the infants' school next door. The school was also built of red brick and stone with many pointy church-like features. It was fusty and chilly but proud of its great age, history and traditions. I could feel the ghosts of the village boys that had come before me in the classroom and corridors. The hall was where our assemblies were held and where we ate lunch and drank our free milk in the mornings, ice cold in winter and curdled in summer. Bill would drink the bottles of the absent boys. There was no waste. Here the headmaster, Mr Bell, welcomed us to the school.

He stood on the podium with a black cape over his grey suit, and I felt great trepidation as if I had been pitched into my very own *Tom Brown's Schooldays* production.

'You will enjoy your time here. This is a great school. Remember you are pupils of Ewell Boys' School now and you carry the good name of the school inside the building and out. If you abide by the few simple rules we have, you will find your time here rewarding. You will learn a great deal; you may excel at sports. We will make you into fine young gentlemen and good citizens. We will make you ready for senior school, wherever that may be. EBS brings the best out in its boys. That's what we *excel* at. However, should you decide to disobey the rules and be disruptive, you will not be tolerated, and you will be severely punished.'

Severely punished? The words struck fear into my heart. I had not experienced physical punishment at home or anywhere else. What could you possibly do to deserve *severe punishment*? I instinctively knew that Mr Bell didn't have a day in the apple orchard in mind. I decided not to be disruptive or break the rules. Regrettably, my friend Tony was not so easily deterred.

A lady with a melancholic disposition and grey hair styled like a man's introduced herself as our class teacher and led us seven- and eight-year-olds off to her little classroom. She was Miss Gentry, and to me she looked the wrong side of a hundred. Of course, she was probably only in her late fifties or early sixties. It was a fact that anybody over thirty dressed decades older in the early 1960s. If you were over fifty you were quite likely to be rocking in a bath chair and holding a trumpet to your ear. Miss Gentry rarely smiled, but over that year, despite her innate dourness, we all grew fond of her.

She was a vegetarian, a term I had never previously heard and would not have understood. Vegetarians in the mid-1960s were as rare as mermaids. She taught us nature study as well as being our form teacher, and although just stopping short of trying to convert us to vegetarianism, her love of animals provoked us to think about the unarguable case for not eating meat. However, we were not making the food-buying decisions and, besides, we were always hungry. Truth be told we would have eaten squirrels if we could have caught them.

At the back of the classroom was a haunting painting called *The Light Of The World*. It showed Jesus holding a lamp and approaching an old wooden door. Miss Gentry told us that the artist, William Holman Hunt, had lived in Ewell and the door was local. She showed us another of his paintings, which was of the old St Mary's Church. She told us that one of Hunt's contemporaries, John Millais, had painted his *Ophelia* at the River Hogsmill which flowed through Ewell. Miss Gentry turned our little village into a wondrous place of history, mystery and charm. Her nickname was Jennywren, and in acknowledgement of this there was a wren's nest on display at the back of the class.

Her lessons were a delight, full of information about the natural world, and for the most part we showed her the respect her gentle and fragile demeanour demanded. However, when a boy called Steven Fisher joined the form and was sat next to me, I saw another side of her. Steve had lank blond hair, had grown tallish quite early and was full of mischief. One day he placed a *Beezer* annual on the floor below our desk by his feet. He turned the pages with toes sticking out of open sandals and kept elbowing me to look down and read the comic strips with him. Miss Gentry rumbled our ruse and exploded. I hadn't seen an adult lose their temper before, and it was alarming. Her face went bright red, and she sprung over to us yanking Fisher from his seat by his forearm and whacking his bare legs with her open hand. I was even more alarmed when she did the same to me.

We were then told to stand in the two front corners of the room, facing the wall, for the rest of the lesson. It was the first time I had been struck by an adult. It didn't hurt, maybe stung a bit, but it was shocking to me that someone outside my family was permitted to smack me. Not that they did very often or at all, but the threat was there. Dad would curse at me – 'You flaming perisher!' – and lift his arm as if he was going to deliver a backhand, but he never did. This particular slap from an ageing schoolmistress was the next defining tug away from my mother's womb following being abandoned at the school gates that first time. Life is a series of such tugs until that final one when your mother leaves you for good.

The school was alert to its place in village life and its Christian values. We sang hymns every morning in assembly, and very soon after joining I could recite all the words without referring to the battered old red hymn book. Some remain embedded in my brain to this day:

> *Far round the world thy children sing their song*
> *From east and west their voices sweetly blend*

or this one because it resonated with my surname:

> *When a knight won his spurs in the stories of old*
> *He was gentle and brave and gallant and bold.*

'Onward Christian Soldiers' was a hymn that was enthusiastically rendered by all. It stirred visceral, patriotic feelings we didn't know we had or where they came from. We boys, at least, felt it was written for us. And I am sure it was. Preparing us for the war we would likely experience in our lifetime. Why not? Very few generations had escaped at least one up until now.

There were scores of these rousing, religious, patriotic songs. At the time I cannot say many of us took on board the messages from them or the Bible excerpts, parables and psalms that were thrust upon us daily. I do not think it made us God-worshipping, God-fearing or God-hating. It was just one of those strange obsessions adults seemed to bang on about – like not placing polythene bags over our heads or not drinking the gravy off our plates. We just went along with it to shut them up.

The old vicar from St Mary's Church in Ewell doddered in once a week in his flowing robe and with his remaining grey hair flung sideways – Ralph Coates style – across his otherwise bald head. His sermons were very boring, and we couldn't wait until they were over, but the teachers seemed to regard him with great reverence. I know now his name was Vincent Davies, and recently I stumbled on his headstone close to the church entrance. I gave him a pat. A belated apology for dismissing him in life.

Vincent's patron was one of the Glyn family, who were our village aristocrats, although by this time their power and reverence in Ewell was a recent memory. Glyn House stood imperiously next to the church, and an old wooden door led from their ample gardens into the churchyard itself. There was a Glyn Arms pub and a Glyn School as testament to their former illustrious status. Sir Arthur Glyn was the last of the family line who was still talked about in the 1960s, although he had died twenty years earlier. Mum told me how Sir Arthur would visit her school, where he was welcomed and treated like royalty. The Glyns had made their money in banking, I understand, and even in the 1980s there was a bank called Williams & Glyn's, which was eventually to be swallowed up by one of the Big Four. I found it hard to understand why people who were born into lots of money or inherited a particular name were treated with such reverence and deference. They had done nothing for it, after all. I put this to my dad.

'That's how it is,' he said rubbing his chin.

'It's not fair,' I countered.

'Life isn't fair. Look at the royal family. They didn't earn their money.'

'They work hard, though,' said my mum, who had been subjected to many years of royal indoctrination by her own mother.

I was still unsettled by my dad's revelation that life wasn't fair. Now he tells me.

There was another man, elderly and small, who visited us in the playground.

'Oh, here he is,' I heard an older boy say once. 'Wee Georgie Wood.'

He was a source of great amusement because he wore casual shorts, like us, but then something rarely witnessed in an adult in civilian daily life. He was there in some official capacity – he must have been – but I never knew what. We were told to be nice to him and treat him with courtesy. He used to ask us about our welfare. Were we eating well? Did we have any concerns? Strange business. As was the nit nurse, who turned up intermittently to pull a nit comb through our hair and wash our scalps in a bowl filled with a strong-smelling chemical. Once an outbreak of dysentery went through the school like a dose of salts, and at every opportunity we were lined up and doused in disinfectant like farm animals.

Mounted on decorative wooden scrolls in the centre of the main wall in the hall were two tabular lists – one was of boys' names who had qualified to reach university and the other was of old boys who never actually grew old because they perished in the two world wars. The latter list was by far the longer.

I wondered who those boys were that reached university. Indeed, on my estate you were more likely to go to borstal or prison than into higher education. I can think of five boys off the top of my head that served time but only two, maybe three, that attended university. The second plaque was far more evocative. These boys had sat at the same desks as me. They had charged around the playground like me. Gathered up conkers fallen from the same horse-chestnut trees. They may even have had younger brothers taught by Miss Gentry. They were innocent kids then, like me. Within five or six short years of leaving the school some found themselves in foreign fields among blood, gore and severed limbs waiting to die. I wondered if they thought about their carefree, happy schooldays in those harrowing final hours of life.

'THESE DIED THAT YOU MAY LIVE' declared the memorial solemnly – and not beating around the bush, I thought. *These are the names of the boys who were killed, and it's partly your fault*, is how I interpreted it. Unlike with the religion here we did take the message on board, and we never took those names in vain. Some of the surnames were still common in the village in the 1960s. That loss of life was still being felt nearly fifty and twenty years on from the respective world wars, and we could feel it too as children. There were people in the village still alive who grew up with the boys from the *first* war never mind the second.

The first name on the tablet is Sgt Robert Wood. Many years later I got access to the headmaster's log of the school for the period around the beginning of the 20th century. Robert Wood figures in it a bit. He was a handful, and the headmaster regretfully records having to cane the boy. When the First World War broke out Robert enlisted, but by October 1914 he had been killed in action across the channel in France. The first old boy to perish in the ridiculously named Great War. One wall in the playground had numerous initials carved into the old red brick, and I would study them and try to match them up with any of the lost boys.

If Miss Gentry's class was a gentle introduction to 'big-boys' school', the second year was to be significantly more brutal and frightening. We were no longer outgrown toddlers to be treated with kid gloves. Our form teacher was Miss Burford, a youngish lady who wore flowery, summery dresses and was a good teacher. She read us *The Lion, The Witch And The Wardrobe*, which transfixed me, and I pestered my parents to get me the sequels from the library. But there was a teacher called Mr Bircham who strode into our orbit, and he struck the fear of God into everyone. Stories about him and his cruelty abounded and, as I recall them now, if true, I find it hard to believe he got away with it for so long. I heard the following rhyme about him before I met him, which filled me with foreboding:

> Mr Bircham was a nasty bastard
> He went to church on Sunday
> He prayed to God to give him strength
> To wallop the boys on Monday

He was tall, thin, balding, with horn-rimmed glasses, and generally wore a black suit, white shirt and black tie done up tightly to accentuate a prominent Adam's apple. Thankfully, my class swerved him as a form teacher, but he did take us for several lessons. His reputation preceded him, and we terrified eight- and nine-year-olds would file into his classroom quietly, looking at the floor, desperately searching for invisibility. His desk was at the front of the class, naturally, and raised upon a small platform, and in front of his desk, placed symbolically on a chair, was a single white adult plimsoll. You could not help but look at it. It would have been more palatable were it just a deterrent, but Bircham used it frequently.

There was a boy in our class who was not a troublemaker. He came from East Ewell. He was the only fat kid in the form and was partial to confectionery. Our only contact with him was to shake him down at playtime for lemon bon-bons, candy twists or whatever sticky delight was stuffed deep into his pockets. He had mastered the art of popping sweets into his mouth during lessons, silently and without moving his mouth, but this fateful day Bircham's antennae picked something up.

'Are you eating sweets, boy?'

A swift gulp bulged his throat betraying the swallowing of a sweet. 'No, sir.'

'Come here, boy.'

The fat kid nervously approached the teacher who had now risen to his feet.

'Do you have any sweets on your person?'

'Yes, sir.'

'Please empty them into the bin, boy.'

The poor kid extracted two or three bags of boiled sweets from his pockets and dropped them into the bin. Bircham meanwhile had taken the slipper from the chair.

'You know it is forbidden to eat sweets in class, don't you? It's disgusting and it's rude. Bend over and touch your toes.'

That was asking a lot of this kid, but he managed to fold his body in half, and Bircham lifted his arm high and came down three times on the poor boy's arse, sending dust and particles into the atmosphere. Each time the boy jolted forward with the impact and let out a whimper of pain. Each time Bircham yanked him back by the scruff of his neck. It wasn't nice.

Not satisfied with beating and humiliating the fat kid, Bircham decided to really exercise his power. He alighted next time on Big Bill.

'Did you just make a noise, Owen?'

'Yes, sir.'

I think Bill may have inadvertently belched.

'Come to the front of the class, boy,' commanded the teacher.

Bill walked among us bravely to the front like a condemned man approaching the gallows.

'I am going to beat you until you make a noise. I will not stop until you cry,' he told Bill.

Bill bent over and touched his toes as instructed and the white slipper came down several times. Eventually Bill let out a sob. Whether he liked it or not Bill now had a reputation, and Bircham made sure that the illusion was violently shattered. Bill was eight years of age. He may have had a big body, but he had an eight-year-old, undeveloped and innocent brain.

For a while Mr Bircham lodged in a house on the Chessington Road, and he used to leave the other slipper hanging from his gate post, knowing his pupils would be passing. What was wrong with this man that he played cruel mind games with little boys? I mentioned him to my parents, but their attitude was to keep out of his way if possible. He left while I was there, and his haunting, evil spectre disappeared from my life.

A decade later, in the 1970s, my eight-year-old younger brother Stephen came home from school, and I overheard him telling Mum about this teacher picking on him. He told our parents about how this teacher had also banged two boys' heads together and it had really upset him. Stephen wanted Mum to complain, but she felt it wasn't her place as she wasn't the parent of one of the smashed boys. It turned out the teacher was Bircham. Our village school had been closed but replaced with a new state-of-the-art replacement. Across the road from our estate. Seemingly, under a new headmaster and staff and in a new building, this bad man had been re-employed.

Some time later Tony and I were walking down Longmead Road, and a man was walking towards us. He had shrunk (we'd grown) and was now sporting a little goatee beard, but I recognised him straight away.

I nudged Tony. 'That's Bircham.'

'Mr Bircham?' asked Tony, side-stepping into the teacher's path.

'Yes', he replied slowly sensing this was not two old pupils wanting to thank him for their education.

'Still bullying kids?'

Bircham stood speechless and a bit scared. Tony, who by now had big, bulging, tattooed building-site arms, advanced on him.

'What goes around comes around. Wanna fight me now?'

The teacher looked down at the ground like we did as seven-year-olds to avoid his glare.

'Only pick on little children, don't you ...?' This, from me, was a statement not a question. There was a silence while we considered our next move. Fortunately, without communicating it we jointly relaxed our body language and Bircham stepped around us.

'Wanker.'

I should not be proud and bragging about the incident, but even today I feel warmed inside by the discomfort and temporary fear we put into this horrible man. I hope he felt a smidgeon of how he had made us feel when we were little more than babies.

11
WONDERFUL CHRISTMASTIME

My third year at Eggs, Bacon and Sausages was a much happier one. I had found my feet and confidence now we had two classes of younger boys below us we could feel superior to and lord it over. Our form teacher was Mrs Galley. She lived just outside the village in a grand dwelling on the main road called Lister House. Her husband was an eminent anaesthetist. Mrs Galley was smartly dressed, played the piano in assembly and was liked and respected. I cannot recall her raising her voice or us playing her up particularly. She introduced us to Michael Bond's Paddington Bear books and a song called 'Football Crazy'. There was a line in it that contained the word 'gob', she insisted we replaced this with 'mouth' even though it didn't rhyme, and she wrote to the educational publishers of the song book admonishing them. She also taught us songs called 'Janko, Janko, Better Beware', 'The Skye Boat Song' and something about being among the leaves so green-o.

She took a personal interest in all us boys but was especially attentive to the pupils she felt might not have been dealt the best cards in life. She encouraged us all to develop any interests we had or any skills we showed any signs of possessing. Big Bill, for example, had an interest in archaeology, Roman history and militaria, and she nurtured and encouraged that in him.

One day she announced that she wanted us all to write a poem and that she would pick the best two and submit them to a national competition being run by BBC Radio. We all dutifully wrote something; I cannot remember mine but do remember Tony's. It began:

> *Snow is white*
> *Snow is light*
> *Snow at night*
> *Is a lovely sight ...*

... or something like that. Mrs Galley said mine and his were good and she would submit them both. In hindsight I believe she was trying to boost us up. I am sure there were better efforts. We thought nothing of it.

One afternoon I came in from school, and Mum welcomed me as I let myself in the back door into the kitchen where she had the ironing board out, pressing clothes, listening to the radio. She rushed forward and hugged me.

'Well done. I'm so proud of you.'

'What?' I asked, perplexed. I was not accustomed to being accused of doing things that made people proud.

'You've just been on the radio. They just read your poem out on *Woman's Hour*. They said, and this a poem from nine-year-old Martin Knight, a pupil at Ewell Boys' School in Surrey. Why didn't you tell us?'

'I didn't know. Old Galley just mumbled on about sending the poem somewhere. I wasn't really listening.'

'Mrs Galley. Not Old Galley. Well, you should be proud. Millions of people listen to *Woman's Hour*.'

'Did they read out Tony's?'

'No, I don't think so.'

I was disappointed Tony's hadn't been featured too. I thought his was better.

Mrs Galley took the class on country walks. One hot day we followed the River Hogsmill from its source at the spring in Ewell all the way to where it joins the Thames at Kingston. On the way an old man was introduced to us. He was closing in on a century in years, and his name was Mr Pocock. He came from an old Ewell family and had attended our own school in the 1870s. It fascinated me that here was I listening to tales of days of yore from a man who would have touched and walked alongside people who had been born in 17-something. And that man or woman from the 18th century he touched could have known people who had witnessed the Great Plague or the Great Fire of London. The centuries shrink when you contemplate things like that. Another time Mrs Galley took us to London Airport on a coach. It had not yet been rebranded as Heathrow.

Trips to London were a real treat. Dad took me to see *Treasure Island* at the Mermaid Theatre. Other than pantomime it was my first visit to a theatre. I was impressed by the character Ben Gunn and the man who played him. A raving nutcase with a long straggly beard. Looking it up now, in 2021, I note it was almost certainly Spike Milligan. Earlier Mum had taken us to Wimbledon Theatre to see *Cinderella*. Jimmy Tarbuck was Buttons, and Anita Harris was, curiously, dressed up as a boy. Both Mum and Dad also took us to the Bertram Mills Circus where the illustrious Coco the Clown performed, but the act that stuck in my mind was a boxing kangaroo. It was led into the boxing ring wearing a silk boxer's robe before chasing a man around the canvas and delivering a left hook, knocking him over.

It reminds me now of an even more alarming story. My Uncle Terry told me that when the fair came to Clapham Common in the 1920s and 1930s there was a sideshow called 'blindfold boxing'. Boys, and Terry was one of them, were blindfolded, placed in a ring and encouraged to smash eight bells out of one another. It was considered highly amusing and entertaining at the time.

I remember well my first bought bicycle; it had been Laurence's. I'd had bikes before but not a nearly new one. Those earlier bikes were self-built mongrels, a frame from the dump, wheels from a neighbour, handlebars from a friend. We painted the finished product, so the hybrid make-up was disguised. This bike, though, had gears and, as with everything he owned, Laurence had cared for it well. I rode it all over. For the first time I would ride to Box Hill in one direction and Kingston and the River Thames in the other. One day I laid it on the ground to join in a mass game of football over Gibraltar Rec. When the game was over some two hours later, I walked over to the fence to where my bike was. But it wasn't. It had gone. Stolen. In the excitement of the match neither I nor anyone else had noticed a thief strolling up and riding off on my pride and joy. It was hard to tell Dad, who was very cross because he had given me a padlock contraption and had said I should always lock it up if I left it anywhere. He reported the theft to the police, and, believe it or not, they came to the house to take details.

That was to be the end of the story, but some months later Dad came in triumphantly and announced, 'I found the bicycle.' He had spotted the cycle propped up against another boy's wall on the estate, and although it had been painted and adapted Dad checked the registration number on the frame and was satisfied it was ours. As we admired and welcomed it home there was an urgent knocking on the door. Dad went and answered it. Mum opened the lounge door slightly so we could hear.

'You just nicked my fucking bike, mate.'

We couldn't hear what Dad was saying as he always spoke evenly and normally without a raised voice.

'I'm going to get the police on you, mate.'

Dad came back in and said, 'I look forward to that. Think it may be some time.'

That boy, the thief, was Liam. I recognised him from behind the net curtain as he stormed off up the garden path. He lived up the top of the main road, and Dad worked with his father at the mental hospital. Liam was an older boy, some four years senior to me, who already had a reputation as a dangerous kid. I was worried he might exact revenge on my dad or, worse still, me.

'You keep away from that boy. He stole your bicycle. I feel sorry for his poor parents. He's trouble. Keep away from him, do you hear?'

Years later I would have cause to wish I had heeded my mum's advice.

Strangely, when England won the World Cup in 1966 I don't remember being overexcited about it at all. Although I was playing football a great deal, I had not yet settled into watching it assiduously on TV or following a specific team. Laurence could not take the tension that historical afternoon and got on his bike and rode around Dee Way repeatedly as that nail-chewing extra time played out. Later Mum took Laurence and me to the Rembrandt in Ewell to see the film *Goal!* which reprised the whole World Cup experience in glorious Technicolor. In those days Technicolor was considered superior to colour, but I think it was a marketing con. It's colour or it's black and white, surely?

We didn't only play football outdoors but also with great enthusiasm and dedication indoors with the table football game Subbuteo. I was an avid player in the mid-1960s through to the mid-1970s. Laurence and I shared a basic infrastructure (a pitch and some goals) but acquired our own teams and accessories. I remember he had the Brazil team, which was the most stylish and exotic around. Yellow-and-green shirts and coffee-coloured players. My elder brother did a paper round every day whereas I only did Sunday and he thus had more disposable income and it was in Dario Gradi's sports shop in Ewell Village where he disposed of it on more and more teams and more and more accessories. Within in a year or two he owned a dug out, advertising hoardings, match officials and, to cap it all, glorious and working floodlights. I became like a guest in my own house when it came to Subbuteo. Many years later I would know how Charlton Athletic felt when they ground-shared with Crystal Palace.

My brother was a meticulous boy, and with Airfix paint left over from a previous model-building obsession he began, very carefully, to personalise his players. A brush of yellow paint, a blob of skin-colour and a stroke of black paint all applied deftly to three Manchester United heads created an authentic Denis Law, Bobby Charlton, and George Best respectively. It was awesome. I tried doing Peter Osgood's lamb-chop sideboards with disastrous smudgy results.

It was supposed to be table football, but we played it on the floor. The disadvantage of this was when I became excited during a fluid attack and heard and then felt that gut-wrenching noise of human knee upon plastic player as I slithered around the room. God forbid it was my brother's Pele. When the players were glued back to their bases they never looked the same and never fully recovered their form.

When I started work in the mid-1970s there was an office Subbuteo league which we conducted in the lunch hour. Only then did I discover that my brother and I had been playing it wrong for all those years. We always used the sides of our crooked forefingers to flick/push the player whereas the pros at the office flicked delicately with forefinger nail.

Dario Gradi was Laurence's teacher at Glyn Grammar School besides being a shop owner. He also played football for Sutton United, who were Manchester United compared to Epsom and Ewell FC in the local amateur footballing stakes. Also playing for Sutton was Larry Pritchard, whose family lived on our estate. In 1970 both Larry and Dario were in the team that drew the mighty and haughty Leeds United in the FA Cup third round at Gander Green Lane. Sutton lost 6-0, but it was a matter of immense pride that Leeds had sent down their best team – including Billy Bremner, Jack Charlton, Norman Hunter and Allan Clarke – to repel the amateur would-be giant-killers.

Larry Pritchard is recognised as one of the best amateur footballers ever. He was capped by England and Great Britain on top of his long career at non-professional clubs. I remember his younger brothers and thought they

Above: Henry Knight Sr, my grandfather, as a civilian and as a soldier

Below: Great-Uncle Bill Judd, the big-game hunter

Above: Dad when he enlisted in the army

Right: New house, new family and me, in arms

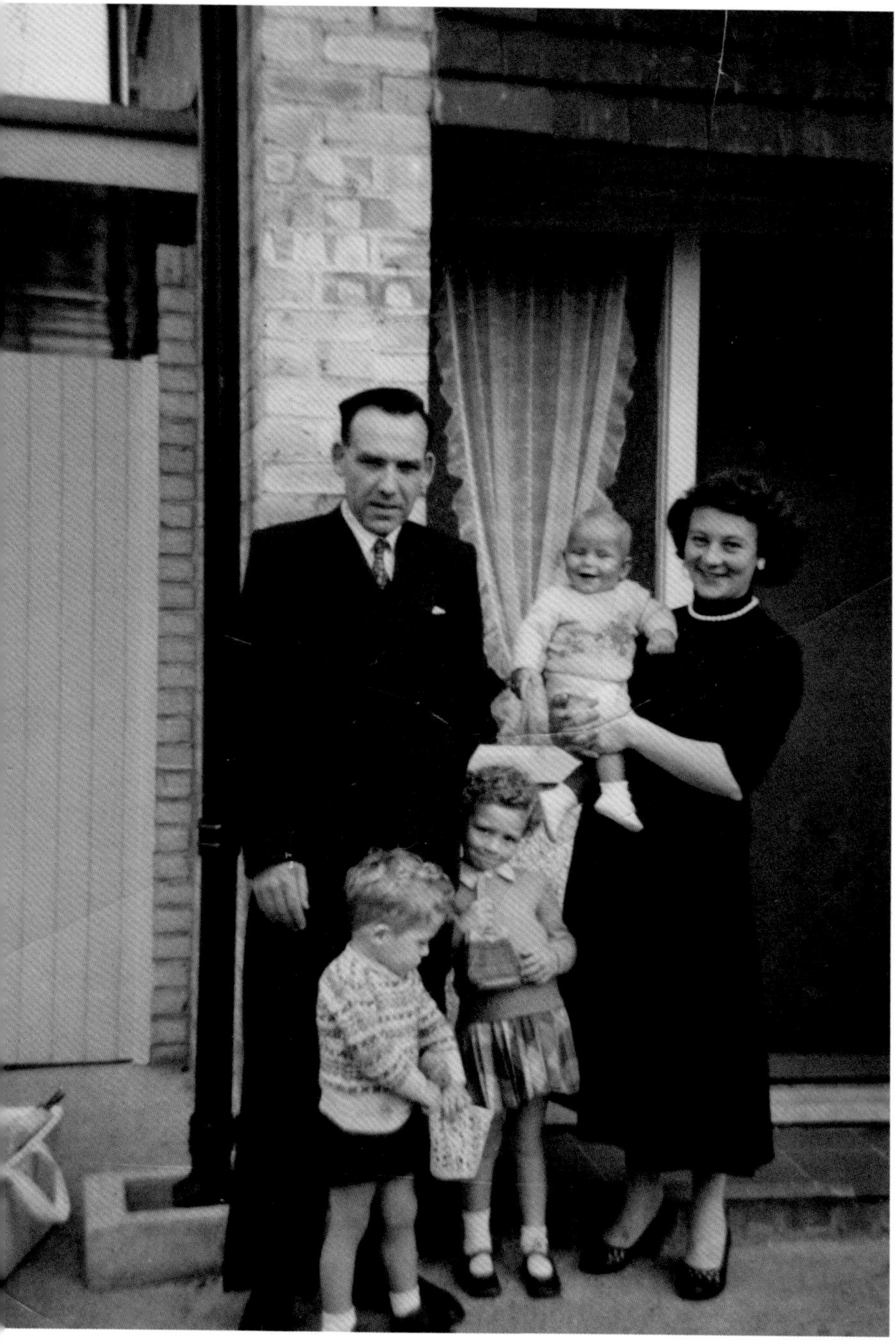

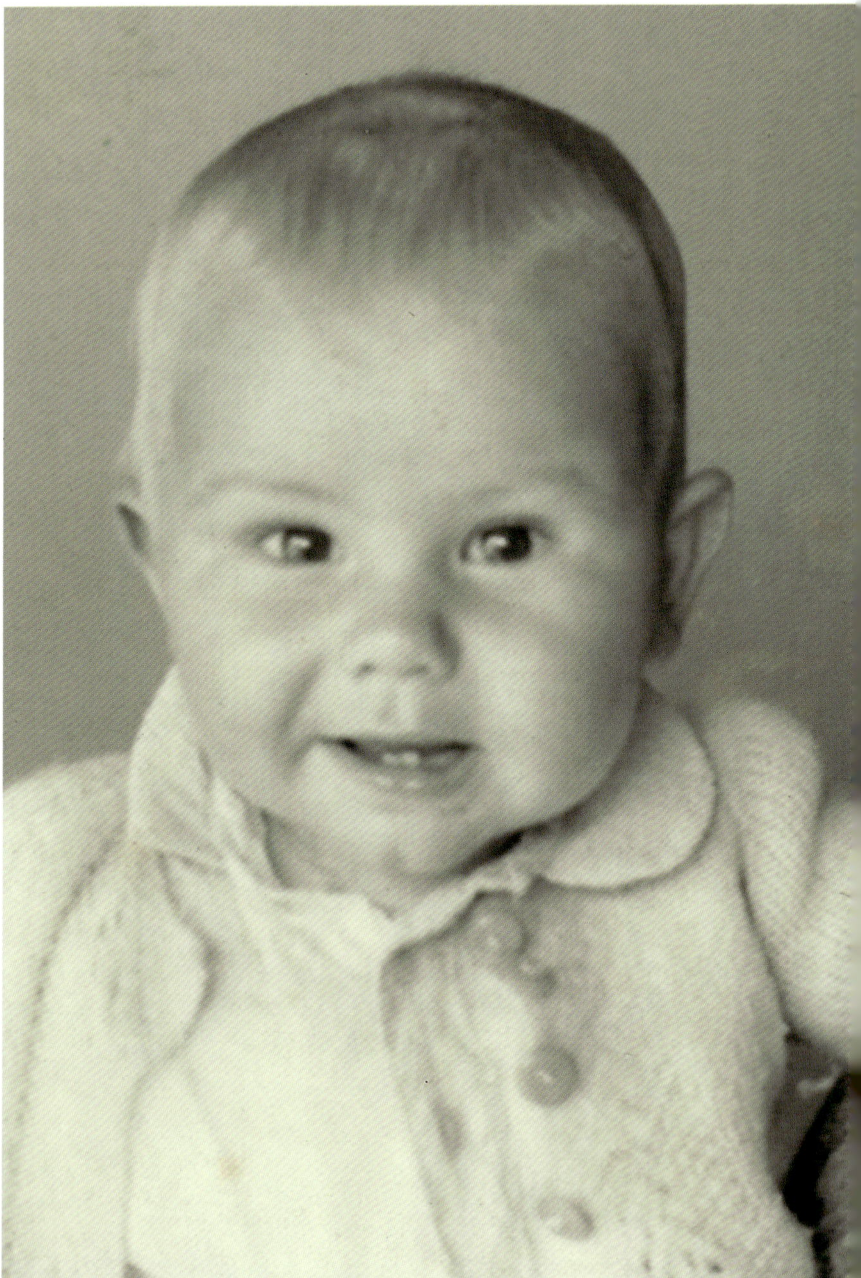

Opposite: Me at three months

Left and below: Back garden adventures

Bottom: Me and Viv

Mum and best friend Eileen

Above: Gibraltar boys 1963

Right: Estate families playing together

Below: Fishing for sticklebacks

Above: The American swing **(top)** and the witch's hat **(bottom)**
Courtesy of Wicksteed Ltd

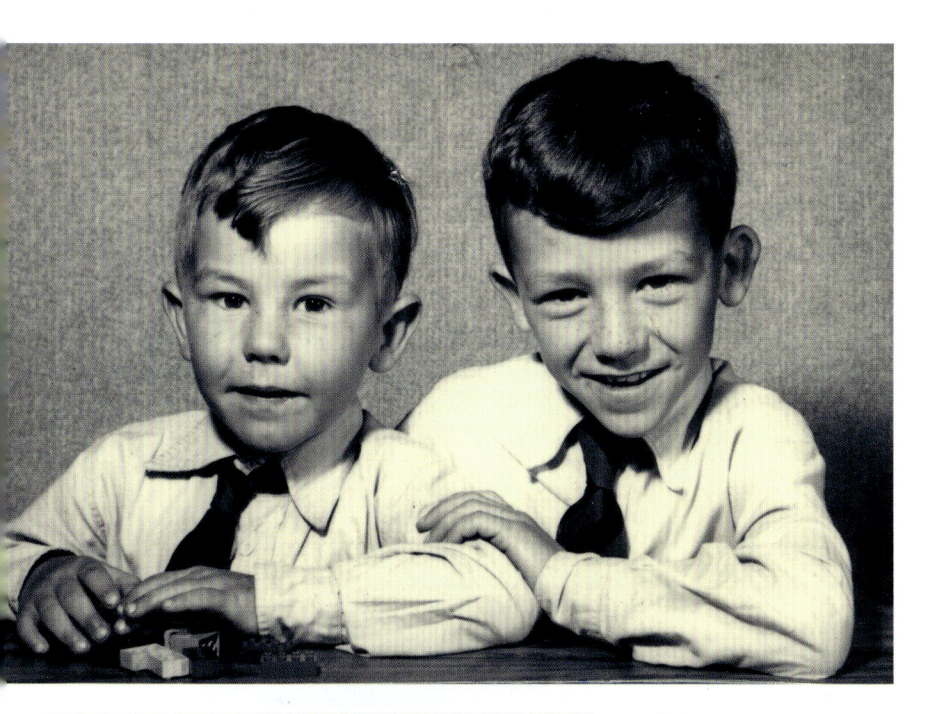

Above: Laurence reassures me as I begin school

Left: Viv looks nervous as he starts school

Above: At Battersea Fun Fair; I don't look too pleased

Below: All of the Knights with Eileen's children

Top: Happy family

Middle left: Grandma's eightieth: the Battersea contingent

Middle right: Before computer games families played Twister – we did, at least

Bottom: Me and my sisters

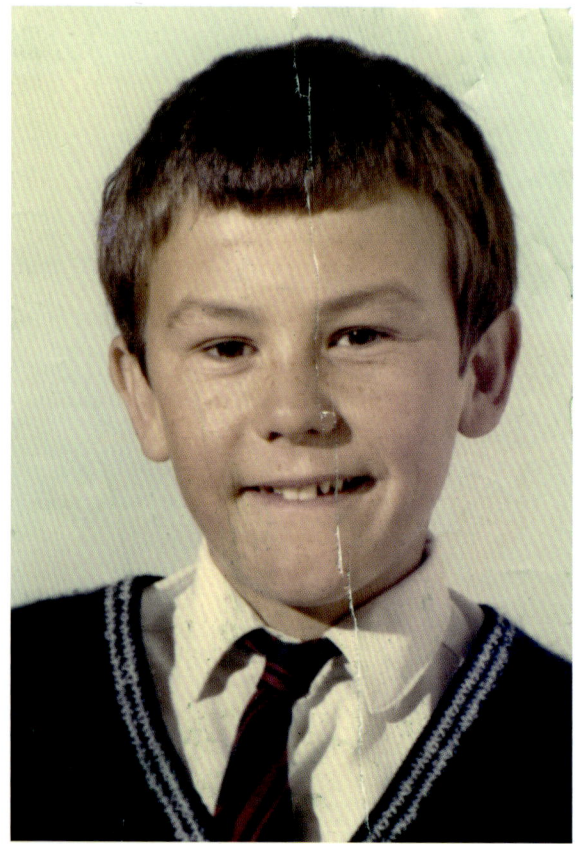

Above: EBS – Ewell Boys' School, aka Eggs, Bacon and Sausages

Left: Starting senior school and in uniform, 1969

Above: New boys at senior school

Below: Mr Rees's class, 1969 – I am the little boy second from left whose feet don't touch the ground; Tony is above me and Eddie above him, while Big Bill is in the middle of the centre row

Above: At nine, still in short trousers

Below: Photobooth images, 1972 **(left)** with long hair and 1974 **(right)** around the time I started work

Above top: My name carved into the wall at West Street School; it's still there today

Above: The old stand at Epsom and Ewell FC where I would lurk below the seating
Courtesy of Richard Lambert www.eefconline.co.uk

Above top: Viv happy and content in later life

Above: Boys to men: Tony and me

were pretty good players too. Micky Cook was another estate boy who made the footballing big time, giving hope to those who came later. Micky played for Crystal Palace and Brentford before enjoying a long non-league career.

Batman was probably what prevented me becoming fully immersed in football in England's momentous World Cup-winning year. I was obsessed with the American TV series, along with millions of other boys my age. A toy Batmobile car replaced the James Bond car in my toy-vehicle affections. I devoured the programme, read the books, bought the bubble gum to collect the cards and eventually had the entire costume. Although I was embarrassed to wear Mum's matching knitted jumpers by now, I was quite prepared to swagger down to the bottom shops in a mask, a cape and tight-fitting trousers at eight years old. I carried my Bat Boomerang in case Burgess Meredith or Caesar Romero – the Penguin and the Joker respectively – were lurking around Gibraltar Crescent. I truly believed I was the height of cool. I was lucky not to be terrorised. When, in later life, it was explained to me that *Batman* was a piss-take, and possibly homoerotic, I felt betrayed. All those Zaps! Pows! and Holy Exclamations! from Robin were part of one big joke played on us children. Nice.

Christmas 1968. Feels like yesterday. The Scaffold were number one with 'Lily The Pink'. A fundamentally stupid song that caught the public imagination and was being hummed, whistled and sung in every playground and workplace in the country. It had been helped along by the Beatles' stardust. One of the members was Mike McGear, brother of Paul McCartney. It would be replaced at the top of the hit parade by 'Ob-La-Di, Ob-La-Da', another jaunty song that embedded itself in people's brains and was written by our Paul but covered by the Marmalade. Also in the chart around that time was 'I'm The Urban Spaceman', a delightful bit of nonsense from the Bonzo Dog Doo-Dah Band, produced by McCartney. The Beatles, six years after their explosive arrival, were still a phenomenon to behold.

The television crackled in the background. Nina and Frederick were on singing their greatest hit 'Little Donkey'. Many years later, as I was researching the book *Grass*, I discovered that Frederick ended up being murdered in the Philippines in a drug-related hit. Talk about childhood images being shattered. Leslie Crowther or Ray Alan, accompanied by Titch and Quackers, were later to be seen on screen visiting sick children in hospital and dishing out presents as smiling, dedicated nurses looking like they had stepped off a *Carry On* film set smiled and cooed.

On Christmas Eve Sally, Laurence and I had been despatched up to Ewell West station to meet Grandma off the train from Clapham Junction. We loved our grandmother, but we were at an age of being easily embarrassed, and she gave us plenty to fill us with dread. She was a formidable woman encased inside a huge overcoat that was as black as coal and as stiff as a suit of armour. It was almost definitely pre-war – First World War, that is. It was adorned with an enormous brooch, as if someone had removed a component of a car engine and welded it to her lapel. And she wore a hat that defied description. The sort of thing that Robin Hood might have worn, one that sported feathers, flowers and what looked like dead ferns shooting out at sharp angles. She clutched an enormous black handbag which, if it weren't for a decorative gold clasp, could have easily been mistaken for Dr Finlay's Gladstone medical bag.

She spoke loudly, complaining about people on the train speaking loudly. Her accent was a memorable blend of Peggy Mount and Kathleen Harrison. Laurence held her bag for her. Sally walked ahead hoping nobody realised there was a connection, and I walked alongside head down, praying to go unrecognised. Once we had her ensconced indoors we breathed a joint sigh of relief. If we kept our friends from coming around we were safe. Grandma was lowered into an armchair and barely moved until when she went home the day after Boxing Day.

Dad gave her a bottle of Guinness from the little bar he had set up in the dining-room. There was also Babycham, Idris ginger beer, Tizer, R. White's lemonade, India pale ale, Harvey's Bristol Cream sherry, Coca-Cola, stout, Sandeman port and various other beers in brown bottles. Packets of Eat Me dates were left out on most surfaces. In defiance of their name, they mostly went uneaten. I have never seen packets of dates any other time than at Christmas, and my hunch is that in most households they went largely unopened and uneaten too. There were also bowls of walnuts with the nutcrackers buried headfirst in them and tins of Quality Street already carefully mined of the few flavours that I liked.

'Don't put the empty wrappers back in the box, Martin. How many times do I have to tell you?'

Grandma would deal with the others. The ones nobody liked. But some of them played havoc with her false teeth, and she occasionally had to prise her dentures apart with her hands.

She had been down earlier in the year when Mum and Dad had surprised her for her eightieth birthday party. Then, in 1968, reaching such an age was considered a remarkable milestone and worthy of great celebration. Most of her peers were long dead by that time. She came from a big family, and the sibling that had died immediately before her had given up the ghost in 1951. It was the first time I had met some of the wider family, grey-haired, besuited Battersea people now flung far and wide but all sharing the same gruelling background of poverty and conflict, but a happier, more jovial bunch you could not meet. Her favourite brother Dan's son Terry Bradshaw was detained elsewhere, although I did not know that until forty years later.

Christmas Day was fantastic. We would crowd around Dad to watch the turkey being carved. It is well known in Britain that only big strong men are able, qualified and permitted to cut turkey. Actually salivating, we could barely contain ourselves as juicy cuts were dropped on to our glistening white adult plates. We could help ourselves to roast potatoes from a bowl. Help ourselves! A bowl! Christmas pudding followed where a threepenny bit lurked within to potentially choke one of us. Then, eating over, we could 'get down' and nip off to the sitting-room to watch the Christmas *Top Of The Pops* or play with our presents.

I would often stay and sit and listen instead to the stories as the adults relaxed, dishes dumped on the side, table cleared. Gaga would roll some tobacco, and Dad would join him. He had a little machine to roll the cigarette, which seemed to me to be unnecessarily complex when Gaga could roll between finger and thumb and with a snake-like flick of his tongue have a cigarette in his mouth in seconds. Mum would light up a rare Guards, Grandma a Weights and Nana would decline, happy with a refillable glass of sherry.

Much of the time Dad would wind his mother up into telling stories or giving her opinions on current affairs as she was unintentionally hilarious and Nana and Gaga couldn't get enough of her. She called Shirley Bassey, Shirley Brassey; Jimmy Tarbuck was Tarbrush; Bruce Forsyth, Brute Forsyth; and John Lennon, John Lemon. Names got mangled somewhere between what they actually were and what she thought they ought to be.

One story she told was how the triple murderer of three policemen, Harry Roberts, was hiding out in the flat above her in Battersea. He carried out the shootings of the officers in Shepherd's Bush and went on the trot for some weeks after. The manhunt for him dominated the news bulletins, his police photo imprinted on our minds with some prominent demonic eyebrows that scared the life out of the general public.

"Er upstairs was sheltering 'im. You know 'er, 'Arry. The one with the 'air an' the make-up. She's on the game, I tell you. Thinks I don't know. But I ain't that stoopid. Anyway, I tell the perlice. I saw 'im walking up the stairs. 'E stared at me. 'E knew I recognised him. I was 'specting 'im to come down an' strangle me any minute. Anyway, they came to see me later and said he weren't there. Has he fled, I says? No, Mrs Tregent, he hasn't been there. I should cocoa, I said.'

'That must have been terrifying, Nell. And how do you get on with your neighbour these days?' probed Gaga gently.

'She don't talk to me. Miserable woman. Good mind to tell the council what sort of racket she's running from there.'

Gaga smiled. Dad confirmed to us later, after Grandma had retired for her afternoon kip, that the neighbour upstairs was a perfectly respectable lady.

I would look at Grandma, at this great age of eighty, having no idea she would plough on for another twenty years, and marvel at the fact that she too could have been held as a baby by someone who was born in the 1790s. My grandma, sitting next to me puffing on a Weights fag, could have brushed shoulders with someone who was in the throng outside St Paul's Cathedral for Horatio Nelson's funeral in 1806.

As Christmas night closed, Dad would announce as if shocked and cross, 'What on earth is going on? It's past twelve. What are you rascals still doing up? It's Boxing Day. Come on, high time you were in your billets. Up to bed now.'

We kids would retire, quietly satisfied that we had taken our parents minds and eyes off the clock and had got away with watching the TV until it ceased broadcasting for the night and the national anthem was played. Dog tired, we would fall asleep within minutes of our heads hitting the pillow, our minds full of what Boxing Day would bring.

12
TICKET TO RIDE

The period around 1968–9 was eventful in many ways, especially in the wider world. I think it was the first time I paid serious attention to the television and media news. The assassinations of Martin Luther King and Bobby Kennedy were big events, and again I remember being mildly disturbed by my parents' concern. I just thought, Well, it's happened in America, so that's all right. 'It could never happen here,' was the reassuring refrain Britons used to soothe each other's fears. The United Kingdom seemed so quaint and undynamic next to the USA. You could never imagine any British protestor or activist being sufficiently aggrieved to assassinate Harold Wilson or Ted Heath, and, if they were so inclined, the choice of weapon would not be a gun, more likely a cricket bat. If America was Mortal Kombat we were Cluedo, complete with Professor Plum in the conservatory with lead piping.

The Vietnam War rolled on and on, and even my parents were not invested in that one. It was America's war, and there was little prospect of it impacting directly on Britain. Germany had been tamed by defeat in two world wars, so the only threat was (allegedly) a belligerent Soviet Union. But even there we were reassured by the widely held belief that our American cousins could sort them out if push came to shove.

I can remember the moon landing, although I was not particularly excited about it. My mum and dad tried to convey the historical import by taking us in the garden at night-time and encouraging us to look up at the moon and absorb the fact that men were walking on it. And ...?

At school we were forced to watch the investiture of Prince Charles as the Prince of Wales at Caernarvon Castle on the new school telly. I was even less interested in this, and most of the school agreed. The royal family was still immensely popular, though, and, although the deference of previous generations was dissipating, we couldn't imagine life without them. There was a rebellious MP named Willie Hamilton who spoke out against the royal family as an institution, but he was a rare voice and treated as a renegade. He famously called Prince Charles a twerp. That was headline news then.

We had been enjoying summer holidays as a family for a few years now. Money must have been a tad easier. Dad was progressing slowly but surely in administration roles at West Park Mental Hospital. He would stay in the NHS for the rest of his career, steadily climbing the ladder and gradually improving his salary and pension. The first holidays were on the Isle of Sheppey in the early 1960s courtesy of my Aunt Margo – the possible communist – who had nevertheless accumulated enough money to own a caravan named Tree Tops on a site at Warden Point. My memories are vague. I don't think it was particularly beautiful, but it was not Ewell, and that was the point. One afternoon my little sister Liz was injured when the heavy caravan door blew shut on her thumb. She was taken to hospital and suffered permanent injury. I had nothing to compare Sheppey to in those days. It was the seaside, and that was all that mattered. But looking back I can see that if Kent was the garden of England, Sheppey was the hard standing where you kept the metal dustbins.

After Sheppey we stayed in a converted railway carriage that sat without wheels next to the station at Walmer in Kent. En route we piled into a single train carriage with wheels as a very happy young family singing 'Ticket To Ride' by the Beatles. 'Concrete and Clay' by Unit 4+2 was also riding high, and through those songs I can date that holiday to 1965. I think the packages could be bought direct from British Rail. The excitement of sleeping in a real railway carriage complete with emergency cord, buffet area and British Rail livery was joyous. Especially for Dad.

Each day we went out from the carriage and visited Deal, Dover, Sandwich, Broadstairs, Ramsgate and beyond. In the evenings we children went next door into the actual station where the stationmaster allowed us to collect tickets from smiling returning commuters. We were the railway children before *The Railway Children* film. The porter who befriended us was called Jerry, and he became our own Bernard Cribbins.

Those daily trips out from the carriage were organised by Dad like an army expedition. He had an army backpack, which he called a valise, that he took everywhere, even to the shops. This would contain among other things an apple and knife to cut it with, a newspaper, his army groundsheet and his army jerrycan from which we all drank squash. When we got up from our beach picnic and folded up the groundsheet to walk back to the nearest railway station he would command us to 'fall in' – only half joking.

We went to the carriage a couple of years running, but then we moved gently upwards again to renting rooms in a grand old Victorian house that had seen better days on the West Hill in Hastings. The top floor had panoramic views across to the East Hill and out to sea. It was a vista like no other to us. Dad had been there as a child, and his love for the town was passed on to us and I hope we have passed it on to our children. We holidayed in that same house for almost the next decade. The owners were a Mr and Mrs Edwards, and I swear that sometimes Mr Edwards wore a smoking jacket like Gomez in *The Addams Family*.

There were some rocks on the West Hill that provided hour upon hour of adventure and playing as we climbed, clambered, leaped and fell. It was a miracle that none of us broke a limb or worse. There was no parental supervision. The rocks included a steep escarpment that led up to the crumbling remains of Hastings Castle. One summer I watched a pair of black redstarts nesting there. At the centre of the rocks was a cave the locals called Cat's Cave, and it was a badge of honour to be able to get in and out. Entry was challenging for a child, but nigh on impossible for an adult due to having to jump over a bit of a drop on to a thin ledge that could only accommodate smaller feet and which you had to shuffle along while holding another ledge above you to edge into the cave. That was the attraction. Once in you could sit imperiously and look down on the go-kart track and the wild, untamed sea lapping in and out. There was still a fishing industry then, and you could see the fishermen sitting outside their black huts repairing their nets with gnarled hands. It was from Cat's Cave I saw mods and rockers in huge numbers walking up and down the promenade preparing to take each other on. From up on the West Hill the rockers looked like a swarm of beetles being washed down the front in an oil slick in their black-leather garb. When they were in town Mum and Dad said it was best not to come off the hill.

In Hastings Dad would have us hiking as usual. The terrain was far hillier than our Kent coast expeditions. He marched us up the East Hill (sometimes if there was just two of us, we took the paid funicular railway) and up to Fairlight Glen. We looked at houses that were perched precariously at the edge of the cliff waiting to crumble into the sea. I found this incredibly sad. We visited the Lovers' Seat where, legend had it, a bereft lady sat at night with a flashlight beaming it across the Channel in forlorn attempts to let her lover who had been lost at sea know that she was there pining for him. The romance and sorrow of this tale made a big impact on me, and it never occurred that it was certainly made up. The seat, I bet, has now been lost to the depths of the English Channel.

One Sunday morning back at the house Dad announced, 'Right, who wants to walk to Rye?'

Rye was about twelve miles away. Sally, Laurence and the others (even Mum) pretended they hadn't heard or sneaked away, suddenly busy, so I, against my better judgement, said I did. So off we went, following the coastal path across Fairlight Glen, through Pett Level, Winchelsea and other places whose names I forget before we reached Rye some five or six hours later. The route was up and down hills with clifftop paths blocked off following rock falls. My little legs were killing me; I was only about nine or ten.

When we reached the charming town of Rye, as if reading my mind, Dad said, 'Don't worry boy. We'll get the bus back,' marching purposefully over to a bus stop.

I saw him running his finger across the timetable grid and then look down at me and then back at the timetable. He was unsure how to break the news. 'NO SUNDAY SERVICE' was clearly written on the bus stop. I could have cried. Probably did. There was no way I could have walked back, even though Dad, had he been alone, would have. It would have pained him greatly, but Dad went to a phone box and called a minicab, a luxury beyond our budget. They were few and far between in those days, especially in the middle of nowhere. The fare would have depleted the family holiday spending money considerably. Dad would have been kicking himself for not foreseeing the hole in his military-style planning.

We had our own cash, we kids. We saved our pocket money, birthday money and paper-round earnings for the holiday each year. Sally had graduated from paper rounds and worked hard in The Newsbox and Reading's newsagent's shops in Epsom. She had the strongest work ethic out of all us kids. This money was ours, and we could spend it how we pleased. Laurence and I would head straight to the pier, where we played the penny machines. It was not unheard of for me to spend (lose) all my brown pennies and halfpennies, threepenny bits, sixpences, florins and even half-crowns in the first couple of days. Laurence lasted longer. Careful with his money, he even held ambitions of making a profit, but the laws of the penny arcades applied even to him in the end.

The amusements were heaven, and I could spend a day in one hall. Even now, as I pass one I experience that frisson of childhood excitement. There was a horseracing game Laurence and I played where you backed jockeys in each race and if your jockey won you doubled or trebled your money. The names of the jockeys gave away how old this machine was even then: Harry Wragg, Gordon Richards and Charlie Smirke among them. If a jockey let me down I chose another in the next race. Laurence would stick with one and keep backing him until he won. He inevitably lost, but not as much as me. I would then gravitate to the 'what-the-butler-saw' machine. Not a lot, sadly. A lady putting on stockings, perhaps. Then there was the grab machine where if you persisted you could win a furry animal that cost less in the shop next door than the seven tries had cost you. Rolling pennies down a slope and hoping they landed in between two lines was good as well, as was the one that pushes the pennies over the cliff edge.

Every hour or so I would fish into my pocket produce a half-crown and take it over to the surly man in the booth. I had to stand on tiptoe to hand it to him.

'Whadoyawannitin?' he grunted while looking over me.

'Pennies, please.'

And the old brown pennies would come hurtling out a long chute into a bowl from which I could scoop the soon-to-be-lost coins into my pockets. Momentarily and entirely falsely I felt like a winner.

We dawdled back to the house, Laurence and me. Pockets lighter. Stopping to throw pebbles into the sea. Laurence could skim and bounce a stone. Mine just plopped in. We loved going down Bottle Alley where a walkway had been decorated with embedded bottles and coloured glass and our voices echoed. We would approach the White Rock Theatre and see who was on, hoping to catch a famous actor leaving or entering. The Troggs were appearing on the pier one year, and mods were beginning to gather across the road. And, as dusk fell, we had one last climb into Cat's Cave before jumping over the wall into the garden and through the back door where undoubtedly Mum would be about to serve up a welcome dinner. Dad would be at the table planning the next day's manoeuvres, an Ordnance Survey map spread far and wide across it, and he hovered over the map with a magnifying glass. Glorious days. I can feel that happiness now. Feel it so much it almost hurts.

I know we were in Hastings on 5 March 1968 because that was the Saturday evening Cliff Richard finished second in the Eurovision Song Contest with 'Congratulations'. Years later I was thrilled to interview Bill Martin, the man who co-wrote it. People took the event seriously in those days, and it ranked along with the FA Cup Final, *Last Night Of The Proms* and Miss World as one of *the* television occasions of the year. The whole family were assembled along the settee and in armchairs pulled close in a semi-circle around the television. Smith's Crisps and Tizer were on the coffee table in front of us. Earlier we had polished off fish and chips around the kitchen table. Rarely was our mixed-race, mixed-age, mixed-sex and mixed-up family more united and happy.

Hopes were high because Sandie Shaw had won it the previous year with 'Puppet On A String' – and, of course, we were British. We were the best. We were always told that, and we believed it. The Eurovision Song Contest was a great opportunity to laugh at the eccentricities of foreigners in their funny clothes, cow bells around their necks, pointy hats and silly beards.

The tension as the results came in and Katie Boyle tried to make sense of it all was palpable, and Cliff, who my sister Sally always adored, was pipped at the post. Lulu would bat for us the following year, and her 'Boom-Bang-A-Bang' was joint winner. It became increasingly hard after that. It seemed that as our kudos as a nation receded so did our performance in the contest. Now we never get a look in, but in those last years of the 1960s judges still voted on merit, not politically.

It is easy to forget just how big Cliff Richard was. Although his trajectory was interrupted by the Beatles, in the period between 1958 and 1968 he was the biggest British male vocalist. I knew all his records, including the B-sides, because of Sally's obsession, and I went with her to see him at the cinema in *Finders Keepers*. By the late 1960s his early films like *Expresso Bongo*, *The Young Ones* and *Summer Holiday* were cropping up on TV on

Sunday afternoons. I stopped taking him seriously, though, when he combed his hair forward, donned thick-framed glasses and went religious.

There was a walkway next to the house in Hastings that dropped down into the new town. I was sent down early some mornings to get fresh rolls from the 1066 Bakery. One day as I walked back up with my shopping bag laden with warm savoury goodies a local boy of about my age and stamp was walking towards me. He was looking me up and down with some hostility I noticed. He had worked out I was a stranger. Don't think the shopping bag helped things either. I tried not to meet his stare.

'D'you wanna fight?' he asked.

'No thanks,' I replied, a little bit too quickly.

He carried on past as if he had just requested the time and I had obliged. It took me by surprise. The fact that a stranger should *want* to fight me for no reason shocked me. It may have been the first time I realised that all boys were sometimes expected to fight. I hoped I might be excused such brutality being small, but the incident made me think. I had no confidence in my physical ability to win a scrap.

With the help of Google, I know that it was one morning in July 1968 when I was outside the back door polishing my shoes with Dad on an old wooden table that stood in our porch. He was a stickler for shiny shoes and taught all us kids how to polish our footwear with gusto from an early age. We used to kneel on the kitchen floor at first and do it with old newspaper laid out, but now the old table meant we could stand more comfortably, albeit outside. We put the Cherry Blossom polish on with a specific brush and then buffed with another and finally got the satisfying reflective shine with a yellow duster.

'Shame about the Cream,' Dad remarked, nonchalantly.

'The cream?' I thoughts perhaps the tinned Carnation evaporated milk in the larder had really evaporated.

'The Cream. They've split up. Haven't you heard?' This was my dad having a joke with me. He had obviously peeked at my *NME* or had heard something on the radio as he carried out his household chores. He would have had no idea who Cream or Eric Clapton were otherwise. I smiled knowingly. He smiled back.

'At least it was amicable,' he continued, parroting a line from the official statement.

He could be very funny, my dad. He had myriad sayings, many borrowed from William Shakespeare. 'Speak now or forever hold your peace,' was one often used. When sister Sally had Cliff Richard singing 'Summer Holiday' on repeat on the record player he'd lower his newspaper and sigh, 'Give it a rest, Clifford.'

Years later it amused him and nobody else to pretend he thought Elton John's name was John Elton and George Michael's Michael George. He was heavily into naval lingo and would often hold his hand over his eyes as if saluting and declare 'Land Ahoy!' He was wont to do this when we were waiting for buses or trains, and we waited for many over the years. He called us kids landlubbers and sea dogs. Upstairs was sometimes the crow's nest. Occasionally and for no reason he would sway from side to side as if he was on board a ship. Seafaring informed his character, although he had served in the army not the navy. Perhaps his family lineage of working on the River Thames was in his blood.

One day we kids walked into the sitting-room, and he was sitting in his chair in my mum's nightie. We thought this hilarious. He enjoyed life to the full. Always busy. Didn't waste time watching television and planned his day meticulously. His thirst for discovery and exploration never left him. I cannot remember him down. If he did have black moods and ever felt despair, he was expert at hiding it from us.

Indoors he wore a jockey's hat long before baseball caps had infiltrated headwear taste this side of the Atlantic. The visor shielded his eyes, he explained. From what? He would often sink into his armchair and lay the then broadsheet *Times* over his face and place his glasses on top to keep it in place. We thought he was having a joke but within minutes the paper would ripple up and down and a nasal whistling sound escaped from below the crossword.

'You were fast asleep,' we told him when he woke.

'No, that is a vicious slur. I was merely resting my eyes,' he'd reply, wagging his finger.

One afternoon he took us down to Sussex to visit a model village. We arrived in a rural hamlet, and Dad marched up to a small cluster of houses. He glared at them as impertinent imposters. The map came out, and he studied it, running his finger along the canvas as Mum rolled her eyes and we kids mucked around. He looked up at the houses and then back at the map. Over his shoulder and to his side. Finally, a man ambled past with a dog.

'Excuse me, sir.' He was always polite. 'I am trying to locate the model village.'

The dog walker laughed. 'The model village? The model village? Crikey, that shut just after the war.'

Dad looked embarrassed for a few seconds.

'What year is the map, Harry?' said Mum.

Dad studied the map. '1926. It was still here when I came when I was about ten.'

'Well, that was 1930,' said Mum. 'It's now 1968.'

Politically Dad had become circumspect by the 1960s. I am sure he still voted Labour having abandoned any Communist Party flirtations. However, he had a low opinion generally of most politicians, believing that many were in it for power, money and vanity rather than a genuine desire to improve people's lives. He felt that the country was poorly served by having to choose between Harold Wilson and Ted Heath. When I would ask who he would be voting for he would shrug and comment that they were both as bad as each other. What about Jeremy Thorpe? He laughed and said, what about him? Later one of the few television programmes he made a point of watching was Mike Yarwood's show, whose bedrock was the mimicking and lampooning of the current crop of politicians. Dad laughed a lot at Mike.

He and Mum never tried to impress upon us their beliefs to such a point that even now I could not say for sure what their political and religious loyalties were. They encouraged us to think things through for ourselves and reach our own conclusions. My parents did, though, impress upon us a set of simple guidelines in the form of sayings and homilies, and they sat above everything else; most parents did the same, and for the most part they worked. They were not strict instructions but were transmitted to us kindly and subtly: Say thank you and please. Do as you will be done by. Treat others as you would like to be treated. Manners cost nothing. Don't lie. Don't steal. Don't hit. Be kind. Share. Read. Learn. Enjoy. Smile. Live and let live.

13
GOT MY MIND SET ON YOU

I emerged from my very early childhood more or less physically unscathed. I attached myself to the back of the ice cream van once and fell off when it started moving and suffered concussion, but that was it. Besides Liz's thumb injury, only Sally among us was badly hurt when she fell out of a tree over the back and broke her arm. When I was nine, though, I was being given a 'backie' on Eddie's bike, and I came off as he took a corner in Gibraltar Rec. Falling off bikes was normal. In fact, it was part of the fun and compulsory. However, this time I fell awkwardly and broke my elbow. The pain was excruciating. I was put into plaster at Epsom District Hospital and had to attend once a week for a long time afterwards for physiotherapy where they gradually persuaded me to stretch my arm fully.

Back at school Tony looked on enviously as I was excused writing and some lessons because of my injury and boys and even some teachers happily signed my plaster with their biros and ink pens. I was awarded temporary celebrity status. I was left in the classroom alone during break times, as there were fears I might get bumped and hurt. All these special measures and attention were beginning to annoy Tony.

The next thing I know is that he invited other boys to jump on his back while he was in the press-up position on extended fingers so he could break them. He succeeded, and his fingers were put into a leather contraption and sling by the hospital, and he too was excused lessons and writing. It reminded me of a prisoner-of-war film we used to watch on TV in which a soldier deliberately hit his hand with a hammer to get out of having to escape.

I had a few rough-and-tumble fights with other boys but nothing of any note and none that left any damage or inflicted too much pain. At school I got into a brawl with an eight-year-old boy from the year above, Stuart. He was as small as I was, but I was taken aback at his energetic enthusiasm to smash my face in. We were in the school library, which was a tiny room, and we crashed around the books and the furniture. It went on for what seemed an age until a teacher broke us up. We were sent to Mr Bell, who warned we'd be caned if there was any recurrence. I have no idea why the fight started, but Stuart and I, who had not known each other well previously, became lifetime friends.

One teatime I was playing football on the green outside my house, and a boy called Mark, who was a year above me at school and bigger, objected to a tackle or something I did and jumped on me. I remember being shocked by his sheer weight smothering me and the panic I felt when I could not get him off. He wasn't a bully, Mark, nor even a scrapper, but he was genuinely mad at me, and I began to scream because I couldn't breathe well. I felt around with my hand beside me and found a stone (what happened to stones; they used to be everywhere?) and smashed his head with it. It must have had a sharp or jagged side to it because it drew blood. Mark jumped off me and ran indoors crying. I sneaked inside fearing repercussions but said nothing to my mum. Sure enough Mark's mum appeared at the front door minutes later holding a bloodied flannel to her son's head.

'Your son has attacked my son with a brick.'

'It was a little stone,' I interjected from behind mum's legs.

'I don't care what it was. Look at what he has done.'

She lifted the flannel to reveal a small gash. I went up on tiptoes to get a better look.

'Did you, Martin?' asked Mum, looking down at me sternly.

'Yes, I did. He was lying on me, beating me up. I was suffocating, Mum.'

Mum was diplomatic but firm. She pointed out that Mark was a lot bigger than me and that he did not deny lying on top of me, slapping and punching, and I probably panicked and wouldn't have known that the stone was sharp. I heard the phrase 'boys will be boys'. Mark was always more careful around me after that, but we remained friendly. I stupidly took the lesson from the incident that a disproportionate response to aggression was a good thing and could scare people off and mean I wouldn't have to fight.

A while later my friend Paul and I committed our one and only burglary, on our friend Dave's house. He and his family had gone away for Christmas, and we decided it would be a thrill to get inside their home. We let ourselves in the back gate and then gained entry by climbing up and opening a bigger window via the fanlight window. Dave's parents would have been relaxed about leaving small windows open or unlocked as burglary was rarer in those days. Once inside we ran around giggling for a few seconds and then sat in an armchair each. On the dining-room table there was a tin with a ribbon around it, and we prised the lid open. Inside was a Christmas cake with delicious looking icing. We took a knife from the kitchen drawer and two plates so as not to make any crumbs and cut and ate a slice each and then replaced the lid. We washed up the plates and the knife and replaced them in the cupboard and drawer. We left the way we had come. When we saw Dave after Christmas it was hard to keep a straight face as he excitedly told us about the burglar who had broken into his house but not taken anything except some cake.

Falling madly in love at the age of nine or ten seems unlikely, but I did, head over heels, and I can still feel the power of it today. There was no sexual engine driving it, but I was pole-axed by the girl's beauty: her hair, her flawless, lightly tanned skin, her smell and her smile. A smile that when she finally awarded it to me made my fucking legs buckle.

Par for the course, I met her at Gibraltar Rec down West Street. Her name was Denise, and she lived in nearby Ewell Court. I knew this because I followed her home. She was a year and a half older than me, and by the time my infatuation began she was reaching the end of her junior-school years. I first saw her on the swings with a couple of friends. She subtly moved her body to make the swing go higher, and the wind rushed through her hair. Finally, she jumped, as did her friends, and landed elegantly near where I was sitting, staring.

I was sat with the soles of my shoes facing her. I was hoping she would be impressed by my new Wayfinder footwear that had a compass embedded in the heel and an animal-track guide on the soles. Some marketing genius had dreamed this up, and boys across the country were pestering their parents for a pair despite no one needing a compass to get around and the fact that wild-animal tracks were spectacularly absent from most urban areas.

A female had not had this effect on me before. I told her I loved her that very first day.

She regarded me with horror, recoiled and said, 'Go away, Titch.' Titch was one of the milder insults aimed at smaller people back in the day. I preferred it to dwarf, midget and even squirt. Some years later another girl I had designs on called me a Munchkin. That cut deep.

But I could not get Denise out of my head. Could not get to sleep. Each afternoon after school that summer I swerved my friends and went to the Rec, and sure enough she would be there. When Denise was in company she would not acknowledge me – indeed, she would throw me a look, warning 'do not dare to talk to me'. When she turned up one evening without her friends I sensed a flicker of interest despite the height and age difference.

'What's the matter with you?' she asked.

'I can't help it. I love you.'

'But you're only nine. You can't fall in love. You don't even know me.'

Slowly, after some weeks of persistent stalking she weakened, and we chatted and met most early evenings, and I would walk her home as it got dark. It was a rule in my house by this time that I had to be indoors by dusk or 9 p.m. whichever came first. One night the tips of our fingers touched, and she did not withdraw her hand. A bolt of romantic electricity coursed through my being. Progress was being made. It was not for public consumption, however. If she saw some girls in the distance beyond the putting green she would tell me to step away in case they were schoolmates. Girls then normally went out with boys older than they were, and having a boyfriend younger was shameful; a suggestion you could not do any better. 'Going out' was a twee phrase used to describe a boyfriend/girlfriend relationship. Where would I be taking Denise? Where would our special date be? The horse show up at Hook Road, the cigarette machine outside Bedford's or Saturday morning pictures, perhaps? We were spoiled for choice.

I said earlier I committed my one and only burglary with Paul. I did, shamefully, commit another with Tony. I made the mistake of mentioning that Denise had gone on holiday with her family.

'Let's get in her house,' suggested Tony, excitedly.

Why I went along with it is beyond me. We got in the same way we did at Dave's. Again, we had no idea what to do once inside. There was no inclination or idea to steal anything. It was all about the thrill of being somewhere we should not have been. We found some aerosol cans of Crazy Foam, which was all the rage at the time, and sprayed it over a couple of mirrors then left. Maybe Denise got the blame. I confessed all to her forty years later.

One evening we saw the sun going down in the distance behind the council yard and set off home. One way out of the Rec was up some stone stairs adjacent to the Ewell West railway platform that led to the main road. A man was coming down towards us carrying his bike with one hand. As I passed him he ruffled my hair as men sometimes did. 'Hello, Sonny Jim,' they would say as they patted my head. But the ruffle this night turned into a tug, and I sensed aggression. It was horrible. I believe he told me to 'hop it'. It all happened in seconds, but he leaned his bike against the fence, picked up Denise who was struck dumb by the turn of events and was interfering with her. I shouted and picked up a stone and threw it at him. It missed but distracted him momentarily, and Denise struggled free and ran past me and straight across the road, adjusting her clothing at the same time. The Chessington Road was a fast highway, and thank God she was not struck by a car.

We ran to the bottom of the hill not stopping until we reached Bedford's, the sweet shop. She was crying, and I put my arm around her. This was something I had been building up to but didn't expect to happen in such traumatic circumstances.

'Don't tell your parents. Don't tell anyone,' she sobbed.

'Why? What did he do?'

I could not understand that she did not want to tell her parents. I cannot remember how much I understood of what had just happened but knew enough to realise that it was serious and wrong. I contemplated kissing her but thankfully decided against it. Instead, we parted at the top of Green Lanes, and I went straight in and told Mum and Dad, despite my promise to Denise. I opened with, 'You'll never guess what just happened.' They were very concerned and shocked, and Dad jumped on his bike and cycled to Denise's house. When he came back he said that she had not mentioned it to her parents. There was no more going to the Rec in the evenings for me or Denise. Whether the events were connected I don't know, but not too long afterwards her family upped sticks and moved to Surbiton. Surbiton was beyond walking – or should I say stalking – distance so there was no chance of resuming our one-sided love affair. It was very sad.

She wrote me a letter that confirmed, in my eager mind, at least, that she had some feelings for me. She drew a picture of us and revealed she had seen me with some mates at Surbiton Lagoon. I treasured the letter and kept it into adulthood. There followed a Christmas card, which I still have, and then she was gone.

The attacker was very distinctive, and I was able to tell the police (they interviewed us separately) that he wore heavy glasses and suffered from weeping acne. Most notably, though, was the observation that his pushbike had a sort of engine attached to it. One afternoon a few months later my sister Sally came in from walking our dog Cindy in a distressed state. She said a man fitting the perv's description had just started following her. Dad jumped on his bike and pedalled furiously up the Longmead Road. I think he apprehended the man and held him while he phoned the police from the phone box in Pound Lane. But there is the possibility my young imagination added that last flourish to give me a happy, safe and dramatic ending. For sure, my sister remembers the incident and Dad biking up the road, but she cannot confirm that he caught the bad man.

The outside world was penetrating my world more and more. I think this was a result of my increased awareness of what was going on around me combined with news and news-based programmes becoming more prevalent on the TV and radio. Early in the 1960s the news was a short ten-minute interval shoe-horned into an evening of entertainment programming; later in the decade it was almost the other way around, with half-hour slots at 6 p.m. and 10 p.m. and other programmes like *Nationwide*, *Panorama*, *This Week*, *World In Action* and many others getting a bigger slice of the schedule.

Around the time I was obsessing over Denise I would have been aware of the big stories of the year. Student riots in Paris and London seemed to be a feature of most weekends. Over here student leader Tariq Ali was the bogeyman or the hero depending on your politics. Immigration was a constant bone of contention. Enoch Powell was a pariah or a hero following his 'rivers of blood' speech, and Ted Heath did his best to distance himself from his MP, but the undeniable fact was Powell echoed the views and channelled the fears of large swathes of the population. Talk of colour bars, racialism, the 'coloured problem' and sending people home were phrases much used in everyday broadcasting.

I even became vaguely aware of what was happening in the rest of the world. America seemed to be one disaster after another; conflict in Rhodesia and Russian tanks rolling into Czechoslovakia filled our screens. But we took little notice. By 'we' I mean adults and children alike. The average viewer or newspaper reader was far more engaged with the rounding up of the Great Train Robbers, the Richardsons' torture trial, with gruesome details of teeth being pulled, and our first introduction to Mad Frankie Fraser and other assorted gory murders. In fact, as a family, we were far more upset by the news of Tony Hancock's sad demise in Australia than any of the aforementioned peace-threatening global events.

Stephen joined our family around this time. The emotional torture of Fiona's departure must have faded, and Mum and Dad agreed to take Stephen, a boy of Barbadian descent, who was in short-term foster care. I went with Mum and our new social worker to fetch him from a large quick-turnover foster-family home in Horsham. From the kitchen Stephen was pointed out to me in the garden sitting on a swing. There were other kids playing, but he sat alone all dressed up in blue shorts and matching blazer in preparation for his next berth. I was encouraged to go out and talk to him. Stephen was three and I was ten. Even then he was strikingly handsome and tall for his age.

'Hello, Stephen. I'm Martin,' I said. 'I'm your new brother.'

Maybe that was not the best way to put it. Stephen did not look at me and just stared down at the floor. How many times this innocent three-year-old had been passed around I do not know. I hope not many. How many 'brothers' had he encountered? Poor boy didn't speak for his first few weeks with us, and I guess he had already learned to internalise his feelings. We were worried he was struck dumb for a while, and the day he first spoke, sitting cross-legged in our living-room, was glorious. He had a good command of vocabulary and just started speaking as if he had been the whole time. We tried not to act surprised, as we didn't want to freak him out. After those first few weeks he settled in and flowered. Stephen was a lovely, beautiful kid.

14
COMING UP

Back at St Mary's School I had entered the final year. Our class was now top of the tree at Eggs, Bacon and Sausages. Not yet five feet, I was now officially a 'big boy'. Yet, as we bossed the younger children around our feelings of seniority were compromised by something coming along the track that would direct, even decide, our futures: the eleven-plus. This was the single written examination that decided whether you went to a secondary modern or to a grammar school. Arguably, it was the test that decided whether you were more likely to be a blue-collar worker or a white-collar worker. The certificate could indicate whether you would own a house as an adult or rent. Even if it did not do any of these things, people believed it did. My siblings Sally and Laurence had both passed their eleven-plus. Sally got into Coombe Girls, a reasonably prestigious school over in Kingston, and Laurence went to Glyn Grammar just over the railway line from the estate. Expectation, therefore, was high.

The boys from Glyn wore a blue uniform and the school had a reputation for academic excellence and had a formidable football team. Each summer a fete was held in the grounds, and the five-a-side football tournament was the key attraction. Here we met boys for the first time who would figure prominently in our lives once we reached senior school. Famous old Glyn boys included the actor David Hemmings and Flash Bob Harris. Bob did not last long at Glyn, but he achieved legendary status first as a hustler at the snooker hall in Epsom and then later on the world snooker stage. Fleetingly Bob was the George Best of the green baize.

Mr Rees was our new form teacher. He was a plump Welshman, balding with a small grey toothbrush moustache. He wore a collar and tie, but his attempt at tidiness was compromised because his outerwear was an old green woollen cardigan, crumpled St Michael trousers and brushed Hush

Puppy shoes on his feet. He struck me as one of those people who could never look smart even if he went to Moss Bros with more guineas than he could spend. He was football mad, and managing our over-achieving school team was his true vocation. To this day I have no idea what subject he taught. There was no detectable curriculum with Reeso (as some called him), but he held our attention. He loved to settle us down and regale us with stories from his childhood in Llandovery, about the legendary highwayman Twm Sion Cati – a 16th-century Welsh Robin Hood with Llandovery connections. Maybe that was the history module. He would tell us such stories if we didn't snitch that he wasn't sticking to conventional lessons. That was the unwritten and unspoken but strictly adhered-to agreement between us. I do not think he cared. His career had peaked long before, and he was now counting down the days to his retirement.

Rees would march us through Ewell Village to the playing field opposite St Mary's Church that was bordered at the far end by the Eight Bells and Jolly Waggoners pubs. He then told us to 'fall in' to two teams and that he'd only be a minute, but there was some broken glass over by those trees he needed to pick up. Yes, he was psychic as well. We watched him at the trees, rocking back, legs apart as he relieved himself. No doubt he'd had a couple of pints in the King Bill at lunchtime as well as a few fags. He smoked in front of us, as did most adults then. But, to mask the smell of the alcohol and the cigarettes, he was a rabid consumer of peppermints, and even now, if I try, I can conjure up the aroma of that questionable cocktail of alcohol, tobacco and peppermint that clung to him.

Sometimes he administered punishment, but unlike Bircham it gave him no pleasure. If he had to he would call you up to the front of the class, wearily ordered you to bend down and then gently clasp your head between his knees and administer the lightest slap imaginable. To maintain the pretence, we returned to our seat rubbing our backside and pulling our suitably admonished face.

He was a kind man too. My mum developed a lump on her breast and had to go to hospital for a week to have the growth removed. It was presented to us kids as a routine operation, but what we picked up on and know now was that there was a period of uncertainty when it was thought that the growth might have been malignant and further invasive surgery needed. Curiously, the word 'cancer' was never mentioned. We kids were coping at home on our own until Dad came in from work, although our neighbour Auntie Pauline would be looking in on us to make sure we had not burned the house down. Mr Rees held me back one day as we were filing out of the class.

'Stay behind, boy. I want to have a word with you.'

I feared some misdemeanour or other had been discovered.

'How is your mother?' he asked when it was only us left in the classroom.

'She's in hospital,' I replied.

'Yes, I know. Well, if you are upset at any time just come and see me.'

That made feel like there was more wrong with Mum than she and Dad were letting on.

'Thank you, sir.'

Rees bent down and picked a large tin from his hold-all and handed it to me. 'This is for you and your brothers and sisters. My wife baked it. I've had a hell of a job not starting on it during the day, I can tell you.'

A beautiful fruit cake, we soon discovered as we tucked into it at home.

There is a picture which shows that Tony, Eddie, Bill and I had long abandoned any pretence of wearing school uniform. I am in my beloved bumper boots. Tony is wearing a defiant polo neck. He was never out of it. A girl had told him once he looked like Ilya Kuryakin from *The Man From Uncle* in it, and after that it became a bit of a fixture. He probably bathed in it. Mr Rees has smartened up for this one. I am not in touch with all the thirty-three boys assembled, but I do know that as I write in 2021, half a century on, at least five are dead. One by suicide following a marital break-up, one helped on the way by drugs, two with Covid-19 complications and another by drink and obesity. At least four spent some time in prison. Two settled in America, one in Australia. Another became the chief executive of one of the biggest food companies in the world. Looking at these classmates, I can recall various nicknames we called each other. Appearance teasing was common. It didn't normally arise from malice, but kids were singled out for being different – or, more accurately, their difference was singled out. It was rare then for children to wear glasses, but one boy did, and he was inevitably called Four Eyes. His spectacles were National Health issue – pink and held together with first-aid-box pink plasters. Only two boys were overweight, and their lives were blighted by too many slurs to mention.

Some of us wore our school shirts for days at a time, even a whole school week. Consequently, dirty tide marks appeared around collar and cuffs. We wore our underpants and socks several days in a row too. One boy I felt very sorry for when he came into school in a pair of grey shorts. Some observant bastards among us could see the hem was uneven and a slightly different length on each leg. It became apparent his mum had cut down a pair of long trousers. Others would be mercilessly baited for not wearing underpants under their shorts. That was common.

Every now and then a 'new boy' arrived. I had been a new boy along with twenty others but never on my own. That must have been a real ordeal for a young child. In that final year Robert joined us. He was paraded at the front of the class. He wore a blazer from another school, short trousers that did not match the blazer and socks rolled down *Just William* style. He had a lopsided grin and an old face on young shoulders. At the first playtime Tony and I decided to seek him out.

The first thing that struck us was his London accent. The floor around him was littered with dropped aitches. He swore casually and liberally, not like us who expected a reaction from every bloody or fuck we sparingly and daringly uttered. He exuded a swaggering confidence that was at odds with a boy who clearly came from an impoverished background.

'Yeah, mate. I just got here. Ewell. Fuck me backwards. Bit quiet, ain't it? I'm from Battersea, me. Been there? Fifty miles away, mate. We just moved here. Abinger Road. Know it? Up the 'ill. Over there.' He jerked his thumb over his shoulder. 'The old man's doing a stretch. Bank robber, 'e is. Luckily he got the 'ouse first. When 'e comes out 'e's gonna retire and come an' live with the ole woman and me an' my bruvvers an' sisters.'

It seemed very rude to me and Tony to refer to your mum and dad as old woman and old man, but his rough-diamond Londoner charm was infectious.

'Do you wanna come to tea at my gaff?'

What to make of this boy? We knew Abinger Road. It was in East Ewell. Nobody we knocked about with lived in a road like that. It was posh. Surely, he was making it up? We had been up there carol singing thinking that the more money a household had the more silver they'd chuck us for slaughtering 'Once In Royal David's City' on their front doorstep. (We were wrong. The more modest homes were normally the most generous.) We took the bank-robber yarn with a pinch of salt. A new boy keen to impress. Trying to make friends. As for the invitation we said we would ask our parents.

When I mentioned going to tea with the new boy Mum was agreeable, especially when I mentioned Abinger Road.

'The one in East Ewell?' she asked in case another one had cropped up on the new Watersedge estate that was then under construction.

'Yes, East Ewell, Mum.'

When I saw Bobby (he said to call him Bobby) the next day, I told him that my old lady was fine about it. Tony's parents were on board too, and a couple of afternoons after Bobby had joined the school we travelled out the village up the Cheam Road together to his house. Sure enough, it was a large, detached mock-Tudor home with a sweeping in-and-out drive. I had never entered a house of this size. To us it was a mansion. Inside there were lakes of shiny parquet floors but no furniture. None. In one corner of a room that seemed bigger than the whole footprint of my house was a television set, and sitting around it, oblivious to our arrival, were three small children, barely dressed, thoroughly engrossed in *Top Cat*.

'Mum,' shouted Bobby towards the kitchen. 'Me pals are 'ere. The ones I told you about. Martin and Tony. They've come to tea.'

The doors of a serving hatch burst open, and like a cuckoo from a clock a lady with flaming red hair threw her head through it.

'Well, you can tell Martin and Tony to fuck off,' she rasped in a non-tipped-cigarette-scorched voice.

I had never heard an adult swear like that. There were lots of bloodys, bleedings and buggers about at the time, but fuck was not a word routinely used by grown-ups in the presence of children. Not where we lived anyway.

'Mam,' pleaded Richard.

'And you can fuck off wiv 'em too, you stoopid bastard, bringing people back 'ere. Use your fucking loaf.'

Bobby shrugged. Tony and I were already walking backwards out of the front door. His mum frightened the life out of us.

Tea incident notwithstanding, Bobby, Tony and I became almost inseparable. He was exciting. There was not a boy like him in the school, perhaps the borough. On a Monday we brought our dinner money in to pay for the school meals for the week. The school should have been paying us, as the food was mainly awful. Mashed potato with hard lumps buried within, gravy with congealed skin, sickly greens and soft carrots and invariably some sort of stew or casserole. Puddings were worse, and I had never seen such dishes at home or anywhere else. Pink semolina, apple crumble, lemon curd, prunes and jam roly-poly. Their pleasant names disguise the awfulness of most of them.

Bobby challenged us. 'Why you buying that shit?'

He led us to the sweet shop in the village and encouraged us to purchase sweets with our dinner money. We loaded up on Toffos, Mint Cracknel, Mars Bars and penny sweets for puddings. We walked up to the Grove, outside our old infant school, to sit down under a large tree and prepared to scoff the confectionery delights, at which point a grinning Bobby emptied his blazer pockets. While we had been innocently occupying the shopkeeper with our legitimate order, he had loaded up with an array of stolen chocolate bars and bags of crisps. We could not believe it. From then on we spent our dinner money on chocolate and sugar, never eating a nutritious, if not palatable, EBS school meal again. Bobby loved it as he was, of course, on the free school meals scheme.

Our newfound alliance with Bobby accelerated our path from mischievous to troublesome, and inevitably this culminated in coming up against the school's severest punishment. Detentions, slaps on the backside and writing 'I must not talk in class' a hundred times no longer held any fear. In that final year the three of us were caned. We had been caught by a grown-up huddled in a phone box ringing numbers at random and swearing down the telephone receiver. We were calling people and shouting down the phone 'Get off the line. There's a train coming.' Kids' stuff. The adult who opened the phone box door and told us off also got a mouthful. How she identified us I cannot remember. Possibly Tony's polo neck, my bumpers and Bobby's purple blazer.

We were stood on the carpet of the headmaster's office. Frank Bell was an angry man. 'When you travel to and from this school you are still representing the school. Do you not comprehend? Your actions have brought the school into disrepute. I have no choice but to cane you.'

At the mention of the word 'cane' Mrs Jerome, the headmaster's secretary, got up and scurried out of the office. She was a kindly lady who dabbed witch hazel on our bloodied knees when we scraped them in the playground. The giddying smell of the witch hazel combined with her perfume as we sat in front of her were worth the pain. She was woman, all woman, Stanley. Mr Bell then sent Bobby and Tony out of the room and told them to wait there. He went into a further individual lecture about how I would soon be going to the senior school and how I needed to improve my behaviour before I got there. As he droned on my eye caught the one small clear pane in the centre of the frosted-glass office door. Bobby had gripped his own hand around his neck and was acting pulling it away with the other hand. It gave the effect he was being strangled by an assailant. I tried not to laugh, but the more I tried the greater the urge became. Then I exploded, expelling spit. Bell could not believe it. He strode around his desk and held me by the back of the neck as he bought his cane down several times on my arse. There is a scene in Ken Loach's superb film *Kes* that practically reprises this event. It is one of the most authentic portrayals of school life in that period I have ever seen.

It didn't really hurt at all. What was more shocking was the temporary loss of control from the headmaster. He was roaring something about it not being a laughing matter. Nevertheless, I was not sufficiently disturbed never to be subjected to other punishments before my days at EBS were out. The problem with deterrents is that once the deterrent has been deployed they lose their deterrent qualities. The cane from Bell hurt less than an elastic band in the face.

With 21st-century eyes it seems brutal that strong middle-aged males were manhandling ten-year-old boys standing less than five feet tall and striking them hard across the buttocks with a long stick. But that's how it was. I caught the final dying days of corporal punishment and thought very little of it. I certainly didn't and don't have any issue with Mr Bell. He was doing his job. He had probably been on courses on how to cane safely. Nevertheless, the thought of having gone from being chucked joyfully in the air to 'A Little Loving' by an adoring mother to being hit with a stick by a big angry man in the space of four short years does make me shudder. I certainly would have been horrified just twenty years later at the thought of that happening to my children.

Tony had a low boredom threshold, and this, coupled with his adventurous spirit, often got him (and me) into trouble. One day he was climbing the trees in the grounds of Bourne Hall. We were shaking down conkers. Tony would always climb higher than was necessary or advisable. Eddie and I stood at the bottom of the tree looking up as he shouted 'I'm Tarzan' and leaped from one branch to another. It was a foolhardy move, and he came tumbling a good thirty feet to the ground with branches only partially breaking his fall. It was shocking as we watched him thud to the floor, but most worrying was that a sharp stone embedded itself into his cheek. He was conscious and seemed to be able to move, but blood pumped from his wound like we had never seen before. I ran into Spring Street for help where Roger Street from the estate – coincidentally Tony's next-door neighbour – was passing. He ran to a phone box and called an ambulance. The upshot was that Tony was left with a gouge-like scar on his face that hardened his features and would later contribute to the wrong impression that he was a boy of violence.

Tony already bore some scars around his eyes. Air guns and rifles were a scourge of 1960s council estates. They were legal but powerful and capable of causing much damage. In the wrong hands they were very dangerous and, of course, people with the right hands had no interest in owning them. Tony copped a pellet in the eye one afternoon. It was never established who did it. A pot-shot from a bedroom window or a sniper behind a car perhaps. Again, stitches were required that left another scar this time on his eyelid. And only days later Tony's dad, a keen darts player, was practising against a board hung on the inside of the garden gate. Tony was watching his father honing his craft when an arrow bounced off the board and landed straight in his eye, reopening the wound. If something bad was going to happen, it normally happened to Tony.

He loved his music, like me. He was not a big Beatles or Stones fan but went crazy over the Monkees when they came along, and we were both caught up in the hysteria that briefly matched Beatlemania. He learned all the words to 'I'm A Believer' and frequently sang it, but he adored 'Daydream Believer', and I cannot hear the 'Cheer up, sleepy Jean' intro without conjuring up images of Tony walking down the road singing at the top of his voice in his best Davy Jones voice. He even banged an imaginary tambourine against his hip. Later he became an early male adopter of the Jackson Five and would regale me with 'I'll Be There' from beginning to end.

The eleven-plus examination loomed large. It was mentioned by the teachers more and more. This served to build a general anxiety among many of us. My parents were certainly expecting and hoping that I would be following in my siblings' footsteps, but they did not exert too much pressure. However, there were boys in my class who knew their parents would be devastated if they failed and there were others who didn't give a toss.

What I did know for sure was that Tony would *not* be passing. He was not an academic boy by any measure. I was therefore forced to decide. I could not contemplate embarking on my senior-school life without my best friends, so I made the decision to fail the test deliberately. To be sure I answered general knowledge questions facetiously. What is the capital of France – F. That type of thing. It worked. I failed decisively, not even being invited for an 'interview' – a mechanism used then to capture capable pupils who might have suffered with nerves on the day.

My father said to me in his final years that failing my eleven-plus was a massive event in my life, and he contended that it spurred me on in adulthood. He said it made me rebellious and angry because my elder brother and sister had both passed and I had failed. Dad spoke many words of wisdom, but he was wrong here. He *was* correct that I avoided a competitive situation with my siblings but for very different reasons than he believed. It was not only my wish to be with Tony and Eddie that pushed me in the direction I took but I strongly felt I would not fit in at grammar school.

From my class of thirty-odd pupils about seven boys passed the exam. Not one was from our estate and all of them lived in the nearby closes, cul-de-sacs and gardens of owner-occupier suburbia. I couldn't work that one out yet. Why would where you lived dictate your level of intelligence or memory or ambition?

Now it was known I would be attending a secondary modern comprehensive school my parents had to decide which one. Longmead School was literally across the road from our house and would be the obvious geographical choice. However, it was an all-boys school and had acquired a deserved reputation for being rough and tough. Mum and Dad decided the mixed Ewell County Secondary School, nearly two miles away, would be a safer choice and offer more ambience. Fortunately, Tony's and Eddie's parents felt the same way. Also Mum had attended the school and had good memories.

Bobby, our new wayward friend, was being sent to Longmead School, joining some older brothers. It was sad, but we agreed to keep in touch. How we were going to do this easily was another matter, as our families did not possess a telephone between us. Inevitably we lost contact. A couple of years later I heard from a boy on the estate who also went to Longmead that a pupil had been expelled from school and sent to approved school for setting a classroom alight. I knew who the arsonist was before the boy said his name.

15
A DAY IN THE LIFE

Before this momentous time of moving up schools, the summer holidays of 1969 were to be enjoyed. Bryan Adams eulogised that particular summer in song. He told us of being at school and having a band where, later, Jimmy quit and Jody got married. He was spot on, at least, when he said that that summer seemed to last for ever and they were the best days of his life. Those six-week interregnums between school years really did feel endless. Friendships could be forged and run their course in those exuberant, halcyon days. Fast-maturing children could even watch in the mirror as their physical appearance changed before their eyes in those long, dreamy weeks. Of course, 'Summer Of '69' had not been written then; the song that, for me, conjures up that time as soon as I hear the opening lyric – 'Call out the instigators' – is 'Something In The Air' by Thunderclap Newman. I had no real idea what the lyrics were about, but with talk of the revolution being here I sensed it was something profound.

For Tony, Eddie and me a typical Saturday that summer would have gone something like this: up early for a fast breakfast of corn flakes and milk dusted with a couple of tablespoons full of sugar. We'd meet at the car park and walk up the 'new road' to Epsom past some gleaming new factories. Under our arms were swimming trunks rolled into a towel like a sausage roll. First stop was Epsom Baths.

The smell of chlorine assaulted our nostrils as we entered the big brown doors. It was a welcome aroma that triggered our excitement. After paying our shilling we then ran down the stairs to the right, which led to the boys' changing rooms, and collected our wire trays that we took into our wooden cubicle where we undressed quicker than a milkman on a promise from a frustrated wife of an oil-rig worker. Reappearing in trunks we handed a tray back to the uninterested attendant who gave us a key in return that we safety-pinned to our trunks. Then we were obliged to paddle through a disinfectant pool – which was a disgusting repository of plasters, scabs, verrucae and detached skin that had floated off other swimmers during the day – and then we rushed up the little stairs exiting to the huge pool like England footballers emerging out of the Wembley tunnel.

The pool seemed enormous and stretched from three feet deep at the 'baby' end to twelve feet at the deep end. Tony was a natural swimmer and would dive in straight off the springboard, curving in the air like a salmon. Here was something he excelled at. Eddie and I were more cautious and positioned ourselves strategically in the middle where our feet still touched the ground, but we were not splashing around with the toddlers. Urban myths abounded. As well as the springboard there was a middle diving board and a top diving board that to me seemed terrifying. Teenagers scrambled up the ladder to queue to dive off it, some making Tarzan noises just to ensure everybody was watching. A story we heard was one of these youths did just this but belly-flopped instead of cutting deftly into the water and his stomach tore open. I was told his name was Alan, a big lad off the estate. People were having to swim hurriedly away from his intestines as they bobbed towards them, and the whole pool turned red. And this was before *Jaws*. A couple of years later I spoke to Alan and mentioned his unfortunate swimming accident. He had no idea what I was talking about and looked at me like I had a screw loose.

After a few hours in the baths, with our skin beginning to wrinkle like prunes, we would return to the cubicles and dress again. In the foyer was a buffet, and a Mars Bar and a hot chocolate never tasted better. Outside on the steps some of the boys would be poncing cigarettes off Cyril, the friendly and entirely harmless mental patient from one of the hospitals. He loved the camaraderie.

From the baths we would walk the short distance into town. Although Epsom was barely a couple of miles from where we lived, we looked upon it as a vibrant, exciting, bustling metropolis. Compared to Ewell Village, where there were still more bikes than cars (and even the occasional horse), it was. We visited Boots, where upstairs there was a record department. You could ask for any single and claim you wanted to listen before buying and the assistant would be obliged to load it up and play it to you in your very own booth.

'No thanks,' we'd say after listening to all six minutes of 'A Whiter Shade of Pale'. Soon some of the assistants got wise to us and would not play ball – or 'Hey Jude', for that matter.

Woolworths next door provided equal amounts of free entertainment. Naturally the charming, chugging, well-polished wooden escalators had to be ascended and descended the wrong ways. The incognito store detective destroyed his anonymity for the day by chasing us and throwing us out of the store.

We would then head up to the clock tower around which clustered a busy outdoor market. By far the most interesting stall for us was Sid the Yid's clothes stall. Everyone called him by that name, and he did himself. Yid, in this case, at least, was not meant or taken in any offensive way. Appearance and clothing was just beginning to become important to us, and within a few months it would be an obsession. The first fashion item I remember hankering after was a monkey jacket. These blue zip-up jackets with their neat red, white and blue collar and cuffs – were popularised in the UK first by being the off-pitch squad attire of the England World Cup team. I pestered my mum and dad for one, and I guess in 1967 or 1968 I was finally satisfied. The day I got it I proudly put it on and walked out of the house down to the shops to make an imaginary purchase. I truly believed that neighbours were rushing to their windows to view the jacket and passing pedestrians were performing double takes and admiring me.

'Ethel, take a look. That boy from over the road, he's only gone and got himself a monkey jacket.'

It was pathetic how a single item of clothing could elevate the self-esteem of a ten-year-old.

That summer of 1969, as we stood in front of Sid's display, we noted older boys trying on shirts with button-down collars and jackets with a wiggly line on the back. These were Brutus shirts and Harringtons, named after a character played by Ryan O' Neal in *Peyton Place*. They also paraded themselves in jeans and jean jackets, which they insisted had to be Levi's. They were using Sid's 'changing-room', a narrow space between the canvas on the back of his stall and his parked-up van, and reappearing to twirl and strut for their mates or girlfriends. We could sense their excitement but hadn't quite got it yet. Desmond Dekker's infectious

'Israelites' emanating from a nearby transistor radio cemented the feel of something in the air. (We called our little transistor radios 'trannies', by the way, enough to have you locked up for a hate crime fifty years later.)

Tearing ourselves away from the banter and bustle of Sid's emporium we would wander up to the Odeon, and, if we had enough money left, go in and see a film. There was a strict censorship code. Not being fifteen feet tall between us and with our swimming gear still under our arms there was no way we were getting into an X-rated show – although, that day would not be too far off. Next down was an A, which meant children could get in with an adult, and then U, which stood for universal, meaning anyone was allowed in. I know we saw *Carry On Camping* there that year. I think the *Carry On* films were AAs – a new classification that allowed you entry if you were fourteen and above. The film sticks in my mind and the nation's because of the single scene where Barbara Windsor's bra pings open during morning exercise and there is a glimpse of her breasts. Or was there? No freeze frame or rewind in those days.

How we all loved Sid James, Bernard Bresslaw, Kenneth Williams and company. *Carry On* films did so much for the country's morale, bringing laughter, pleasure and titillation to millions for nearly three decades. As far as I know not one of that little firm ever got a knighthood, yet people like Kenneth Branagh – a man most people outside his family would be hard pushed to name any production he has ever been in – is Sir Kenneth. That's Britain's embedded snobbery for you.

When we left the Odeon we swerved next door to Marshall's, the fish shop. It was a long shop with beautiful glazed-tile walls. We would buy a piece of the cheap option – rock salmon, the new rebranding of dogfish – and a large portion of chips between us. The meal came wrapped in newspaper, and we were invited to smother it in salt and vinegar before heading outside to wolf it down.

As we walked out of Epsom the market would be packing up. Shoe-shop girls would be queueing at the bus stops to head home. I wonder if people had more feet then, for there were footwear shops galore. I can remember the following in Epsom High Street alone: Ravel, Dolcis, Lilley & Skinner, Clarks, Tru-Form and Freeman, Hardy & Willis. Market traders and other male workers were pushing open the doors of the pubs – the Marquis of

Granby, the Albion, the Wellington, the Spread Eagle, the Magpie, the Rifleman, the White Hart and the Charter – to spend some of their hard-earned dosh.

By the time we arrived indoors it would be past 6 p.m., and we had been away from home a good nine or ten hours. Mum and Dad would not bat an eyelid. This was normal in the summer holidays. I would have tea of Marmite sandwiches (not disclosing the fish and chips and sweets that had been consumed earlier) and biscuits and join my siblings in the sitting-room watching *Dr Who*. I could take or leave that programme, although I did get a bolt of excitement seeing Daleks gliding around London landmarks exterminating at will.

Later Mum and Dad would end their gardening and household chores and settle in their chairs, and we would watch *The Lulu Show* and then *Morecambe And Wise* as a family. Bedtime would be around 10 p.m., although that didn't necessarily mean sleep. Up on the top bunk I would insert my earpiece and navigate the fuzzy frequencies and high-pitched whistles on my tiny transistor radio and find Radio Luxembourg, where the likes of Tony Prince – the Royal Ruler – was playing the records that would be making *Top Of The Pops* in a few weeks' time. A couple of hours later my mum or my dad would pad silently into the room, carefully take the plug from my ear, lift the radio from the pillow and place them on the chest of drawers below the bunk as I slept like a dog.

There was no such thing as fast food in the borough besides fish and chips. Home delivery of hot food was a concept as foreign as Botswana. The first fast-food chain I do remember was Wimpy, and when they opened in Epsom it was a cause of great local excitement. It was a little piece of America brought to our town. Burgers were exotic, and flourishes like tomato sauce in a squeezy red-plastic-tomato container were revolutionary. Ice cream floats, Brown Derbys and Knickerbocker Glories the height of indulgence. The Wimpy became a magnet for teenagers and the place to be. It was a pub without beer, a disco without music and a cinema without film. Occasionally we bought some food.

I didn't experience Chinese or Indian cuisine until some years later when I first left school. I remember ordering the family's first takeaway meal –

probably in 1974–5 – and being thrilled to be showing my parents something new rather than the other way around.

'Chow mein? What is it?' said Mum nervously wrapping some around a chopstick and gingerly placing it in her mouth.

'I don't know, but it's nice.'

Meanwhile, Dad had got the hang of his chopsticks and was shovelling rice down his throat.

In 1967 the family invested in a reel-to-reel tape recorder. The wonder and entertainment it brought to our house for a few months was immense. Recording and hearing our own voices for the first time in a very homely way connected us to the technological revolution that was going on all around us. Colour televisions, washing machines and refrigerators were beginning to be taken for granted by some (not us), and we had started to hear the word 'computer', so this machine we were all kneeling around on the floor was a tiny taste of what was coming.

Recently my sister was sorting Mum's things and found several tapes she must have converted to CD before her stroke. Here we are introducing ourselves one by one. Dad has his guitar, and he and Mum sing 'We Shall Overcome', surely influenced by the Martin Luther King race protests. I screech 'My Mind's Eye' by Small Faces from beginning to end. Laurence reads a poem. Sally is reticent; she is of an age where she realises that something incriminating may be left to embarrass her in her teenage years.

Mum has recorded one entire tea time as we sit around competing for toast and chocolate fingers. By this time we are our natural selves, the novelty of the technology has passed. Mum berates me about my table manners.

'Don't speak with your mouth full. Put your food down while you are chewing. Don't speak so fast.'

I volunteer that I don't like a certain teacher at school.

'You don't like anyone,' observes Mum.

Then the conversation moves on to football because Ian Wilson has appeared at the front door asking if Laurence is coming out to play a game on the green.

'You will be playing football soon, Viv, when you go to the big-boys' school,' says Mum.

Viv was six or seven, but even by then I knew he had no interest or aptitude for football or any other sport for that matter. I took him on to the green outside a few times, but he stood there, still, his eyes squeezed shut hoping that ball or boy did not come near him.

And then Liz, his older sister, but closest in age to him asks innocently, 'Mummy? When Viv goes to big-boys' school will he be the only black boy there?'

Mum avoids answering. Liz's question comes from a place of genuine sibling concern. There is a silence except me crunching on toast. I am oblivious, but I am hoping now, fifty-plus years on, that poor Viv was not too scared. Because, yes, he was the only black boy at big-boys' school.

Besides the moon landing and the investiture of Charles as the Prince of Wales, the other event that Ewell Boys' School appeared very excited about as we prepared to leave was the arrival of decimal currency, which was officially two years away. Advance coinage was being sold in display boxes, and we would look in awe at the new 50p bit with its revolutionary heptagonal shape, and we were already spending 5p and 10p coins in the shops. It was going to be sad to lose the old penny, halfpenny, half-crown, tanner and the threepenny bit. I was particularly fond of the latter, which was normally pronounced 'thruppenny', and even recall the last few farthings in circulation. I feel like I should start talking about groats now, but, on checking, I see they were discontinued in the 1850s.

Many adults viewed decimalisation as a ruse to put prices up, and judging how confectionary prices increased, it was. It was explained that it was part of aligning ourselves with European measures and the gradual adoption of metrication. I was not alone in wondering why Europe didn't align with us. Hadn't we saved them in the war? That is what we were taught. My gran in Battersea held the line until she died in 1988. She could never get her head around the change, and right up to the end of her life she was a familiar, if not welcome, shopper on Lavender Hill who demanded of exasperated shopkeepers to know the price of goods in 'real money'.

I deduce that Mum and Dad decided to foster Stephen because it would help Vivian. With Fiona gone he was not just the only black kid on the estate and in Ewell Boys' School, he was the only black kid in our family. Viv was a sensitive soul. He took things to heart, and the older he got I think it became more difficult. One afternoon he told me that a boy on the estate was bullying him. I knew the boy. He was only Viv's age and size, but he knew that Viv would not hit him back, so in my book that was bullying. When Viv told me I knew where the boy would be.

'Come with me,' I said, and marched Viv over the rope swing.

The boy knew something was amiss when I approached him purposefully with Viv reluctantly trailing along behind me.

'Hit him, Viv,' I ordered.

Viv looked unsure.

'Smack him. Gary's not going to hit you back, are you, Gary?'

Gary shook his head. Viv stepped forward and punched Gary in the face. It was a half-hearted, nervous blow, but it made the point, and as far as I know Gary never bothered Viv again.

Viv's best friend was an Italian boy called Lorenzo, who endured similar ribbing, teasing and bullying. There was a significant Italian community in Epsom, so Lorenzo was not as much of a novelty/target as Viv, and he was lighter skinned. His other friend at the time was another quiet boy called Perry. His claim to fame was that his grandfather or uncle was Tommy Godfrey, who played Arthur in TV's *Love Thy Neighbour*. This was an early 1970s sitcom, now long banished from our screens and practically erased from the public's memory, the poor actors and people associated with the programme forever shamed for being part of an endeavour considered by many now to be hideously racist.

Well, Viv adored the programme. I can picture him now contorting himself with laughter as the white, small, tubby, bigoted idiotic Englishman, Eddie Booth, portrayed by Jack Smethurst, was always outwitted and humiliated by his tall, good-looking black neighbour played by Rudolph Walker. So in my opinion the sitcom is wrongly maligned. It did depict attitudes at the time that we now decry, but I bet Viv was not the only black kid it gave great pleasure and confidence to. And Nina Baden-Semper, who played Rudolph's wife in the series, had every red-blooded male, regardless of their skin hue, lusting over her. *Love Thy Neighbour* was an important, groundbreaking programme of its time.

This is not to detract from the everyday and sometimes cruel racism my brothers Viv and later Stephen were forced to endure. Such was the climate at the time that white people believed they were demonstrating their lack of racism by using 'playful' terms to and for black people such as sambo and darkie instead of nigger, coon and wog. It got worse for my brothers as they got older and they began to realise the backdrop to their 'difference'. There is nothing worse for teenagers than being different. But most can do something about their difference. They can buy those fashionable clothes, cut their hair in that style, follow that football club, become a fan of that band. But for Viv and Steve their difference was being black in a white world, and there was nothing they could do about that.

I would watch Viv and his friends Perry and Lorenzo sometimes, playing, sitting on the floor with their Hot Wheels cars. Gentle and easily pleased. There was no rough and tumble. No desire to climb over fences, to steal apples, to knock on people's doors and run away, to pinch eggs from nests, to play raucous games of football. I am sure Mum thought about me – why can't he be like that? I know I sometimes did.

As the summer holiday ended, I got myself into more trouble than I had ever been in before. It started so innocently. The Mills brothers and I had wandered down to Epsom and Ewell Football Club to watch a pre-season friendly one sunny Saturday afternoon. As usual we had scrambled up the small hill behind the hole in the fence behind the away end. This was a grand term, as there were fewer than a hundred away fans over a whole season. Once in the ground we had split up and tried to meld in so it wasn't obvious we hadn't paid. Up at the home end the Mills boys seemed to be in a mild confrontation with three boys I didn't recognise. I swaggered into the middle of them.

The smallest one turned to me. 'Do you like ice cream?' he asked.

'Yes.'

'Well, lick this,' he said and kicked me up the arse. This was all very sudden and unexpected. The boy was now poised, fists raised to receive my reaction. I was being humiliated, and his lack of fear provoked mine. I felt I needed to up the ante to scare him off. I fumbled in my jeans pocket and pulled out my penknife. You know, the one we used to play splits with. The situation was running out of control.

My opponent looked at the pathetic blunt penknife and laughed.

I had a choice now. Walk away and look a complete idiot and have the

Mills brothers see my complete and utter cowardice and collapse and doubtless tell all and sundry or attack. So I lunged at him.

The boy clasped his coat and fell to the floor. In utter panic we ran like the clappers, the brothers and I, out of the ground, past the Rec and down the Chessington Road. As we entered the estate I threw the blasted knife into the river. The Mills brothers ran into their house, and I carried on to mine.

Laurence was sitting on the sofa watching *Grandstand* as the teleprinter brought in the football results from around the country. This was my brother's favourite time of the week. He said Mum and Dad were out shopping. I sat down next to him, frozen with horror with what was about to unfold. I thought about committing suicide but had no idea how to do it. I considered putting my head in the gas oven, but what then? I had visions of a dead boy lying in a pool of blood being comforted by Epsom and Ewell players from the pitch. I was trembling. But Laurence didn't notice – the teleprompter was poised at White Hart Lane.

A knock at the door. Two policemen in uniform. A panda car parked outside. 'Martin?'

'Yes.'

'Are your parents in?'

'No.'

'We need to come in.' They followed me into the sitting-room. Laurence looked up, looked at me and looked back at the television. Nothing really perturbed him.

We sat in silence until Mum and Dad returned from a shopping trip to Epsom laden with bags of groceries. We had no car then. We then went into the dining-room. The police started to tell Mum and Dad what had happened, and I could see the blood drain from their poor faces. Then another knock at the door. This time it was the boy's parents with two of the Epsom and Ewell officials. There had never been so many adults in this small room. Six grown-ups, two in uniform and eleven-year-old me.

It transpired that the boy had not been stabbed or anything like it. But he thought or pretended he had. Thank God. I had been praying in my head for a way out. My mum was crying. The boy was completely unhurt. However, his mum could see the utter distress in my mum and said there and then she wished no charges to be brought against me, which was kind and charitable. The police agreed and gave me a good ticking off. Relief flooded through my bloodstream, and I started to cry too. Minutes earlier I had been contemplating a life in prison and the murder of an unknown boy on my conscience.

My mum started to faint when our visitors left. Dad caught her, sat her in a chair and gave her a glass of water.

'What *is* this matter with you? Where have we gone wrong? What have we done to deserve this? Go on, get to your room. I can't bear to look at you,' she sobbed.

I did not protest. What *was* the matter with me? I lay in bed wondering what next. Dad came into the room. Shut the door quietly behind him. Is he going to batter me, I thought? He never had, but I had pushed the boat out with this one, and there's always a first time. He sat on the end of the bed.

'Don't worry yourself too much,' he said, unexpectedly. 'These things happen. Fortunately no harm was done. It's not the end of the world.'

He could not have said anything more reassuring, because I was thinking it *was* the end of the world. That I was a bad person beyond rehabilitation. He asked me where the knife was, and I told him I had chucked it in the river. Best leave it there, he said. And no more carrying knives. You are too old for splits. His kindness and ability to diffuse the situation with some humour has stayed with me. What a decent and far-seeing man he was. I could have been criminalised then. I guess my dad could see that it might have been a fork in the road. He must have spoken to my mum because the next day even she was all right with me. Still flushed and distressed, but she was OK. They handled it well, and I don't remember the incident ever being mentioned again except for my mum ordering, 'I don't want you going around with those Mills brothers any more.' That was not very fair. They were completely innocent.

16
GETTING BETTER

Dad had moved from West Park Hospital to a better-paid managerial job in a hospital over at Croydon, and he commuted there each weekday. His promotion and relocation to south London coincided with the local football club, Crystal Palace, being promoted to the First Division, and, although Dad was not a big soccer fan, he got caught up in the excitement. This was apparent to us as he spent a few months walking around the house barking 'Up the Palace!'

On 23 August 1969 he took me to Selhurst Park to watch my first professional football match. He escorted me, Laurence and his school chum Paul. It was against Spurs, Laurence's team, and they won 0-2 with Jimmy Pearce and Martin Chivers scoring. Jimmy Greaves did not hit the back of the net, uncharacteristically, but I was thrilled to see him in action. He was my hero. My allegiance then was still not to clubs but to players. George Best and Jimmy were my absolute footballing idols.

There were 40,000 people packed into Selhurst Park that afternoon, and I was enchanted. I loved the way they played 'Glad All Over' by the Dave Clark Five through the Tannoy, and the crowd, adults included, marking the beat by banging the hoardings and stamping their feet. I relished the hot dogs, the journey to and from via Ewell West, Epsom, Sutton and Selhurst railway stations and the football. Palace did not have much of a team and were not expected to be able to survive in the First Division, but they had a boy wonder in Stevie Kember and a criminally underrated goalkeeper in John Jackson who did more than anybody to keep them afloat. We stood so close behind his goal that in winter we could see the breath leaving his mouth, and occasionally he'd turn around and speak to us.

I wanted more of this and pleaded with Dad to let me go alone or with my mates, and he agreed. I would travel with Paul, Kevan McIlroy and Tony Jones, although not all at the same time. The spectacle of seeing the faces I knew so well from my 'Soccer Stars' sticker collection come to life was one of the most exciting experiences so far in my tender years. I was fortunate enough to see the game between Palace and Manchester United in 1971. Mighty star-studded United were beginning to crumble and no longer the dynamic force that had won the European Cup three years earlier. Bobby Charlton played but was close to retirement and had dropped further back into midfield, but Law and Best were on vintage form. The Reds won 5-3 with the mercurial Law netting a hat-trick and E for B and Georgie, Georgie, Georgie Best slotting in the other two. I was so lucky to see some of these legends just as they were slipping into retirement and pub ownership.

At first it was the thrill of seeing the games and all the football icons, but after a while, I realised, I was a Palace fan. I bought a silk Palace scarf that was tied around my wrist or hanging off the hoops around the waist of my Levi's. Even after I started supporting another club I sneaked back when I could. Don Rogers arrived from Swindon Town, and he was magical. The feeling of electric expectancy when the ball was pumped out to him on the wing stays with me today.

One Saturday afternoon Chelsea came to Selhurst Park. I had never seen anything like it. It was post-skinhead, but Dr Martens were on mass display. The police could not control the Chelsea mob, who were in the home end, the away end and the enclosures. They sang and surged throughout the game and after the match practically knocked down the big gates in their haste to get out on to the streets and cause havoc. Hugely adrenalised by the raucous, dangerous mob and discarding my Palace allegiance, I placed myself among them and watched with sheer astonishment as they charged away towards Norwood Junction leaving snapped-off wing mirrors, broken windows and shoppers scattered in their wake. We bumped into some older lads from Epsom and tagged along with them as they seemed to know the drill. I had just experienced my first football riot. A few months later I presented myself at the Chelsea Shed for the first time. I visited Selhurst Park less and less but did see the arrival of Peter Taylor, a talented barrel-chested winger, who I prayed Chelsea would sign.

*

The whole family were avid readers, which is to be expected with parents who had met and worked in a public library. Initially, we used Epsom Library, an imposing converted Victorian house with a parking place for our bikes down the side, but in 1970 Bourne Hall opened to much local excitement. It was a futuristic design that looked as if a substantial flying saucer had landed from the sky slap bang in the middle of Ewell Village. Instead of becoming an out-of-place eyesore, the building and its new facilities – which included a museum and function rooms – were embraced by the villagers, who grew to love them.

When I had moved up to the junior school, aged eight, my reading world really and truly opened up. My classroom in the second year housed a large bookcase, and I sat in front of it so soon knew the contents and geography of every shelf. I discovered a dusty row of red-covered Just William books by Richmal Crompton, and the rebel inside me was immediately awakened. Here was a boy of about my age then who deliberately rolled down his long school socks, fired catapults, had a gang that was at constant war with another, wound up his parents and knew his older brother was an idiot and his sister deluded. It wasn't until I reread them as an adult that I realised the stories were shot through with dry humour. I would say that William was my first literary hero. It would be interesting to know how he fared as an adult. If he were alive today he'd be 105.

There were also the Jennings books written by Anthony Buckeridge, who worked as a schoolmaster. They told of the adventures of the boy Jennings and his chum Darbishire in their provincial boarding school. I lapped it all up even if their school had little in common with the schools I was attending. There was a television series too, and the boy who played Jennings was Mitch Mitchell, later the drummer in the Jimi Hendrix Experience. The Jennings and Just William books were the only ones that made me laugh out loud until Tom Sharpe in the next decade.

My younger sister Liz was a voracious reader and digested the Enid Blyton back catalogue at an early age. Mum still borrowed a few books every week, but Dad was now short on time as the demands of his new position swallowed up his time and energy. I read about five books a week at one stage, using other family members' library tickets. I gobbled up the Sherlock Holmes canon and then moved on to some of Sir Arthur Conan Doyle's historical novels but preferred his dinosaur romp *The Lost World*.

We were also hefty spenders at Bedford's newsagent's to satisfy our reading appetites. Every Thursday they delivered the *TV Times* and *Radio Times*. This was the only sure way of knowing what was on television, as BBC's listings were in one, ITV's in the other. Mum had her weekly *Woman's Own* and the glossier, heavier *She* once a month. Liz also took *Look-In*, a *TV Times* for kids.

At the age of nine I became obsessed with Dennis Wheatley. It was the cleavage that was on display on some of his black-magic-genre covers that first attracted me. *The Devil Rides Out, The Dark Secret Of Josephine* and *To The Devil – A Daughter* jump to mind. Then there was the Roger Brook historical series, Gregory Sallust, secret agent, and the Duke de Richelieu. I think he wrote over a hundred books, and I read most of them. They all contained sex, or hints of it, and alluring descriptions of women's bodies and should really have been X-rated. Certainly not the sort of thing a nine-year-old boy should be devouring so eagerly.

I became Wheatley's stalker. I wrote to him, and he made the mistake of replying. I said I wanted to be a writer (which I'm not sure I did) and asked if he had any advice for me. He did. He said only write about things you know and had experienced, which I thought a bit rich from him considering his books were about Marie Antoinette, Napoleon and Satan. Nevertheless, armed with his address in Cadogan Square, Chelsea, which was printed at the top of the letter, I travelled up on the train to look at his house. Bizarrely, Dad came with me, but I went up again, alone, at least one other time. Thankfully, I never bumped into him because I know I would have spoken and pretended it was an absolute coincidence that a boy from Epsom who had written to him happened to be wandering around Cadogan Square on a Sunday lunchtime.

Dad took me to London a great deal, and he would point out blue plaques on buildings to Charles Dickens and various other authors. I was fascinated. One Sunday afternoon we went to Speakers' Corner in Hyde Park where we stood around watching and listening to an array of apparent eccentrics heralding the impending end of the world, the second coming of Jesus and warning of the terrors of communism or the dire threat of the 'permissive society'.

'Shut up, you daft old git,' shouted one middle-aged lady.

'Put a sock in it.'

'Jesus was a junkie.'

The abuse and heckling the speakers endured appeared relentless, but they ploughed on, undaunted.

'Why do they do it, Dad?'

'Because they believe in what they're saying. The important thing is they can say it. Anybody can come here, upturn a crate, climb up on it and say what they want. It's a free country and we have free speech. The minute we can't do this we have a problem. A big problem.'

A turning point in my reading journey was when I picked up a book called *A Start In Life* that my mum was reading. If I ran out of my own books I would read her pile. She liked a man called Howard Spring and J.B. Priestley and later Leslie Thomas. I remember Priestley's *The Good Companions* and Thomas's *Tropic Of Ruislip*, which was an early introduction for me to the curious practice of wife-swapping. But this book by Alan Sillitoe about a young man from Nottingham who comes down to London and gets tied up with the swinging sixties, gangsters and countless lusty women really transfixed me. It was a literary *The Likely Lads* with an edge to it. My mum was puzzled I liked it so much and said that it was not Sillitoe's best work and explained it was comedy, which I hadn't picked up on at all. She brought me home *Saturday Night And Sunday Morning* and *The Loneliness Of The Long-Distance Runner*. Blimey, did they knock me for six. They introduced me to the north of England beyond *Coronation Street*, to abortion, to working-class rebellion, to the world of work, and I never wanted to read anything lightweight again.

From Sillitoe I moved on to George Orwell, to the *Brave New World* of Aldous Huxley and to the *Lord Of The Flies* by William Golding. I read books about books just to find material I should read. I read the full-length versions of Dickens's catalogue again instead of the abridged editions we had dipped into at school. How I got time to have all this leisure activity I describe in this ramble through my early childhood I cannot fathom because my nose must have been stuck in a book for many of my waking hours.

As the change of schools loomed things were moving on around the house. America led the way. The modern domestic appliances we saw with curious and jealous eyes on the TV in the likes of *Flipper* or *The Dick Van Dyke Show* would get to us about five years later. Eventually we became the proud owners of a telephone and a refrigerator. We had been on the waiting list for a phone for nearly a year, but the GPO were now ready to install it. Of course, it was initially a party line, which meant we shared the outside line with a neighbour and only one household could use the telephone at any one time, but this was a minor inconvenience to endure in exchange for being wired up to the rest of the world. If we picked up the receiver and our neighbours were on the line we would politely replace it and try again later (or put our hand over the receiver and listen).

The phone sat proudly in the hall on a small decorative table with a lace cloth over it. The number was soon indelibly printed on all our minds. Of course, nobody rang us, as most people we knew did not have telephones either, but Nan and Gaga down in Portslade did, and this was one of the reasons I think my parents approved the expenditure so there was a way of them contacting us as my grandfather's emphysema worsened.

In the early days when it rang it paralysed the front room. We all looked at each other expectantly. One of we kids would jump forward and turn down the volume button on the TV. Mum would stand up and pat her apron down and position her hair and step purposefully into the hall. It was like she was composing herself for an important job interview.

'Ewell 9-5-9-1. How can I help you?' Mum was no cockney, but that was said with such diction and so precisely we thought it was another woman out there in the hall. As if she had stepped out of our television set.

On Christmas Day we introduced Grandma to this stunning new technology. Dad had rung Uncle Charlie and Auntie Jill in Brentford. Such a distance. Must have been a trunk call. Grandma could not cope with it. She twisted the receiver in her hand somehow getting her fingers tangled in the lead.

'You hold it like this, Mum. No, speak into this bit,' explained Dad, exasperated.

Then she started shouting.

''Ello! Charlie! 'Ello. Are you there? It's Aunt Nell. I'm at 'Arry's. Can you receive me? Over?'

We were in hysterics, rolling around the floor laughing. How she had got to the early 1970s having never used a telephone or noticing how they were operated on the television is beyond me. But it is true. Dad said that at one point she was holding the receiver to her forehead, and he was wresting it out of her hand.

After a while its hallowed status waned, and we children were permitted to use it if we didn't spend time chatting and 'running up the bill'. What was the point then? Later the GPO ingeniously and uncharacteristically entrepreneurially dreamed up Dial-A-Disc, where you dialled 160 and could listen to a current chart hit on repeat all day if you so wished. I thought this signalled the demise of the record player. It was via 160 that I learned the preposterous lyrics of 'Hot Love' by T. Rex off by heart: 'Well she's faster than most, and she lives on the coast ... / Well she ain't no witch, and I love the way she twitch ...' This practice ended quite abruptly when the quarterly bill arrived.

The introduction of the refrigerator was another tangible sign that our lives were becoming easier and more comfortable. We experienced cold drinks in summer for the first time. Now we realised that what we thought was cold was not. Modest amounts of ice cream could be held on site and not purchased from Peach Bar, and we walked around the house sucking on ice pops. We were in heaven. My brother Laurence was so taken with it that for a while he made himself ice cube sandwiches.

Things were also literally more comfortable underfoot too, as 'wall-to-wall' and 'fitted' carpets entered the vocabulary for the first time. Instead of a patchwork of mats and rugs around the house we had fitters come in and lay carpeting across the lounge, and it seemed like the height of luxury. Others talked about shag pile, but we never quite got there. Soon the council would be installing central heating across the estate, and the coalman, paraffin heaters and electric fires would slowly disappear.

Some estate families had even got themselves colour televisions, even though half the output was still broadcast in black and white. Incredibly, we didn't get there until 1976 when Björn Borg first won Wimbledon. Me and Mum sat there luxuriating in it.

'Look at the green turf.'

'Look at his blond hair. He's a real dish.'

If we had looked out of the window we would have seen green turf and blond human beings, but on our television it was like a miracle. There were some downsides – like discovering that an actor in *On The Buses* had yellow nicotine stains on his teeth – but over all it was a magical journey of discovery.

As the new decade approached there were changes outside the house too. From an almost complete absence of cars at the beginning of the 1960s, now most households owned one. We didn't, but most did. Sunday was car-washing day, and the boys and men would be outside with their buckets, soap and polish spending hours getting their vehicles pristine. The smell of Turtle Wax combined with roast lamb pervaded the estate. A lot of men seemed to spend more time petting their motors than their wives and girlfriends. On the Chessington Road, a newly opened motor spares shop called UCS (Universal Car Spares) was doing great business and fed the need for intensive car care.

Ford was the dominant manufacturer. Zephyrs and Zodiacs, Cortinas, Capris and Corsairs and Anglias, Escorts and Populars. There were also Morris Oxfords and Minors and Austin Cambridges and 1100s and a few Minis. Occasionally someone would cruise into the estate in an American car – a Pontiac or a Buick – and we kids would crowd around and salivate over it. There were a couple of greasers who drove around in open-topped models, big tattooed arms leaning on the door, jet-black hair slicked back, courting girls off the estate.

Harold Macmillan may have been right when he declared 'You've never had it so good' in the year of my birth, but it got better and better after the prime minister made that claim. The early and mid-1960s were, I can see now in hindsight, still very austere compared with today. Rationing may have ended before I was born, but not in our house. Our food, our clothes, our warmth, our toys were all rationed. We didn't really recognise the gentle rumble of hunger until it was sated as we got older, but most of us had it. That was why scrumping and blackberry picking were so popular with children and a blind eye turned to by parents. I think the changes that Macmillan heralded filtered down to the council estates and the working classes and became apparent from about 1966. From that time most families started acquiring the mod cons I have mentioned in this chapter. There was more money around. The rise in the standard of living continued year on year until the materialistic momentum got rudely interrupted in the austere early 1970s before resuming its rise at the end of that decade.

The 1960s was a great period from where I stood, although I would argue the decade started in 1963 and ended in 1970. Culturally 1960, 1961 and 1962 belonged to the 1950s. England won the World Cup. Football had never been so rich in personalities and blessed with talent. We had Best and Greaves, Bobby Charlton and Bobby Moore and Pele and Eusebio and Osgood, Hudson and Cooke at Chelsea. At the cinema there was James Bond and *Carry On*. On the TV there was *The Man From Uncle* and *Batman*, Tony Hancock and *Morecambe And Wise*. On Fridays we had fish and chips and Tizer from Mannings at Pound Lane. We got pocket money and earned more with paper rounds. We were happy. Everybody around us seemed happy and content and, most important of all, nobody died.

17
HELP!

We stood in a group, the fifteen or so boys from EBS, in the playground of Ruxley Lane School in West Ewell. It was a modern school, only a decade old in 1969, about two miles from our house in the direction of Kingston. We were trying to appear relaxed, but we were all apprehensive, even a little frightened. We were one of several similar clusters. The biggest was the boys and girls from Ruxley Juniors, the natural occupants of this secondary modern comprehensive school, and their self-assuredness showed. Then there were the kids from Riverview School, an equally confident group, many of whom lived on the Cox Lane and Watersedge council estates that were literally on the other side of the main road from the school.

We looked each other up and down, or rather we looked over at them, and when they looked back we averted our gazes. Big Bill had caught their eye. At eleven he was surely the largest boy among the new intake. He would not be able to remain anonymous, and I could see he had clocked that fact.

Before starting at Ruxley I had never visited the Cox Lane estate even though it was nearby. There was good reason for this: I was scared. It was an older, bigger estate than ours, and legend had it that the boys were stronger and tougher. A Gypsy site ran off the bottom by the river, and Hardwick's breaker's yard was attached to one side. The caravan site had come to national prominence a few years earlier when it was the setting for the semi-dramatised documentary *Cathy Come Home* aired by the BBC. It highlighted the problems of homelessness and the struggle to get out of a caravan into a permanent home. Some of the boys and girls at school with me now had managed to sidle into many of the background shots.

The sheer size of the school was intimidating. EBS now seemed quaint and tiny with its 130 or so pupils and staff in single figures. Ruxley Lane was a sand-coloured brick cluster of buildings with playing fields, tennis courts, science lab and car park for the teaching staff. We Ewell boys were resplendent in our shirt and ties, long trousers and blazers. The blazer breast pocket boasted a picture of a swan in flight underlined with the school motto – *Power Through Grace*. Nobody ever explained what it really meant. A master came into the playground with a loudhailer and ordered us into the main hall where we were sat on arranged benches and waited to be addressed and instructed.

We filed in and sat down again with our own. Not a word had been exchanged across the groups, although those of us in the Ewell contingent could not stop looking over at something we had not seen at school since we were infants: girls. They were everywhere. They too were wearing blue or white shirts and ties but sported cardigans, hip-hugging mini-skirts and tights. Many of them were clutching wicker baskets as if on their way to a picnic.

A middle-aged man with swept-back hair that curled up on his collar, suggesting a hint of individuality, took the stage. This was Mr Bowerman. He was the headmaster of this school that just catered for the first and second year and the sixth form. The third and fourth years were down the road in another older school called Danetree Road. We were all part of the same school, but the growth in the post-war population of Epsom and Ewell was running ahead of the educational-building infrastructure.

Bowerman did a lot to calm our nervousness. He said that if you behaved yourself there was nothing to fear and all to gain. He seemed very human and cracked several jokes. He wore flannel trousers, a tweed jacket with leather patches on the elbows and a small woollen tie. I had been fearing and imagining fierce men in gowns and mortar boards swishing knobbly canes. Bowerman introduced the teachers and the subjects they taught. Then he got down to the nitty-gritty.

We were each allocated to a 'house', and these houses were set against each other in terms of sport and other activities. The houses were Scott (as in Captain), Livingstone (as in David, not Ken), Keller (as in Helen) and Nightingale (as in Florence). Children today would have little idea who any of them were, but I am amazed, looking back, that they chose two women role models in what was then still a very male-centric world. Each house had their own colour, and this matched up with the tie we had been allocated. It was all very random. I was in Livingstone and had a red tie.

Then we were told which class we were in and to follow our teacher to our new classroom.

We had all been streamed. A and Alpha were for the children deemed academically intelligent enough to follow an O- and A-level curriculum. It was expected that some of these pupils would go on to further education, which in those days meant university. Then there were T and S, no idea what they stood for, but they were for the kids who would follow a CSE trajectory. (A grade 1 CSE was the equivalent of a C grade O level.) Then there was B and Beta which was for the rump who had shown no particular aptitude or academic enthusiasm or attainment. These children were expected to work in manual trades, factories, typing pools and shops. Finally, there was 1R. Shamefully, the R stood for remedial, and the pupils were often casually referred to as the 'remedials'. It was shocking, condemning them to probable failure and definite discrimination and ridicule from day one. If you didn't have learning difficulties before you were shoved in there, you soon would have.

I was put in 1A. My form teacher was a Mrs Quarrel, and our classroom was a hut next to one of the main entrances to the school. Mrs Quarrel's subject was English. On what basis the streaming was carried out I will never know. It could not have been on the eleven-plus showing or I would have been in R with the rest of the marginalised. I wonder if Mr Rees was asked to give a personal assessment of each pupil. I was not happy with the allocation, as I had little intention of excelling or working too hard, but Eddie, my close pal, was also in 1A, so we took comfort from being together in this scary, vast new world. Tony and Bill were reunited in 1T. I like to think Rees maybe did what he could to keep friends together.

Mrs Quarrel was a middle-aged prim-and-proper English teacher who laid out her stall straight away. She took no nonsense from anyone. We were here to learn, and we were the cream of the year and should not allow ourselves to be distracted by standards and behaviour we might see elsewhere. What she was getting at soon became apparent. This hut was our classroom, and although we would travel around the complex it would be here we returned to during breaks and at the end of the day also for our English tuition. She did not exude the warmth of Mrs Galley, but I didn't mind her. A few years later an upcoming politician named Margaret Thatcher put me in mind of Mrs Quarrel.

Meeting each new teacher was an ordeal. Mr Clayton we encountered for double woodwork once a week. I was useless manually and remain so. While boys happily planed planks of wood throwing off shavings like shearing a sheep, I stood there struggling with how to hold the tool properly.

'Knight, it's not a cricket bat, you idiot.'

Through the school year we (they) learned about joints and grains and dowels and dovetails and produced ever more intricate trophies. I was stuck with the toothbrush holder that we had embarked on in the first week. Mr Clayton wasn't much bigger than me, but he frightened me at first. When he introduced himself he felt like he had to compensate for his lack of size: 'And if any of you lads think I might be a soft touch, just to let you know I was a boxing champion in the army.'

Again, we worked each other out quite early on, and I never had a problem with him. He showed my toothbrush holder to later classes as an example of what not to do.

Mr Bowerman taught us art, and I learned from him. I was not much cop, but some tips about pencil shading and drawing human faces have stayed with me. He was a nice man who I would soon get to know a little better. Mrs Dancer taught us geography, Miss Hocking was maths and Miss Bradford was history. Mr Sutton, who sported a walrus moustache, taught English and was inclined to write 'Easily Distracted' in my school reports.

Our games master was Vincent Blore, who had been a goalkeeper for West Ham, Crystal Palace and Derby County before the war had interrupted his career. My mum remembers him joining the school when the war ended and said there was great excitement at a footballing celebrity joining the staff. Now he was at the end of his teaching career, and his body language revealed a general counting-the-days demeanour. He was perfectly pleasant, and one day, because I signalled an interest, he took me into his room and showed me his scrap-book of press cuttings. He said there was a period when there was talk of him playing for England. Shyly proud as he was, I saw a sadness in him. He walked like there was a huge weight on his shoulders. After a while Mum told me his only daughter had fairly recently died as a young adult. Because of this knowledge I never really played him up. Unfortunately, others did.

Incredibly, looking back with 21st-century eyes, the enthusiasm vacuum on the games-teaching side was taken up by a groundsman called Joe Taylor. He probably had more impact on the male half of the school than any teacher. Joe was a lantern-jawed old guy who had been a boxer and without fail wore a quilted green goalkeeper's jersey. What hair he had was silver, and most of this jutted out from his prominent chin. He never had a beard, yet we never saw him clean-shaven. It was the eighth wonder of the world. He had a hut that he shared with some lawnmowers and petrol cans, but rarely did you see him groundkeeping. He had all but taken over the school football team from Mr Blore, coaching them, picking the players and going to watch them when they played. On occasions where a trophy was going to be presented he changed into a smart black blazer.

Joe loved boxing more than football, and he was a well-known local trainer operating out of Pitt House in Ewell Village. At Ruxley Lane he selected some likely lads, took them under his wing and nurtured them as fighters. The school had had some success not too long before I arrived with Eric Blake, who represented Britain in the 1968 Olympic Games, and a boy called Johnny Evans who was also highly rated. However, Joe extended boxing to all of us because should a fight or an argument develop among the boys in the playground it normally came to Joe's attention, and after school he would arrange for the beef to be settled in the ring. He laced up the most unlikely contenders in ill-fitting, tired old gloves and set them against each other within a ring formed by us spectators, who stood around urging one or other on and generally baying for blood. Most matches were declared a draw, and Joe would always step in before any serious injury occurred, the idea being that the dispute would be settled and the bad feeling expended under adult supervision. In retrospect the practice was astonishing. The teachers must have known all about it but allowed it to continue.

Even in 1970, imagine little twelve-year-old Barnaby coming home with a black eye and his parents asked how he got it.

'I fought another boy in the boxing ring.'

'You did what? Who organised that?'

'The groundsman. His name is Joe.'

Nowadays there would be a scandal and heads would roll. But it worked. I saw some fiery, well-matched fights in the ring, which always took place on school premises, and I dreaded ever being challenged or coming on to

Joe's pugilistic horizon. Unfortunately, that was not to be. The details have become very sketchy, but it was a boy in my class who I had a minor argument with, and I cannot remember over what. He was small like me, and somehow Joe decided we were size-matched and needed to step into the ring to settle our differences. Neither of us relished the prospect, but Joe had announced us on the card, and it was almost unthinkable to back out.

He called us together as he tried to tighten the laces on our gloves, because there was a genuine prospect of them falling off, our hands being so small. He tried to teach us in thirty seconds a little about technique. Something about keeping guards up. We raised our little fists and imitated what we had seen on television. Stepping around each other. I could see the other boy was going to fight a defensive bout and didn't want to rile me by attacking. That would have been fine with me, and I would have happily passed the three rounds without either of us laying a punch on the other, but the crowd were having none of it.

'Get stuck in.'

'Clock him.'

'Couple of fairies, these two.'

The humiliation of doing nothing was worse than a boring, cowardly fight, so I dropped all pretence of keeping my guard up and just walked over to the other boy and hit him with a flurry of blows, carrying on when I landed on top of him as he fell to the ground in submission. Joe hurriedly jumped in, pulled us to our feet and held an arm each aloft declaring a draw. It was an unsatisfactory experience for all involved.

Not long after this a boy from the year above 'offered me out'. That was the term widely used. I had no idea why. I had never spoken to this bloke and did not even know his name until this happened. He shoulder-barged me as we passed in the corridor and jumped back as if I had been the aggressor.

'Do you wanna fight?'

No, I didn't. If I declined, though, I suspect he would have seen that as a sign of weakness and beat me up anyway, so I chose the most pragmatic option.

'In the ring,' I suggested. I figured that if my enemy could bash me up in a bad way then better it be moderated by Joe. My pals Paul and Stuart, who were also in the year above, assured me the bloke was 'nothing'.

'You'll do him, easy,' Stuart said.

Thanks, Stu. A healthy crowd had gathered for the bout, and I was very nervous, but there was no going back. Like before, I just wind-milled forward with no technique. The older boy did not fold, though, and traded punches, his having some aim. However, in the third round he too collapsed into the human ropes as my momentum overcame him. Joe grabbed our arms and called a draw.

'You fought well. A real battle that one,' praised Joe.

Joe had a habit of grabbing you in a friendly headlock and rubbing his stubble on your face. This is a fact, as he did it to me many times. I never saw anything suspicious in this at the time and not sure if I do now, but if a teacher did it you might be quite alarmed.

To be fair to Joe, he was at the school when Mr Blore, the official games master, had abdicated much responsibility and enthusiasm for his charges and Joe saw himself as stepping in and developing and encouraging the boys. The school realised this too, I'm sure, and that is why his unconventional ways were tolerated. I liked him, and many pupils thought highly of him and were forever grateful for the way he brought on their sporting abilities.

Because I was small, thankfully not many people bothered to pick a fight with me. I was hardly a feather in anyone's cap unless that someone was even smaller than me, and there were not very many boys in that first year who fitted the bill. But for my friend Bill life was becoming more difficult. There was nowhere for him to hide. Conversely, his size made him a target. He already looked like a man dressing up as a boy when he wore the school uniform. An XXL Jimmy Clitheroe.

There really wasn't anybody in our year who was going to take him on, but the school hard nuts in higher years saw him as easy prey. A boy from the third year, for example, his gang in tow, would encounter Bill at the Poole Road fish and chip shop at lunchtime and challenge him to a fight. Bill would politely decline. We were new boys and strict observers of the hierarchy that dictated that you didn't cheek or hit back boys from older years. The chasm between thirteen years of age and eleven was immense. A couple of times these boys nutted Bill or shoved him, and it was horrible to see. We ached for Bill to hit one back, but he, as did we, knew his life would be hell if he did. Bill had not really used violence before, but it was coming his way whether he liked it or not, and I felt sad for him. Only a few months before he had been happy excavating for Roman earthenware and pottering around Ewell Village, he now found himself having to learn fast how to navigate a new world where a small bunch of bullies wanted to hurt and humiliate him for no other reason than he was bigger than them.

18
THIS BOY

It was in that first year of Ruxley Lane school that the skinhead youth cult swept the country and became for me and almost everyone I knocked about with all-consuming. Only a couple of summers before I was dreaming of Action Men and Johnny Seven guns and now I was pining for Ben Sherman shirts, Levi's jeans, Dr Marten boots and Crombie overcoats.

It sort of crept up. We all knew about mods and rockers, but I had been too young to become caught up in all that. I should have been too young to be caught up in the skinhead subculture really, but by the age of twelve in late 1970 I was converted. Peer pressure was a big factor. There was a terror of being different, and if you didn't have the look you stood out. At least, that is what we thought. Again, the pressure was on my poor old mum to kit me out. Levi's were brought from Millets in Epsom. My mum was horrified when I promptly jumped in the bath with them on to shrink and fade them. Brand-new Levi's were frowned upon. Later I added splashes of household bleach as this also enhanced their authenticity and allure, apparently. Mum was then instructed to add an outer turn-up which had to be exactly the right depth. Then I purchased my first Fred Perry from Bells in Tolworth. My Dr Marten boots I managed to get free off a boy on the estate who had already outgrown his, and the rest came – Brutus shirts, Harrington jackets, Levi's Sta-Prest trousers, Levi's cords, thin braces, yellow socks – as and when I could afford them, mainly from Sid at Epsom Market. Sometimes we would help Sid set up and pack up his stall for a couple of shillings and the smell and touch of two-tone tonic trousers.

Eventually I took the plunge and walked into the arcade in Epsom and had my hair cropped in Fisher's, the barber shop. It was a significant plunge because I had been battling my mum for the past few years to allow me to grow my hair longer, and I was at last winning. I wanted Beatles hair. Or George Best hair. But now the whole lot had gone.

The wardrobe was vital to the new identity, but there was an essential accompanying associated culture. My sister Sally had by now left school and entered the world of work, her grammar-school education helping her land a job as a trainee supervisor at Marks & Spencer in Kingston. Marks were a wonderful company to work for then, and my sister loved it. Mum did too because at the end of the week the staff could swoop around the store and buy up the 'waste' – food items that were about to exceed newly introduced sell-by dates – at knockdown prices. It was a valuable perk that saved the family money and improved our diet and food variety no end.

Sally now had her own cash and started to buy records that I pounced on. She introduced me to the *Motown Chartbusters* series and reggae music via the *Tighten Up* albums. The latter were laced with sexual references and innuendo that were sparking much erotic thought in my fast-developing mind that, in turn, was sending signals to other parts of my body. One song by a lady was about her boyfriend who boasted 'barbed wire in his underpants', and another female sung a line in 'Wreck-A-Buddy' where she moaned, 'And if he's ugly, I don't mind / He's got a dick and I want to grind.' The single that Sally brought home that I associate most with the dawning of my baby skinhead phase, though, was 'You Can Get It If You Really Want'. He was a cool man, was Desmond Dekker, and I automatically assumed that tune was about sex too.

I was envious of Sally and her exciting life. Each weekend her friends would come to the kitchen and flit around getting ready for their night out. Trying out clothes. Applying make-up. Smoking cigarettes. Playing 'What Becomes Of The Broken Hearted?' by Jimmy Ruffin and 'Tears Of A Clown' by Smokey on the record player. They were off to the Purley Orchid, the Kingston Hotel or the Foresters' Hall in Epsom. They had girl-skinhead haircuts with the compulsory hair slide, mohair skirts, Fred Perry tops, and some wore surfing beads around their necks.

In Kingston she met a strapping skinhead called Steve. I hero-worshipped him for a while. When she brought him home he strode into our front room like a colossus in a sleeveless V-necked pullover, tartan Ben Sherman, ice-blue Sta-Prest and the heaviest, shiniest pair of Ivy brogues I'd ever seen. As he plonked down into an armchair his trousers rode high up his leg revealing quality-cotton red socks. He flicked open a pack of Piccadilly from his pocket and leaned over to my dad.

'Wanna fag, guvnor?'

My dad declined. He squinted at the television.

'Mind if I switch it over? Want to see the racing.'

My bemused father told him to go ahead.

However, Steve coming on to the estate was problematical. He was a leading face in the Kingston skinheads, and their sworn enemies were the Epsom boys. Also there was a showdown in an altercation that became known locally as the 'Battle of Ewell West Station'. The Kingston chaps and a group of skinheads, mainly off our estate, clashed on the approach to the platforms of Ewell West railway station one day. One boy, Mark, one of ours, tried to clamber over a spiked fence, slipped and ended up with the spike piercing his calf. It was the talk of the town. Mark lost a lot of blood but recovered to tell the tale. Steve stopped coming, and I next heard of him nearly half a century later when sadly he died. Steve's death was widely reported on social media, as he had become one of Stoke City's most famous fans where they knew him fondly as Cockney Steve.

Some of the older Epsom boys got involved in another fight that became big news locally, but this time the outcome was even more grisly. A brawl erupted in the Drift Bridge Hotel with some lads from another town, and a boy I knew slightly was stabbed in the neck with a bottle. Tragically, he died at the age of just nineteen.

The family finances were improving significantly. Hence my ability to bend Mum's arm to kit me out. Housekeeping from Sally (and soon Laurence) along with the M&S food was a boost, but also Dad was now in a senior management position at Springfield Mental Hospital in Earlsfield and earning good money. Springfield was a big institution looking after psychiatric patients from across London and the south. Dad rarely talked about his work, but I remember him being stressed once when a patient, who had previously murdered someone, had absconded. These were the days before press officers in the health service, and it fell to Dad to deal with some of the fallout.

Dad came across several famous people in the hospitals he worked in. At various times *Z-Cars* and *Coronation Street* actors were resident in the Epsom cluster. Comedienne Hylda Baker was in for a while, as was Peter

Green, founder of Fleetwood Mac. Most famously in Long Grove Hospital, Reggie and Ronnie Kray fooled the security to allow Ronnie, who was being detained securely, to abscond. They probably adapted their ruse from a Sunday afternoon WW2 prisoner of war film.

Sometimes Dad brought patients home to the house. There was one old chap who came to Sunday lunch occasionally. He was a sweet fellow who dressed up in a suit and tie and waistcoat for his visit. A gold watch hung from his waistcoat. He reminded me of Dr Cameron from TV's *Dr Finlay's Casebook*. I was confused at first, as I expected mental patients to look deranged, and I carefully eyed the knife and fork in his hand. Of course, he was completely harmless. Dad said he did something when he was a young boy that resulted in his being sent to an institution, and now he was so dependent he couldn't live on the outside. I liked to imagine that *something* was killing his parents, but Dad would not say. He just replied it was nice for the man to experience some normality.

During my first school year I was by far the worst-behaved boy in 1A. This is not to say I was very bad, but nobody else in the class was inclined to muck around much. Eddie laughed at my antics but kept on the right side of school law, and Andrew Munro, an identical twin already embracing the hippy culture, was the only other who was rebellious. It fell to me to entertain me. I cannot think what it was I did, but teachers often trotted out the line 'Just because you don't want to learn, Knight, you have no right to disrupt the education of people who do.'

I liked to challenge the teachers in a subtle way, and with a couple of them I had a personal war going on that kept me engaged but kept them enraged. I endeavoured to annoy them in ways that weren't easily punishable. I strove to show them that they might be teaching me, or trying to, but I was as clever, maybe even cleverer than them.

There was a master called Mr Dimelow (which was an unfortunate name as *dimlo* was Romany slang for a very stupid person) who taught us civics – no idea – and I think viewed himself as a progressive teacher introducing new methods and ideas into the school. He said he was a Liberal – whatever that meant at the time. He liked to pull up a chair and sit among us rather than in front of us to signal that he was an equal rather than a master. He wore a corduroy jacket. I disliked him, and as he invited debate I normally argued the toss. One day he snapped – I was probably dissing Jeremy Thorpe or Roy Jenkins or whoever he was lauding at the time.

'Shut up, Knight! Just shut up.' His face was reddening. I thought he might strike me. 'Do you want to learn? Do you want to take anything away from this school after five years? What job do you think you are going to do? Really, what profession will *you* be entering?' He smiled and looked around the class. He thought he had me on the ropes. Some giggling encouraged him. 'What will you become, Knight? Don't tell me – you're going to be a scientist. Or a brain surgeon. Yes, that's it, Knight the brain surgeon. Dr Knight. Come on, boy, enlighten the class. We want to know what you're going to be. What are you going to do? Come on, Knight. Cat got your tongue?'

I milked the short silence as if I were struggling with my answer. 'Well, sir, actually, I do know what I want to be.'

'Oh, pray, tell.' Dimelow swung around and smirked to the class as if to say – this will be interesting.

'Yes, I would very much like to become a dustman when I leave school.'

It was the answer Dimelow had dreamed of. He literally guffawed and smacked his leg. 'A dustman. A dustman. So that's the extent of your ambition is it, Knight? You want to cart around other people's putrid, steaming rubbish for the rest of your life, do you?'

I waited for the laughing to die down. Timing would be everything. Dimelow stared hard at me searching for my discomfort.

'What's wrong with it, sir? Rick's dad's a dustman. Ain't he, Rick?'

Rick nodded happily. His dad *was* a dustman, and he didn't care who knew.

Dimelow was lost for words. He stood up and walked back to his desk and shuffled some books. He was severely embarrassed. 'There is nothing wrong with it,' he finally muttered into his silly little beard.

Our eyes met later, and he knew that I knew exactly what I was doing. I had sprung a trap and proved that Dimelow was a dim low.

The school summer holidays of 1970 were an exciting time. Our little gang had expanded. Tony and I remained close despite being separated in school, but we had become friendly with some boys who lived halfway between the estate and the school: Roy, Kevin, Frank and Tony Jones among them. We were already knocking about regularly with Paul and Stuart from the year above who also lived in the same few roads.

We got into scooters and mopeds and rode them illegally over the back. I bought a stripped-down Lambretta from my neighbour Lee, and Tony Brand, Tony Jones and Keith had a Vespa they christened Totoke, an amalgam of their Christian names. Although I was markedly unmechanically minded I was forced to learn about technical things such as HT leads, flywheels and carburettors. I was forever traipsing up to the Burmah garage on Ruxley Lane to fill my little can with two-stroke petrol.

The police knew we were all riding bikes over there, and some of us were as young as ten, but they generally didn't interfere. We had hours and days of uninterrupted fun, although the petrified pheasants and skylarks didn't agree. One day I felt emboldened and tore through the estate on the Lambretta taking corners like Barry Sheene, but as I turned my handlebars to enter the car park the bike itself maintained the same course. I smashed into a shiny Ford Corsair, scratching the doors and ripping off the wing mirror. The owner was out of his house in a flash. Interfering with a man's precious Ford was on a par with interfering with a man's wife at the time. He cuffed me and took me by the arm back to my house where he demanded compensation from my weary parents.

After my Lambretta I acquired a Honda 50 motorbike from a local tearaway called Peter Lawrence. It cost £10. We bought it between three of us – me, Derek and Dave – but it was decided to keep it at my house as I was closest to the fields. One lazy Sunday afternoon I was riding the bike alone along the cinder path that intersected the main field, and a policeman showed up on his push bike. I recognised him as PC Crossley. He was a beat officer who was particularly hated because of his over-enthusiastic application of the law.

'Come here, you,' he shouted.

I looked at him and looked beyond him and behind me. He was on a pushbike, and I was on a motorbike. No contest. I could have some fun here. I revved the engine, let the clutch out and roared off up one of the paths. I stopped a safe distance the other side of him and waved before shooting off again. It was a stupid piece of bravado because I hadn't considered radio communications. Before I knew it a police panda car had pulled up in Hollymoor Lane and a Black Maria on the scraping that would soon become Sefton Road. The officers had jumped out and were running towards me – they seemed very angry. I got off the scooter and waited.

They put the bike in the Black Maria – or meat wagon as we called those vehicles then – and me in the police car. They drove me the few yards home and interrupted Sunday lunch. My mum and dad were not pleased. Dinner being disrupted was not the problem, but a Black Maria and a panda car escorting me home and being parked outside the house was a cause of great shame. To make matters worse the law had done some checks, and apparently the Honda had been stolen from Epsom railway station some weeks earlier. They told my parents they would be looking at charging me with receiving stolen goods and that an appearance at juvenile court could be on the cards. I never heard anything more and was quite put out the police never returned 'my' bike.

Our gang of little skinheads competed with clothes and records and wandered around the area – our boundaries, geographical and personal, ever expanding. 'In The Summertime' by Mungo Jerry was undoubtedly the song of the summer with 'Spirit In The Sky' by Norman Greenbaum pushing it close. The lyrics to 'In The Summertime' have come under attack in recent times, particularly 'Have a drink, have a drive / Go out and see what you can find.' Ray Dorset, who wrote the song, doesn't say drink ten pints, so I don't see the problem. The lyrics were clearly written by a testosterone-fuelled heterosexual in an age when there was no shame in that.

Down on the Isle of Wight Jimi Hendrix had electrified a massive open-air audience and the grammar-school boys over at Glyn were embracing the burgeoning hippy scene enthusiastically. Janis Joplin also made waves at the concert, and within a few months they were both dead from over-enthusiastic ingestion of drink and drugs. Flower power, San Francisco, the Grateful Dead and the whole American-led hippy culture had hijacked *Melody Maker* and *NME*, but on the estate and at our school hippy culture never went much beyond a tiny minority interest.

Chelsea won the FA Cup following a replay against Leeds United, and a whole generation of boys became fans on the back of the muddy romance of those two Cup Final ties. On our estate the oldest boys generally supported Spurs, as they had been converted by the double-winning side that contained Danny Blanchflower, Dave Mackay and John White nearly a decade earlier, and the younger boys were mainly Chelsea, drawn in by Peter Osgood, Alan Hudson and Charlie Cooke. There was also a rump of Manchester United because the magic of Bobby Charlton, Denis Law and

Georgie Best transcended local loyalties. Meanwhile, England failed to retain the World Cup in Mexico. Chelsea's goalkeeper, Peter Bonetti, got the blame. Suddenly the Esso World Cup coins we had all been manically collecting lost their lustre.

Ron 'Chopper' Harris, the Chelsea captain, lived in West Gardens off West Street and was regularly seen riding his bike around the area. He had also bought a sweet shop for his parents on Ruxley Lane. He was encouraging to my friends Paul and Stuart. They were both slight in build but nevertheless skilful footballers. Unlike many of my fellow park players (and me) they understood about releasing the ball and distributing it. Ron encouraged them and invited them to his nearby bungalow, where he lived with his wife and children. You could do things like that in those days without triggering a vigilante mob. He gave them tickets for both the quarter finals and semis of the 1970 FA Cup. Paul and Stuart were tremendously excited because Chopper had also promised them tickets to the Wembley final against Leeds United. However, when it came to it, he couldn't quite manage it, so he told them that they could have the boots he played in instead. One each. As good as his word, Ron presented them to the boys after the famous replay at Old Trafford. Paul and Stuart brought the football boots to school. Boys gathered around. Touching the boots. Gaping at them. If there had been camera phones, then they'd have been having selfies with them. A Chelsea-supporting school, Ruxley Lane had never seen anything like it. Paul and Stuart were the bee's knees.

I remember Mum being upset by the actor Jimmy Hanley dying. He meant little to us, but he was the son in the radio and film series *Meet The Huggets* in the 1940s and 1950s, and my parents' generation were very fond of him and his on-screen mum and dad, Jack Warner and Kathleen Harrison. Jack was a national treasure and entered our living-rooms early every Saturday evening as the genial, geriatric policeman Sergeant Dixon of Dock Green police station. Every episode he would greet the audience with 'Evening all' and sign off at the end with 'Goodnight all', always with a gentle salute, warming the hearts of families up and down the country. Within just a few years my generation would come face to face with the Special Patrol Group on our town's streets on a Saturday night, banishing the illusion of a

Dixonite police force for ever more. Kathleen Harrison was still around too and had made a welcome TV comeback in *Mrs Thursday* about a charlady who comes into money. For our family the programme resonated because my grandma was a charlady into her eighties, and very proud of it too. Sadly, she never came into money.

Late in 1970 the whole country willed on athlete Lilian Board, who had been winning Olympic medals only two years before, as she battled cancer, and at Christmas we mourned her tragic death nationally. We had watched on television as she was flown out to the clinic of a Dr Issels in Switzerland, which was presented as her last chance of survival. Years later Bob Marley would also turn to Issels for help. It was the first time I can remember cancer being talked about openly on television. I know the theory is that people just didn't talk about cancer in those days, and it was still as prevalent as today, but I'm not buying it. If it was affecting one in two as it is does today, they would never have been able to keep a lid on it like they did.

Girls were becoming almost as important to most of my group as clothes. They were much discussed, and we lied to one another about the sexual experiences we had had, normally on a holiday where the veracity of the yarn was difficult to disprove. Nobody wanted to be left behind. The Four Fs – *Find 'em, Finger 'em, Fuck 'em, Forget 'em* – was a bullshit-bravado mantra we learned and quoted at one another, and I, for one, was stuck embarrassingly on the first F.

I had been fortunate earlier, though, because I was having some sexual experimentation with a girl from Epsom called Jenny. She was very pretty, with short blonde hair and flawless olive skin. She was aware of her developing sexuality before she even got to senior school. Fortunately for me, Jenny, who was the same age, had a very early appetite for and curiosity about sex, and sometimes she used me to sate that curiosity. It started with playing a game called Truth, Kiss, Dare or Promise. This involved sitting on an old flat gravestone down at St Mary's Churchyard with another couple of friends and spinning a stick.

'I dare you to touch Christine's tit from the outside.'

Some dare. If Christine wasn't agreeable, Jenny was. She was up for being touched almost anywhere, shrugging and making out she had no choice, as if the rules of the game were sacrosanct. Most of the time it was her dreaming up the dare. By the age of eleven or twelve we were meeting over the back after tea and before dusk, lying down in the long grass and exploring our bodily impulses more and more. Cider with Jenny. We even attempted intercourse but failed down to my lack of grasp of genital geography. By the age of thirteen Jenny had left me behind. She had become very pretty, voluptuous and flirtatious. Predictably she came to the attention of older, more experienced boys who were able to give her what she craved. My early sexual dawn proved to be of the false variety, and some excruciatingly barren years lay ahead as I watched in terror, shame and envy as one schoolmate after the other bagged a girlfriend and kicked off a genuine intimate relationship.

In September of 1970 I moved into 2A with a new form teacher, whose subject was music. She quickly came to detest me, and I her. She could see I was a threat to her authority, and I could see she was a threat to my quality of school life. She tried to get me to sing in front of the class as a punishment for talking. It was a direct attempt to humiliate me, and I refused. She backed down. She called me the 'class clown' but warned me that she and my fellow pupils would not be my audience.

I had had enough by now of life in the A stream and had reached a decision. I was missing my mates and envied the lack of curricular pressure being put on them. My musical form teacher thought she had the ultimate threat and used it several times, but one day I was ready for her.

'Knight, if you don't settle down, I will be recommending to the head that you be put down to the B stream. How would you like that?' Strangely, she thought this was the ultimate shame for a pupil.

'If you could, miss, that would be great.'

'I beg your pardon?'

'If you could recommend I be put down to the B stream, please.'

'In that case I most certainly will.'

Wheels were set in motion. Mr Bowerman sent for me. We had a chat in his office. He was a fair man.

'Are you finding the work too much, Martin?'

'No.'

'Why do you wish to be demoted then?'

'Because I don't fit in. I'm not meant for the A stream.'

'Has someone said this to you?' said Bowerman, suspecting that the piano woman or another teacher had got to me.

'No. All my friends are in B and Beta.'

'OK.' He smiled benevolently, thinking this kid finds the work too much but is too proud to admit it. 'We will have a word with your parents. It is a big decision. It may impact the rest of your life.'

At home my mum asked, 'Are you finding the work too much?'

'Yes,' I said.

I knew it would take a different tack with my parents.

So, by Christmas 1970 I was out of 2A and placed in form 2B. Mrs Dancer was the form teacher. Her husband was a master over at Danetree Road and had allegedly been a Japanese prisoner of war. My mum remembers him coming back to the school after the war ended and how they were told not to play him up because of the ordeal he had suffered. He was thin-lipped and tended to speak quietly through a semi-closed mouth – one of the more doubtful rumours about him that was treated as fact by us was that the Japanese had sewed his lips together while incarcerated. Mrs Dancer scanned the classroom, saw an empty seat next to a boy and told me to sit there. His name was Derek. Any hopes he had of academic advancement or a quiet life were dashed that day.

Tony sadly was not in B, nor Bill, but Keith was. Keith had joined St Mary's in the final year and lived on the other side of the Chessington Road from the estate. Good looking and confident by this second year of senior school, he was well established as one of most unruly boys in the school. Along with a few others who came off the Cox Lane estate, I had at last found the bad company I craved.

19
I SHOULD HAVE KNOWN BETTER

Inevitably, I soon received the cane at senior-school level. Stupidly, I played a practical joke on my new desk-next-door-neighbour Derek that backfired. It involved sending a note to a girl, ostensibly from Derek, which didn't go down very well. Derek and I were summoned to Mr Bowerman's study. The headmaster weighed it all up and concluded that we should report to him after assembly in the morning and we would be caned.

It would be mine and Derek's first corporal punishment at Ruxley Lane. My new classmate was not at all happy. He was a quiet boy who had thus far managed to remain almost invisible in school and had done nothing wrong. Keith, however, was already a regular visitor to Bowerman's study.

'Don't worry about it. It don't hurt. Couple of whacks on the arse and that's it,' he counselled.

We didn't look convinced.

'You got Levi's cut-downs at home?' I nodded. Levi's cut-downs were simply Levi's jeans that had passed their use-by date with much of the leg cut off to create frayed summer shorts. 'Put your cut-downs on under your trousers, and wear three pairs of pants. Seriously, you won't feel a thing.'

The following morning we stood through assembly apprehensive and worried that the new layers around our girth were blindingly obvious. We must have looked like a pair of fidgety and sweating Michelin men. Three pairs of Jockey Y-fronts and denim jeans under cotton C&A trousers had me walking the short distance from the hall to the headmaster's study like Wyatt Earp. I went in first. Bowerman looked me up and down and a faint smile twitched on his lips.

'Good try, Knight. Go to the changing rooms and take off whatever it is you have padded your trousers with.'

He ordered Derek to do the same. We went back in the study feeling almost naked now and took our rightful punishment. It stung, but it didn't really hurt. My feeling is that Bowerman was going through the motions and applied minimal power. It was no worse than an inoculation, which was another trial the school put us through. The deterrent value of the cane had now been negated, and I would visit Bowerman's study at least a couple more times before the school year was out.

In the T class Tony had made friends with another boy called Tony. Tony Cruse. He lived adjacent to the school, and it was to his empty house we would rush at lunchtimes. There was a rope swing over the River Hogsmill at the bottom of his garden, and sometimes we would muck around there too. His neighbour, little Ray Curran, wasn't even of school age but patrolled the swing as if he owned it. If we had enough money we would buy some chips first from the Poole Road fish shop. If we didn't, we would ponce. If you took one chip each off ten boys that might be enough to satisfy your appetite until later. Tuesday was a special day, for it was then that Radio 1 unveiled the new music chart, culminating with the number-one song at 1 o'clock. This was heady stuff. For some reason, hard to summon up now, it really mattered who was going up and down the chart. We would argue and banter over who would be top of the charts.

'I'll have two bob that 'Telegram Sam' comes straight in at number one,' said Tony C.

'You're on,' I said, confident because I had read in my *NME* that the record had only been released on Friday, and one weekend of sales might not be enough, even though the popularity of Marc Bolan and T. Rex was becoming stratospheric. I was wrong and Tony was right. It was an exciting time in music, as in the wake of Marc and his corkscrew hair, Slade, Gary Glitter, Rod Stewart, the Sweet and the whole glam-rock movement all broke through.

Top Of The Pops (*TOTP*) was another music-related ritual enjoyed by most. As a family we gathered around the television set on a Thursday evening at 7.25 p.m., after enduring a normally boring half-hour of *Tomorrow's World*. It was great for us kids to put face, flesh and motion to people we had only heard on the radio or seen on the pages of a music magazine. *TOTP* debuts were national events to remain imprinted on youthful minds long into adulthood. Marc Bolan wearing glitter around the eyes was copied in schools across the country. And once the teachers did it, the pupils followed. Noddy Holder's rasping voice echoed across that maligned decade. Rod Stewart and the Faces kicking a football around the studio while miming to 'Maggie May' was a new height of BBC-protocol irreverence. David Bowie clasping Mick Ronson to his sweaty, bare, hairless chest breaking down post-war mindsets.

Mum and Dad would look on in puzzlement. Androgynous pop stars challenging the status quo they grew up with. Brian Connolly of the Sweet confused Mum. 'Is he a she? Or is she a he?'

Dad was not taken with Gary Glitter. 'Isn't he a bit old for this lark?'

'He's really good, Dad,' I replied.

'Umm.'

Fast forward thirty years or more, and I vividly remembered that conversation when Gary Glitter's sordid secret became public knowledge. Yes, it was now official – that bouncing bouffant had been a wig all along.

Watching television as a family in the early 1970s reminds me of the happiest times. We watched *Match Of The Day* together on Saturday night and normally *Parkinson* afterwards – if there was someone decent on. We would laugh at all the acting luvvies talking about their 'art' and referring to each other by their surnames – 'Olivier said to me ...' – but some of those interviews are as memorable to a generation as those *TOTP* debuts: Muhammed Ali, Peter Sellers, Peter Ustinov, Peter Cook, Kenneth Williams, George Best, James Cagney and Pat O'Brien. All the guests were top drawer, and the show allowed the interviewees to tell stories and answer questions in a leisurely way. No rushing, no plugging films, books and shows. No grandstanding by the host. If you grew up on Parky it was hard to adapt later to the style and substance of Jonathan Ross and Graham Norton.

A national love affair was started when an unknown Scottish comedian called Billy Connolly came on *Parkinson* and told a joke about someone parking their bike in the crack of his murdered wife's bum. We had not heard anything like it. Only a couple of years earlier the country (or the media, at least) was up in arms because a showjumper called Harvey Smith had thrown a V-sign on live television. The furore went on for days.

On Sundays we would settle down again and watch *The Big Match*. Brian Moore's voice soothing us while Jimmy Hill's lofty opinions and over-engineered analysis made us laugh. *The Golden Shot* followed with Bob

Monkhouse and the lovely and dizzy Anne Aston. For a while I took to answering the house telephone by saying, 'Hello, who's calling *The Golden Shot?*'

During the week we all laughed together at *Steptoe And Son*, *On The Buses* and *Till Death Us Do Part*. History has been rewritten about these shows. Somehow, although *Steptoe* aired the everyday prejudices, sexism and bigotry of the time, it has been left alone by the revisionists. Not sure why. The way *Till Death Us Do Part* is dealt with is to claim that people were laughing *at* Alf Garnett, not *with* him. The narrative now is that scriptwriter Johnny Speight created this odious, racist, working-class character to hold a mirror to society and its right-wing, reactionary values. Bollocks. People loved Alf. The further he went, the more he swore and cursed, the more he attacked, the more they liked it. There were Alfs everywhere. Vast swathes of the population *were* Alf. People may not like this uncomfortable truth, but it is a truth nevertheless.

On The Buses, however, has been bullied almost out of the national consciousness. It never attracted the level of attention from intellectuals that was given to *Steptoe And Son* or *Till Death Us Do Part*, but the general population of Britain loved it. It was as English as fish and chips, and we in the Knight household liked to watch it with our fish and chips as we gathered around the box at 7.30 on a Friday.

The sitcom was anchored around Stan Butler, a randy bus driver forever trying to seduce the young teenage clippies working from his Luxton bus garage. Stan was played by Reg Varney, who was already by then about fifty. We had to suspend belief when he chased and captured these sexy, miniskirted, dangly ear-ringed beauties. We had to suspend belief even more when his colleague Jack, played by Bob Grant, pinched the 'bird' off him. Jack was lanky, balding and looked as if he had a permanent cold. Both men were always trying to pull the wool over Inspector 'I'll get you, Butler' Blakey's snake eyes. Now the programme is dismissed as sexist, offensive bilge. Well, there were about twenty million people who enjoyed being offended by it every Friday night, and when I hear people spouting this view, pouring scorn on it and patronising the people who enjoyed it, it irks me.

Coronation Street was religiously followed by seventeen million households, which accounted for pretty much the entire nation. People who claimed they had never watched it I filed in the same drawer as post-pubescent males who claimed never to have masturbated. It only aired in those days on a Monday and a Wednesday, one hour a week. The characters were well rounded and the storylines believable and often shot through with humour. There was barely a person alive in the UK then who was not familiar with Annie Walker, Elsie Tanner, Ena Sharples, Albert Tatlock, Stan Ogden, et al.

In my opinion it all went wrong for *Coronation Street* when it increased its output from two episodes a week to six. This had the effect of accelerating the previously gentle and nuanced character development three-fold and exhausting storylines in much quicker time. To illustrate this, between 1960 and 1980 there were only ten character demises. The next two decades saw seventeen deaths, and in the last twenty years it has gone crackers with seventy-five poor souls dying, often in increasingly bizarre circumstances. It has become almost as dangerous to live on Coronation Street as it is to reside in the rural village of Midsomer, where two people are murdered every Sunday.

There were some special TV moments that happened now and then that made a nationwide impact and would be the main topic of conversation the next day at school – and in workplaces too, no doubt. Most people remember where they were when Valerie Barlow got electrocuted – in front of the television watching *Coronation Street*. One other such event was when an unknown, unpredictable comedian called Freddie Starr appeared on the *Royal Variety Performance*. It was 1970, and the entire country had a choice of only three channels. More than twenty million people would have watched the Liverpudlian do a sublime impression of Mick Jagger. Nobody could take Mick as seriously as he took himself after that.

A couple of years earlier the population had become addicted to *The Forsyte Saga*, the *Downton Abbey* of its day. The scene where Soames raped Irene, played by Nyree Dawn-Porter, scandalised the country, but the viewing figures rocketed. Churches rescheduled their services (people were still going then) so the congregation could be home in time for the Sunday-evening start.

The freedom of sitting around Tony Cruse's listening to the radio, smoking fags and watching television became seductive. Tony Brand started to persuade me to play truant for the first time since infants' school.

Sometimes we would walk into Baker's Field as if going to school, wait a while and then turn around and go straight back to his house. This allowed enough time for his mum to head off on her bike to another school where she worked as a dinner lady.

Once the novelty wore off it became boring sitting in Tony's empty house afraid to touch anything in case we left traces of our presence and ducking down as we passed the window, so we ventured outside. This was more exciting because you could then play cat and mouse with the truancy officer. For us this was a man called Mr Lake, who had replaced a Mr Whitehead.

'Lakey's coming!' was a familiar cry as the middle-aged man would appear out of a copse and grab one of us by the arm and frogmarch us to his car and deliver us back to school. He never tried to talk to us or persuade us of the error of our ways. His job was to catch and return, and that was that. A caning was the standard punishment. Barely anyone was ever expelled from school while I was there. They call expulsion 'being excluded' now to make it all sound more inclusive.

Tony and I went up to Epsom Downs one time. Lakey wouldn't search for you up there among genuine race crowds. It was sparsely attended, so it could not have been Derby week. We were hanging around by the winning post when a man came over to us and started chatting. It was a hot day, and he was wearing a no-sleeve jeans jacket, buttons undone to reveal a tanned hairy chest. A medallion hung around his neck. He was in his thirties with a mane of shaggy black hair. He reminded me of Patrick Mower, who was riding high on TV at the time in *Callan*. He struck up a low-key conversation barely looking at us, playing it cool. He told us he was a stunt man and had an American car. How stupid were we? Did we know the way into Epsom town? Just down the hill, mate. You lads going that way? I'll give you a ride. He really did have an American car. An open-topped Cadillac. Tony jumped in the back, and I sat next to macho man in the front. As he drove down Ashley Road, Tony perched on the front of his seat leaning between us. Suddenly I was aware of Tony poking me in the shoulder. I looked at him and he nodded to the man's crotch area. It looked like a small rolling pin was stuffed down his tight velvet hipsters. Something wasn't right.

'This'll do, mate,' said Tony as we cruised up to the traffic lights at the White Hart. He was clambering out the back already.

'Don't you want to go for a drink, boys. I know a ...'

I had opened the door and was out. We ran down the high street laughing hysterically. We thought it exciting and hilarious and couldn't wait to tell our mates. Writing these memories now I am astonished just how many of these potentially dangerous experiences we found ourselves in. How many of these weirdos were out there?

The summer between the second and third school year Mill Reef won the Derby, and we were up there for that too. Geoff Lewis rode him. I was not a horseracing fan, but there was a buzz about Mill Reef at the time along with another horse called Brigadier Gerard. The previous year Nijinsky had become the nation's favourite horse ever. The Derby was special for Epsom people. We were given the afternoon off school to be able to get home in advance of the crowds, and that saved us playing truant. It was an enormous occasion, like the FA Cup Final, that the whole country loved. A million or more souls would descend on Epsom, and the carnival atmosphere that was created was unique. Rich and poor rubbed shoulders. Pubs would shut through fear of trouble from rowdy racegoers and marauding Gypsies. The local paper would openly warn readers to lock their houses and garages as the Gypsies were in town. It was mostly in their heads. Those publicans brave enough to stay open would likely be rewarded with record takings.

On the racecourse, characters abounded. Prince Monolulu, an African chief, who gave out tips for money shouting 'I gotta horse' was well known. He may have been African, but he was no more a tribal chief than I was. Police and pickpockets mingled with the crowd. Toffs in top hats showboated down the course while the Queen and her mum looked down from their pod in the grandstand. Tic-tac men in white gloves communicated with others across the track. I wondered if it was all a show. Bookmakers cried the odds from an upturned crate while their partner snatched banknotes off eager punters. Gypsy men with tanned, leathery skin and large bellies wearing white shirts and trousers suspended by black braces threaded their way through the crowds to the beer tents where they sat down on crates swigging from brown beer bottles and renewing old friendships or family bonds.

For we kids there were opportunities to make a few bob. We learned the art of identifying drunk, affable men who were flushed with ale and a winning bet. The men with their pockets hanging outside their trousers we learned to give a wide berth.

'Spare us half-crown, mister?' We started high and worked down. After the last race had been run teams of mental patients were bussed up, and they earned pocket money (I hope) to spread out in a line and pick up the litter across the hill and in the dip. Some unkindly called this the second Derby. We did a similar thing, but we were looking for dropped coins and sometimes notes. We always found something.

There were two fairs in those early days. One in the dip and one across the road opposite Tattenham Corner. The smell of chips and industrial engine oil assaulted your nostrils as you entered. Rock 'n' roll was in the air and candy floss trodden into the ground. Fairground music seemed stuck in the late 1950s and early 1960s. You would rarely hear the Beatles or the Stones. It was all Del Shannon, Ricky Valance and the Tornadoes. Already the grass had been worn away by the footfall. On the outer perimeter were the gentler rides – the horses on a pole, the kiddies' trains, the coconut shies – so as not to put anybody off, but deeper in you would find the Rotor where you were stuck to the wall as the floor disappeared beneath you, the dive bomber that took you so high you were level with the steeple of Headley Church on the horizon and the dodgem cars patrolled by lanky youths showing off their dexterity as they effortlessly stepped around the moving cars in almost balletic fashion. Later the film *That'll Be The Day* perfectly encapsulated the whole experience.

In 1974 Mum gave me a pound note to place on a rank outsider in the Derby. The horse was called Snow Knight, and Mum said she wouldn't be able to face life if it won and we hadn't backed it, given Knight was our surname.

'It's a fifty-to-one shot, Mum. Don't waste your money.'

She insisted, and I stuffed the note in my pocket. At the course I walked down the row of bookies, and there was no movement in the price. Satisfied that there was no coup under way, and Mum's wager had no chance, I moved over to the fair where I very quickly spent her quid. Later I was standing furtively by a stall where a showman was rounding up a crowd by promising to throw knives at a nude lady and wondering if I looked old enough to enter his mysterious and alluring tent, when two boys I knew came up to me. They had just walked over from the course.

'Who'd believe it, eh? Fifty to fucking one.'
My heart began a rapid descent down my body like a broken lift. 'What?'
'The Derby winner, fifty-to-one outsider. Bookies had it off.'
'What was it called?'
'Snow Knight. Did you back it?'
No I fucking didn't.

I thought of Mum at home. She would have come in from the kitchen and sat down and watched the race for sure. She'd have been on cloud nine. Fifty pounds could well have been more than a week's wages for my dad. This was a significant family windfall. How would I face her? For a moment I contemplated jumping off the Big Wheel or running away with the fair. They might be looking for a dwarf. Could I carry a story about being robbed? Then I faced up to reality, peeled off from my friends and headed home.

As I walked in the door Mum's big smile dropped seeing the crushed and guilty expression on my face. 'You didn't place the bet, did you?'

'I'm sorry, Mum.'

She turned her back to me and immersed her hands back into the foamy washing up bowl. 'I'm very disappointed in you. That's no different from stealing.'

I hadn't seen it that way, but those quietly spoken words and seeing Mum's shoulders sag found my conscience guilty.

20
I DON'T WANT TO BE A SOLDIER

The trepidation of starting my third year at Danetree Road was almost as intense as leaving junior school for senior school. Danetree had a reputation for brutality in the playground and a harsher regime among the teachers. All sorts of stories filtered down to us freshly anointed teenagers, most of them patently untrue. We would be the babies again at thirteen in a school of battle-hardened fourteen- and fifteen-year-olds.

First, there was a bunch of new teachers to become acquainted with. I couldn't help noticing they were predominantly male, reflecting, I felt, the requirement for stronger discipline. The headmaster was Leonard Bradbury. He was a troubled-looking man with grey hair parted in the middle. He had a habit, much imitated, of running his fingers through his locks to reposition the two curtains that regularly fell on to his forehead. Another quirk of his, where he addressed most people as 'folks', was also keenly mimicked. He was known as a progressive head with a keen social awareness. Some of his staff, who watched as discipline in the school slipped term by term, saw that as a weakness. Over all he was well liked by the pupils – having been a centre forward for Manchester United and his promising career having been ended by the Second World War helped. On the 28 January 1939 he made his first-team debut against Chelsea at Stamford Bridge and scored the only, but winning, goal. A few months later a declaration of war changed everything. I wonder now did Mr Bradbury and Mr Blore ever play in a competitive match against each other?

Our first form teacher was Mr Denham. He taught mathematics. He was a tall, angular middle-aged man with a distinctive nasal inflection to his voice. His introductory speech to us was a revelation. 'I want a quiet life. I will not give you a hard time if you don't give me a hard time. That's not too much to ask, is it? Some of you want to learn, and I am happy to teach you, but those of you who don't want to learn, I am not going to waste my precious time on you. Is that clear? I ask those of you who do not want to be educated to sit down the back and play quietly among yourselves. Hangman. Battleships. Whatever takes your fancy.'

After a debate about the practical uses of algebra in everyday life it was amicably agreed that I would be one of those boys sitting at the back playing hangman. He wrote in my first term school report: 'Has no interest in or aptitude for mathematics.'

I never crossed Mr Denham, but Keith did. He breached the informal ceasefire and insulted him by responding to a question by pinching his nose and mimicking the teacher's nasal speech. He had mistaken Denham's unconventional approach for weakness. Denham lost control, and it was frightening. In his haste to get at Keith he knocked over chairs and dragged him from his seat, simultaneously smacking him around the face and head with his open spare hand. We were stunned into silence, and Keith broke free and ran out of the classroom.

'Good riddance!' shouted the teacher.

He was not a bad bloke, and all of us, including Keith, became good pals as the school year wore on. He once called me an incorrigible rogue, which I quite liked.

'If the headmaster calls in,' he would say, 'try to look like you're working, for heaven's sake. Try to look like you're learning. It'll be easier for all of us.' When Mr Bradbury did visit, Denham would pull faces as he was following him out to the door. We loved that. He adored gossip. If there had been an incident in the school between a pupil and a teacher he would pull up a chair and ask us about it. Sometimes he would even comment on other teachers, gently taking the piss out of them. He would tell us to speak quietly, 'Walls have big ears.'

Another master was a diminutive grey-haired man who was nearing retirement. The story about him (that Mr Denham did not dismiss when we asked him) was that some years earlier he had made a sixth-form pupil pregnant and married her. If this was true it brings into sharp focus how times have changed.

Mr Thomas was barking mad. A Welshman, he swept around the place in a cloak like something out of a Billy Bunter book. Thomas, whether he realised it or not, was a laughing stock. His nickname, unimaginatively, was

Boyo, and, inexplicably, he called most boys Flyer. He had been there when my mum attended so was another about to retire. He used to walk into his stores cupboard, which had a small inset window. He would then bend his knees and crouch down and then come back up again slowly and mechanically to give the impression to the class that he was going up and down in a lift. Bonkers. Between these displays of insanity, he taught English.

Mr Foster was an English and religious education teacher who was married to the school secretary. He would become our form teacher in the fourth year. His nickname was Religious Monkey. I could see why. He taught religion and had a round friendly monkey face. He had the knack of being able to keep order without resorting to violence or even threatening to. It was a rare gift among teachers at that school.

Music was taught by a Mr Deal, an insular man with a bald head and a small toothbrush moustache. One day Keith (who else?) let out a trumpet-like fart. We were (not) listening to some classical music at the time. Deal looked up and said calmly to Keith, 'Was that you?'

'It was Knight, sir.' I think this was a reflex reply from Keith. We normally blamed things on each other, and there was no malice intended. Deal strode over to us menacingly and walked past me, lulling me into thinking the danger had gone and then ... whack! I had never been hit so hard in my whole life. It was a shock, and my head smashed down on the wooden desk and bounced back up. Painful and dangerous to a young skull. He then did the same to Keith. Nothing was said, and even though a nasty bump sprung up on my forehead I did not think to complain to the school or my parents.

Nearly twenty years later, while at work, I was reading an edition of the *Yorkshire Post* for my job. I turned the page, and there was the discombobulating image of Mr Deal staring out at me. He had done much the same thing to a boy in the Midlands but had gone further. This time the pupil and his parents had reported him to the police, and times had changed. Deal had been criminally prosecuted. I had no sympathy for him.

Mr Calcutt taught religious education too. He was a well-groomed, serious man in a smart suit who was heavily involved in one of the local churches. He encouraged debate and did not teach *at* the children. That ethos would eventually result in a showdown between us.

Geography was taught by Mr Nye. He was not very tall, overweight but pugnacious looking with a sandy moustache and hair and, as he often reminded us all, had served in the Royal Air Force. Nye was arguably the most important teacher in the school. He appeared to be keeping the edifices of discipline from complete collapse almost single-handedly. He was not afraid to go head to head with any boy and showed no fear, even of Bill, who had grown to be comfortably the biggest boy in the school and was by this time prepared to use his fists if he really had to. Bill was not a troublemaker, however, although trouble sometimes came to him because of his high visibility, and Nye recognised this. There was a mutual respect. Other teachers struggling with order would sometimes threaten to fetch Mr Nye, which normally worked. I always thought this was a sad indictment of their teaching abilities, especially the men. Bradbury was the headmaster in name, but Nye was the *head master* in practice.

At Danetree they were still teaching art to us, but instead of Mr Bowerman, who had the ability to tune us in, we now had a Miss Bell, who was uninspiring and lost the class very early on. A boy at the front (Keith?) lobbed a blackboard rubber backwards over his shoulder, and I picked it up off the floor and threw it back down the front. I chucked with a bit too much force, and the rubber landed at Miss Bell's feet.

'Knight, pick up that rubber and take it to Mr Bradbury and tell him I sent you because you threw it at me.'

'I didn't throw it *at* you. I threw it at Keith.'

'Get to Mr Bradbury's office now,' she screamed.

When I arrived Stuart and Paul were queueing there with some other boys waiting for the cane. Stuart said to me to hold the tap of the central heating radiator if I could because it would numb my hand and the cane wouldn't hurt so much. Hand? I was expecting and not much fearing another couple of swipes on the bum. Hand was different, and suddenly I was nervous. We could hear the thwack from the inside the office as one of Paul and Stuart's lot was being corporally punished. We winced but started giggling, and Stuart put his white handkerchief over his face so his mirth didn't show.

'Get in here, Leitch.'

Paul followed, and then it was my turn.

Mr Bradbury sat down and asked me to explain why I had been sent to him. I said I had thrown a blackboard rubber because someone had thrown it at me, but that Miss Bell thought I was throwing at her. Bradbury shook his head solemnly as my sorry story unfolded. All the time I was clutching the wooden backed blackboard rubber which now felt like an offensive weapon in my hands.

'I am disappointed to find you here. You are not one of these boys [he meant Paul and Stuart]. You are a sensible boy. You need to have a really good reflection on the company you keep ...' – Bradbury paused as he gathered his thoughts; I interpreted this to mean that I was going to be let off the cane, which was a good job because the heat from the radiator on my hand had long since dissipated – '... but you leave me no choice but to cane you.'

'The cane doesn't work, though, does it, sir?' I don't know where that came from, but it took the headmaster by surprise.

'What do you mean it doesn't work?'

'Well, it doesn't, does it? You cane the same people nearly every day. Jones, Fisher, Owen, Brand, etc. It's not changing anyone's behaviour, is it? If it worked they wouldn't be here each morning.'

This uncomfortable truth coming from the small, polite boy opposite unsettled him.

'What do you suggest then, Knight?'

'That's your job to work out, but just because you cannot think of an alternative does that make it right to carry on with a failed punishment?'

That was it. He sprung out his chair grabbing a gnarled straight cane from what looked like a quiver in the corner. He asked me which hand I wrote with and then asked me to extend the other. Clutching my spare arm tightly so I couldn't run away (which I thought was over the top, but then again there was a story that one of the Merchant brothers had jumped out of his window and escaped through the quadrant) he whacked the thin piece of wood down on my poor fingertips three times. His curtains hung down, and he seemed genuinely embarrassed and remorseful.

'Go back to your classroom and apologise to Miss Bell and tell her you have been punished.'

'Yes, sir.'

If this was 1971, which I think it was, I knew Mr Bradbury would be feeling uncomfortable about caning, and I was probably seeking to exploit that. A boy called Martin Woodhams had made national headlines when he refused the cane from his headmaster at another school. He was sent home, forbidden from returning until he agreed to accept his punishment. His 'crime' was to write an essay that the head deemed 'flippant', and there was a stand-off assiduously followed in the press. The next year London secondary-school pupils took to the streets in a protest against corporal punishment that also captured the imagination of the newspapers and television. The march through the centre of the city turned violent, and there were images of scruffy kids being headlocked and dumped into open-mouthed police vans. The tide had turned, and the cane would soon join the mortar board and gown to exist only in the pages of *The Dandy* and *The Beano* – and even there for not much longer.

Violence, authorised and unauthorised, though, was all around. Playground fights were commonplace and, no longer moderated by Joe Taylor, sometimes ended in much blood, missing teeth and tears. Two boys in the year above – Peter and Jeff, both with reputations for toughness – fought for over an hour once, the fight migrating around the playground and along paths and corridors and taking a huge crowd with it. It was blood sport. Bullying was rife, and if you were unfortunate to be a bit different, had no back-up or in the wrong place at the wrong time, it could be you. I saw things that haunt me to this day.

By this time I was a frequenter of youth clubs in the evenings. These clubs were set up by well-meaning social workers to keep children off the streets and out of mischief. The nearest one to us, and the first I used, was the Boys' Club on Longmead Road. Here we played table tennis, snooker, cards and football. The young blokes that ran it allowed us to smoke, which made us feel very grown up at eleven or twelve. However, the clue was in the name – it was a boys' club. No girls. I graduated to the Javelin Club in Epsom, which soon changed its name to the Samurai Club, cashing in on a growing youth obsession with kung-fu fighting. Girls gathered in corners, moving on to the floor to dance to 'Stoned Love' by the Supremes. We boys played a fruit machine and showed off our latest tonic trousers or Ivy loafers. The nearby Foresters' Hall was a dangerous place on a Friday night where the older boys fought battles with interlopers from other towns and, failing that, one another. A crop-haired bouncer called Louis Barfe attempted to keep order. I sneaked in there once or twice.

Finally, me and my pals Paul and Stuart settled on the disco club run by the Ewell Congregational Church, which was more commonly known as the Congo. The boys here weren't quite as threatening as those at the Foresters' and there was no alcohol, although older boys did turn up to admire and court the girls. I think the church types that ran the place nursed aspirations of converting some of us, like the Staneway Sunday-school evangelists. One evening I showboated past an older boy from another school called Pat, deliberately letting a door to the dancefloor swing back into his face. I think we had taken a dislike to him because he had a particularly smart light-coloured Crombie with a velvet collar. He was not amused, stepped in front of me and knocked me clean out. It was a good punch, and when I came around I went home with my tail firmly jammed between my legs. The following week Tony very loyally and with no fear confronted Pat.

'What did you pick on Martin for? He's only small.'

'You'll do then,' said Pat, and proceeded to knock three of Tony's teeth out.

There was another small youth club in a far corner of the Wells estate in Epsom, and for some reason war was declared on it. One early evening as many as fifty boys from Danetree Road School travelled across Epsom Common to ambush this unsuspecting little group. When we arrived there was barely anybody in attendance, so we made do with some low-key vandalism and setting some dustbins alight. A bored Epsom police force got wind and turned up *en masse* in a fleet of cars and vans. We ran on to the common and were chased by the police. As I curled up in a bush deciding that was my best bet I could hear barking dogs nearby and I felt like Hardy Krüger in *The One That Got Away*.

I was now in 3T, the stream that was targeting us at taking CSEs, the poor-man's O level, just about better than leaving school empty handed. I made some good friends in this class, and we would stay together for the remaining three school years. Keith was the one I knew best, but I palled up especially with Terry, who lived on the Cox Lane estate. Terry was an absolute scream. He laughed all the time, was always up for the craic and generally didn't give a fuck about anyone or anything. We sat next to each other in most lessons. I was also friendly with Clive and Jeremy, both smashing lads. There was another boy in the class, Robert, who was also up for anything and good value.

One day some of the boys secretly got into the loft above one of the classrooms and were entertaining us by poking digits and appendages through a hole in the ceiling. When they came down they said there was huge stuffed stag's head up there, complete with antlers. We decided to steal and sell it. We went up at lunch-break. Two boys held an antler each, and with a crowd around them to hide the booty we strolled nonchalantly across the school field and put the trophy in Jeremy Peach's house until after school. Then we adopted the same method to walk the stag's head down to Ewell Village and Maldwyn's antiques shop. Maldwyn was a little fat man in a cardigan, balding with fluffy grey hair at the sides. Fag in his mouth. He would have known we had come across the mounted head via nefarious means, but he didn't care.

'I'll give you £10,' he grunted.

'We'll accept £20,' I countered.

'That is my final offer,' he said dismissively.

'OK. A tenner.'

We salivated as Moggy (his nickname) counted out ten grubby green one-pound notes. Outside we congratulated one another on our good work, dished out £2 each and headed for the bus stop. The fair was in town.

My school days were by now unrecognisable from only three years earlier. The harsh realities of life were barging in on me. The realisation that your parents could not necessarily protect you was a Father-Christmas-is-not-real moment. The fact that grown men were permitted to hit you with their bare hands, a chilling shock. The reality that there were other boys who would happily smash your face in for no reason, very worrying. And the constant presence of girls who were becoming prettier and more desirable by the day but were largely untouchable, achingly frustrating. By now I also had this impudent new companion who lived between my legs and woke up every morning before I did.

Things were darkening in the wider world too. The Troubles in Northern Ireland dominated the news. Calling the maiming and murdering of soldiers and civilians the Troubles I always thought was deliberately downgrading the reality, as if the terrible situation in Belfast was on a par with Michael Crawford's Frank Spencer confessing 'I had a bit of trouble' in *Some Mothers Do 'Ave 'Em*.

In addition to Ireland was the relentless diet of strikes and industrial strife. The same old names on the TV every day: TUC, Joe Gormley, Vic Feather, Hugh Scanlon, Tom Jackson, ACAS. Dull men in suits entering buildings giving updates on negotiations. Relishing their time in the sun. Dad was quietly full of foreboding. He didn't like the way the country was going. Unemployment was mentioned more and more. There was a joke at the time:

Q: Why does Edward Heath wear his underpants in the bath?
A: So he doesn't have to look down on the unemployed.

He didn't say it because he didn't want to worry us, but Dad was concerned about the employment prospects for us kids who were soon to be entering the job market.

Moreover, there was news from Bangladesh, where children were starving to death. Their parents were too, I imagine, but it was the babies and infants with flies crawling over their eyelids and out of their nostrils that were beamed into our homes to prise open people's wallets and purses. Charity workers came to the door asking for money. George Harrison organised a fund-raising concert. It was the first time I remember being pressed by television to care about famine in far-off lands and dig deep. It was a sign that wealth had trickled down to the ordinary working-class people and they were able to consider donating to charity rather than seeking it for the first time.

If the news flow was dark and dim, our lives were lit by up by the fizzing music scene, albums especially. Only much older siblings called them LPs now, and our parents still mumbled under their breaths about 78s. Brother Laurence purchased *Electric Warrior* by T. Rex, featuring 'Get It On' and 'Jeepster', which became lasting anthems of that year of 1971. He also bought *Every Picture Tells A Story* by Rod Stewart into the home. It was generally accepted that with most albums there would be some dross to wade through before unearthing the gems, but Rod's breakthrough solo album was quality from beginning to end. 'Maggie May' tapped into every schoolboy's fantasy about being seduced by an older woman against a backdrop of hustling in pool halls – of which there were none in the UK yet. I managed to get the funds together to buy Cat Stevens' *Teaser And The Firecat*, which was already being declared a masterpiece. That and John

Lennon's *Imagine* were my only owned albums for a long while, but they could be used as currency at school to borrow others: *Sticky Fingers* by the Rolling Stones, *Hunky Dory* from David Bowie and *Who's Next* all guested at home at various times.

Going to record shops to buy an album or just to look at them was a leisure pursuit in its own right. Epsom's Harlequin was the place to go. Row upon row of albums sorted by genre and then alphabetically within that genre. There was a section called 'Easy Listening', which included the likes of Mantovani and Des O'Connor, but no boy (Harlequin was a 95% male preserve) would be seen dead flicking through that. Most would cluster around 'Rock' or 'Heavy Rock', and here were the delights of *Fragile* by Yes and *Tarkus* by Emerson, Lake & Palmer. (I privately thought the category here should have been 'Hard Listening'.) These teenagers would move slowly in their long trench coats and fingerless gloves (in summer), lovingly tipping the record out of its cover and admiring it. It's a circular piece of black plastic, mate. They're all the same.

I had now moved into the fourth year at school. By rights this should have been my last year of formal education. I, and nearly everyone I knocked around with, should have been finishing up at fifteen years old and getting out to work. Paul and Stuart were already out there. Paul was apprenticed as a painter and decorator, and Stuart was training to be a toolmaker at Ronson's.

My year, though, was the first to be impacted by a new government act – the Raising Of The School Leaving Age (ROSLA) – which ruled that we had to stay on an extra year until sixteen. I don't know what was behind the new law. Why keep kids who would not be achieving anything academically on at school? It was commonly perceived to be a Government ruse to keep a lid on rising unemployment. Instead of leaving school in the summer of 1973 we had to now wait until the summer of 1974. This was a source of growing resentment for many of us. We wanted money in our pockets, and most parents wanted money out of our pockets. Paul and Stuart were already living in the big world – buying clothes, walking into betting shops, getting into pubs, taking girls out – and there we were walking to school to be shouted at by teachers who would really have preferred us not to be there. It seemed very unfair and pointless.

The careers officer came in to do sessions with us one week. We were allotted quarter of an hour each with him. I remember his name, incredibly as he was only in my life for just 15 minutes: Mr Rowton. He wore thick-rimmed tortoiseshell glasses and had glued down his remaining tufts of hair to his scalp. I settled down in the chair in the office next to the headmaster's study that had been requisitioned for him.

'Now, Martin, have you had any thoughts about what you'd like to do when you leave school?'

'Yes. I'd like to be a reporter.'

'A newspaper reporter?

'Yes.'

'It says here you are not sitting any O levels. I think it would be a prerequisite that you have an English O level at the very least to become a reporter on the local paper, for example.'

I shrugged.

'What are you good at?' he asked, searching for a route forward.

I thought about treating him to the owl noises I could make with cupped hands that generally went down well but decided against it and shrugged again.

'Have you considered the army?'

Had I considered the army? Yeah, sounds a great idea. Go to Ireland and get my fucking head blasted off. The look on my face gave Mr Rowton his answer.

'Have you thought about the GPO?'

'What's that?' After his effort to pack me off to conflicts abroad I thought it might be a Middle Eastern militia organisation.

'The General Post Office. They are currently keen for young men to train as postmen.'

No, I had not thought about being a fucking postman either. I've nothing against postmen, it just seemed such a random career path he was trying to send me down. Rowton had decided from a cursory glance at some paragraph or other about me that shoving letters through doors and dodging dangerous dogs was my destiny. He stuffed some pamphlets into my hand depicting smiling posties in pristine uniforms and caps, and I noticed more leaflets for careers in the army, navy and RAF fanned out on the table. He had decided that I would be more suited to carrying a postbag than a rifle. And there, in the space of fifteen minutes, my life was mapped out for me.

201

Speaking of examinations, it was now that we were being told to choose which subjects we wanted to drop, if any. For me that was easy – most of them. I had made my mind up only to sit three CSEs, and they were the subjects I had an interest in and where I had a good relationship with the teacher: English, history and art.

Before entering Mr Calcutt's religious education lesson one afternoon I had canvassed the class first. Even the word 'lesson' summed it up for me. It smacked of punishment or revenge – 'I'm going to teach you a lesson.' I had had an idea. Calcutt kicked off his usual earnest teachings. He would read a passage from the Bible and then invite us to discuss it and perhaps relate the underlying message to modern life.

'And Jesus walked on water ...'

I shot my hand up.

'Yes, Knight?'

'How did he do that?'

'It was a miracle, Knight.'

'I don't believe that is possible.'

'It's a miracle, Knight. I told you.' The back of the teacher's neck was burning red. We knew from experience that was a sign of imminent loss of temper.

'How do we know it happened?'

Calcutt held his Bible aloft and patted it triumphantly. 'Because, Knight, it's here in the Bible. The Holy Book.'

'Just because someone wrote something down in a book that doesn't make it true, does it? Biggles isn't real, is he, sir?'

That raised some laughs.

'Knight, you are a non-believer. That is clear. However, that does not give you the right to hijack the lesson.'

'I'm not saying I'm a non-believer. You are asking us to accept a story that you have no proof or evidence ever happened. Why should we believe that any more than we should believe ... *Black Beauty*?'

The class giggled louder. Calcutt slammed his Bible down on the desk making the half of the class who were dozing jump. 'That's it! Enough! You may have no interest in this subject, and I therefore suggest you leave the lesson immediately and allow the rest of the class to proceed.'

'They don't want to learn neither, sir. Nobody here is going to be a priest or a nun, so none of us can see the point in doing the exam or listening to all this mumbo-jumbo.'

I knew this was the dangerous part. I thought he might hit me. I saw him whack Derek once and wanted to say then 'that's not very Christian-like' but held my tongue.

'Really, Knight? So, you are the form spokesman, are you? You've been elected to speak on behalf of the class, have you? OK, hands up, please, those of you who will be taking the religious education CSE next year?'

One hand, maybe two or even three, were slowly raised but no momentum built. It was a resounding no. He didn't look at me. He was in shock. He knew I had ambushed him. His face burned as he picked up his Bible and notes and pushed them into his briefcase, and then he turned around and walked out of the classroom.

I felt no guilt at the time. Even though Mr Calcutt was a decent man I genuinely believed it was a waste of our time pursuing religion as a subject to the exam stage. Seriously, in what way was learning all that Bible stuff (whether it was true or not) going to benefit any of us ever in the world of work? The *Evening News* didn't have a section for vicars in the job ads.

However, I did feel guilt later in life. When I was about sixty years old, somebody told me that Mr Calcutt was, remarkably, still alive and residing in the same house by the church where he had lived when we were kids. I deliberately started riding my bike past the house until early one summer's evening I saw him bending down tending a flowerbed in his front garden. I had decided to apologise. He would have probably forgotten anyway, but I felt it was something I should do. I pulled my bike up.

'Excuse me.'

Mr Calcutt looked up. He had aged well. I calculated he must have been mid-eighties, even ninety, but he had kept his hair and his face had not altered much. But he was clearly old and looked vulnerable. Perhaps he didn't want to be reminded of an unpleasant experience and an even more unpleasant boy.

'Do you know the way to Poole Road, please?' I bottled it but resolved to revisit and try again. Sadly, before I got around to doing so, I read in the local paper he had died. A late-life lesson learned about acting sooner rather than later.

21
HERE COMES THE SUN

Late in 1972 Mum took me down to Portslade on the train to visit Nana and Gaga. I knew my grandfather's emphysema was worsening and that he was now bedridden, but I didn't really appreciate that I was being taken down to say goodbye. When I saw him I was shocked to the core. He was propped up in bed by a small mountain of pillows. He reminded me of a little fledgling bird scarcely out of the egg with his scraggy neck and emaciated frame. His eyes were wide and bulging, and when he spoke he stared into a space beyond me. I wondered if he had gone blind. There was a jungle of breathing apparatus, medicines and pills all around him.

'Dad, Martin's here,' my mum whispered into his ear. She took my hand and placed it into his. Despite his weakness he gripped my hand like it had never been held before.

'Hello, Martin. How are you?'

'I'm all right, Gaga.'

'That's what we want to hear. You watching the soccer results?'

'Yes, Gaga.' I was trying to keep in the tears. He continued to squeeze my hand. Tried to say something else but struggled for breath, and Nana leaned over and placed an oxygen mask over his mouth. I watched it steam up. I felt I was looking at a dead body that hadn't quite died yet. Mum gently prised my hand out of his and motioned for me to give him a kiss, which I did and then went next door to sit and watch *Grandstand* with Frank Bough. Later, through the crack in the door, I saw Mum's brother, Uncle Ken, carrying Gaga to the toilet. The son carrying the father like a baby. I am recounting an event of almost fifty years ago, and I can feel again the fear and raw grief I felt that Saturday afternoon as it dawned on me my grand-dad was about to die and nobody could do a thing about it.

I prayed for him that night in bed, pleading with God to save him. I had only ever prayed at school. I said the Lord's Prayer too and added a list of names at the end of other relatives for God to look after in the interests of fairness. I did it again the next night and then became worried about stopping in case they all started dying because I was not keeping it up. I still do it now if I do not fall asleep first. Sadly, but inevitably, my mum is the one name still there of that long list of my elders, but I can't bear dropping them now.

Although there was low-level indoctrination at EBS, I was not religious. Far from it. I was pulling out the stops for my granddad. A desperate little boy. But something must have lodged inside me from those St Mary's school and church days, and in some periods of my life it triumphs over my logic. I strongly suspect that when my time comes I will be saying prayers, hymns and psalms, anything that might get me an easier ride to the other side – just in case there is one.

A few weeks after that miserable visit to Portslade we were all sitting at home watching *BBC Sports Personality Of The Year*. Mary Peters, our pent-athlete who had won a gold medal in the Olympics, was accepting the award from Princess Anne when the telephone rang. Mum got up to answer it. A few seconds later we heard a heart-rending wail from the hall, like an injured animal. Dad jumped up, and we children looked at one another terrified. He brought Mum back into the sitting-room with his arms wrapped around her, supporting her, as she sobbed uncontrollably.

'Gaga has died,' he explained.

Gaga was the first person I loved who died. The gamut of emotions I went through are now well trodden, but then, at fourteen years old, they were crippling. The first one was, why him? Why us? It didn't occur to me it was part of the natural scheme of things. He was sixty-six and had gone a bit early, but the average lifespan was still being measured then as three score years and ten. Then there was the shock that I would never see him again. I couldn't believe there was no recourse. Nobody to appeal to. No way of getting him back.

The first two emotions I came to terms with over time, but the third emotion remains unresolved. It dawned on me then how quickly in the scheme of things Gaga would disappear. This man who was so kind and gentle and special and meant so much to us would gradually be forgotten. He is remembered by a few of us in the family, but when we go then he completely goes. When the last person to remember him dies, then he is gone. That sad fact is the killer. By 2040, for example, the only indication that my lovely grandfather ever existed will be a few lines on an ancestry website. That's what I struggled with then and still do, especially as that day is now that much closer for me. At the time of writing I am three years younger than he was then. The finality of death is shocking. When we hear at funerals and see written on gravestones – His Memory Will Live Forever and suchlike – it is simply not true. His or her memory will live only as long as the last person who knew them survives, that is the truth of it. And, for Gaga, read each and every one of us.

The decline of the country was writ large daily on our television screens. The IRA had bought the 'armed struggle' to our doorsteps, detonating bombs and killing people across England. Now it was close to home and very scary. The miners' strike was also affecting us directly by way of power cuts, and the three-day week was the big talking point. Previously I for one had miners' disputes filed under 'up north', so nothing to worry about. I and most people I knew had never visited the north and doubted if we ever would. It might as well have been Siberia.

But the power cuts spooked people. They highlighted the fragility of the status quo, although we kids loved them and saw in them the opportunity for increased mischief. Blackouts were ideal for creeping behind off licences and stealing their empty bottles to take in a few days later to get the refund money. There was a wartime feel or so our parents told us, but Dad was worried. Really worried. Labour MP Tony Benn particularly gave him sleepless nights. He was convinced that Harold Wilson would come to power once again and that Benn – who he believed was a dangerous communist – would wrest control from Wilson. I asked him once what was so bad about the three-day week. The way I saw it was that people were getting the same money for less work.

'We're not producing goods when the factories are closed. Heath has lost control, and Wilson is no better. We're on the road to bankruptcy'.

Dad had moved from contemplating Communist Party membership in 1946 to fearing the Labour Party in 1974. Although his austere working-class background stopped him from even *thinking* about voting

Conservative, if someone with a bit of backbone replaced Heath he'd consider it. Needs must, as he would sometimes say.

'What happens then?'

'I really don't know. I dread to think. Complete economic collapse? Anarchy? Invasion?'

Mum could see me sliding down the armchair with fear and horror.

'Harry!' Mum interjected. 'What are you doing to the boy? You're scaring the living daylights out of him. You're all doom and gloom.'

Dad tried to back-pedal. Not very convincingly. 'I suppose you're right. We got through the war ... just.'

He wasn't one of those people to sit and moan. He would try and act. The next thing we know was that he had dug a hole in the back garden and was storing canned food.

'What are you doing, Dad?'

'Just keeping the food cool,' he didn't want to provoke Mum's ire again.

'But we've got a fridge now.'

'Yes, but there's not a lot of room.'

We laughed about it then and sometimes still do, but now, as a parent and grandparent, I can feel his fear. Five kids to support single-handedly and the country falling apart before your very eyes. Poor Dad, he must have felt a heavy load weighing on him alone out there in the garden digging holes.

Meanwhile, in school, discipline had broken down even more as far as our year went. No longer did Lakey drive all over to round us up – they didn't want us in the school. We were the ROSLA year; a bunch of uninterested, disruptive, dysfunctional bored kids who wanted to be at work. That tedium and resentment manifested itself more and more in vandalism and anarchy.

We had been moved back down to Ruxley Lane for this final term to some hastily erected buildings called the ROSLA units, constructed exclusively for this extra rogue year. They are still there now. We had to use them earlier than planned, as one day we arrived at school in Danetree to find two of our classrooms gone. They were huts of the type built across the country to cope with growing pupil numbers after the war. One of the huts was my form class where all my school paraphernalia was stored in my desk. The huts were burned down, and a still-steaming black patch was about all that was left when I turned up one morning. How would I cope without my protractor and compass, two compulsory accessories I never used or saw used?

A boy from my year and a boy from the year above had broken in the previous night poured paraffin all over and flicked a match. Mr Bradbury held another morose assembly wondering, what next? He had done another just a few days before bemoaning the fact that one of the girls had placed a sanitary towel on the bonnet of a teacher's car. The ordered, respectful world he understood was degenerating around him. Not long after, Mr Bradbury retired. He had become a husk. I felt sorry for him and Mr Blore, who also, to his great relief, finally went. I saw Bradbury a few years later on my television screen as an audience member in Robin Day's *Question Time*. The colour was back in his cheeks.

It had become the thing to throw parties, and as we were all hitting sixteen there seemed to be one every weekend. On most occasions accommodating or absent parents provided an empty house, and the invitees would roll up clutching their red Party Seven cans of Watney's Pale Ale, tin openers at the ready. The legitimate guests were normally swelled by gatecrashers.

The idea was to drink as much as you could as quickly as you could and get a girl upstairs for some fumbling around and perhaps more. Or vice versa. If the stories recounted later have an ounce of truth a lot of girls and boys lost their virginities in an upstairs bedroom to the beat and warbling of the Rubettes singing 'Sugar Baby Love'. The fast drinking helped everyone loosen up, and it was also a handy insurance policy against the more likely outcome of failing miserably with the opposite sex.

'Did you shag anyone?'

'Nah. Too pissed, me.' / 'What? And waste valuable drinking time?'

In January 1974 Tony and I set off to the Cox Lane estate for a sixteenth birthday party. Tony was resplendent in his purple-and-black Budgie jacket – named after the character in a TV programme we all adored, *Budgie*, starring Adam Faith. Adam played a petty criminal wide boy who was manipulated by a Scottish gangster called Charlie Endell and terrorised by his personal heavy, Laughing Spam Fritter. It was broadcast on a Friday at 9 p.m., and even Paul, who by now had the money and freedom to be out late on a Friday night, preferred to get home at the same time as me to watch it. I was wearing new check Oxford bags – very baggy, but smart strides with a neat turn-up. Undoubtedly, I would also have been donning my Prince-of-Wales check Harrington jacket. I was proud of this because, although Harringtons were two-a-penny, this pattern was rare in Epsom, and I never saw anybody else with one. I was hugging our Party Seven can and Tony was clutching a bottle of Bell's Scotch he had stolen from home. We considered this more than the admission price.

Inside it was dark, and the turntable had been commandeered by the girls. 'Ghetto Child' by the Detroit Spinners and 'Daydreamer' by David Cassidy set the mood. A single set of flashing traffic lights was meant to signify that a disco was in operation. Boys and girls were coupling up and moving into the centre of the room and smooching. I decided to chat to Jane. I knew her well. She was a pretty olive-skinned girl. I do not think I was trying to 'pull' her, but no doubt if she had shown the slightest hint of being interested in me I would have tried.

A boy from my year who I considered a mate was leaning against the wall swigging from a can, and he leaned forward and said, 'You got as much chance with her as I do with the queen.'

I thought he was having a joke and turned away. I think I laughed the comment off. I genuinely have no memory of what happened next, but I have been told many times. The boy hit me with a fierce uppercut that lifted me off the floor and knocked me clean out, and while I lay on the floor he delivered some kicks to my head until others managed to pull him away. I was still out cold. Somebody had run upstairs to fetch Tony (his party was progressing well), and he came down and remonstrated with my attacker. We all knocked around together. I think I was in the front garden by this time being checked over by a couple of concerned girls. Tony came out, and we left the party as it didn't seem wise to stay.

I never really knew why the boy did it. I doubt it was anything to do with me chatting up Jane. I saw him at school on the Monday. I guess he didn't like me. He only said, 'How's your head? Do you want to carry it on?' Carry it on? I had no idea there was a feud or an issue. No, thanks. I knew I would have no chance beating him even if I was prepared. I didn't fancy the same again and this time in front of the whole school.

'No.'

Much to my relief he turned away. My humiliation was complete.

On the day after the party Mum had called me down from my bedroom for Sunday dinner. I had been sitting up there mulling over the previous night's events. Feeling sorry for myself. Worrying about what would happen at school the next day. Ashamed and embarrassed that I had not hit back. Distraught that everyone had seen me for the weakling I was. I was now the bloke who had sand kicked in his face, except I wasn't going to turn to Charles Atlas to build my body up and pay him back. I was going to sit there and take it. I was metaphorically smothered head to toe with sand.

'You're quiet,' said Mum as I chewed half-heartedly on a roast potato. She could read me like a book.

'I'm all right,' I replied, but I wasn't, my head hurt as I chewed, and when I ran my fingers over my scalp, I was alarmed to feel three or four tender bumps.

Curiously, I felt sad for them, my mum and dad. If they had known that the previous evening their little baby, who they had held in their arms and rocked to sleep, had been kicked around somebody's front room like a football a few hours before, they would have been distraught. It would have broken their hearts if they had known I was frightened to go to school the next day in case it happened again, but knew I had no choice.

Ironically, it was with that boy and a few others that I had my first experience with drugs. The 'drug' in question was actually shoe conditioner! We purchased bottles of it from the local launderette machine and poured it on to a handkerchief and then smothered our faces, inhaling deeply. The result was entering a dream-like state and losing bodily control that seemed to last for ages but in reality was only seconds. We sniffed it inside the cinema while watching *Shaft*, an early 'blaxploitation' film starring Richard Roundtree. It was a massive hit with white people. The shoe conditioner craze swept the country among delinquents like us, and eventually they took the chemical out of it to render it harmless and thrill-free. God knows what damage it did to our brain cells.

I soon recovered mentally and physically from getting my head kicked in, and life, as it does, was looking up again. I saw Jenny regularly as she was still at school and we lived close by, but our sexual fumbling had long since ceased. She had moved from older boys in the school to even older boys outside the school. Her boyfriends had sideburns, motorbikes, cash and cars. One day, as our schooldays were finally ending, Jenny and I walked home together. It was nice to chat with her again.

Out the blue she said, 'What are you doing this evening?'

'Nothing.'

'Mum and Dad are going to the social club. Come around at eightish.'

That was interesting – but I still didn't trust in my good fortune and thought she was simply bored and wanted some company while her parents were out. When I arrived she asked me if I was still a virgin. I was expecting a cup of tea. I denied such a scurrilous allegation.

'Who, then?'

I trotted out some nonsense about someone I had met on a day out. She threw her head back and laughed loudly. Had she got me around to take the piss and rub my nose in my pathetic sexual naivety?

'Do you want to lose it?'

I nodded cautiously. I was expecting her to say 'tough' next.

'OK. But if you tell anyone your life won't be worth living.'

I did not need to be told that. Her current boyfriend was built like a brick shithouse. She sank back on the sofa and beckoned me towards her. My body felt like it was about to explode.

'Come on then. We haven't got long. My sister could come home at any minute.'

That snippet of information didn't help my state of mind. I dropped my jeans down and waddled towards her. With some guidance we managed the act. It lasted a fleeting few moments, but it was like a huge burden had been lifted. I had been raised out of purgatory.

'Thank you.'

'You better hope I don't get pregnant.' Jenny saw my worried look. 'Don't worry, I'm only kidding you.'

I was not reassured, but my euphoria was such that I didn't care. I walked back to my house from hers like I was walking on air. I wanted to announce to my parents 'Guess what? I'm not a virgin any more. I've had it away. I'm a fucker I am' but decided against. I am forever indebted to Jenny – gifting me my manhood was one of the sweetest things a friend ever did for me. She freed me from a prison of embarrassment and shame.

As our schooldays reached the end, the boys in 5T decided to make a final trip together to sleep the night under the stars. We knew our lives were about to change radically and that many of us would drift away and some would never see the rest of us again. We met at Epsom railway station and walked up to the Downs and from there threaded through woods, fields and footpaths to Headley Heath. We pooled our money, and the older looking among us, some of whom were now boasting bum fluff on their chins, had been into the off licence and purchased big bottles of cider, cans of Long Life, sweets and plenty of cigarettes. We sat around a fire, a transistor radio crackling, telling stories, laughing, joking and singing. Terry treated us to 'Bollocky Bill The Sailor', a ditty that went on for so long we started to doze off as the alcohol anaesthetised us and the fire burned out. We were all rudely awakened before we achieved deep sleep when the roar of motorbikes and the raucous shouting of men could be heard. 'Hell's Angels,' someone whispered. We peered through the ferns down into a dip where the motorbikes were circling. Our bravado and faux drunkenness suddenly checked. There were girls with them too. We furtively watched, wide-eyed, hoping we were about to witness some initiation rituals that didn't involve us being tortured but did involve some hanky-panky with the girls.

I think about that night. Nothing really happened, but I treasure it. Boys of varying heights, from varying backgrounds with varying personalities who had shared the same classroom and existed in close proximity to each other for three years engineering one last event all together. All nervous about what life held in store. All sad about breaking up but none wishing to articulate any of this because we were aspiring adults and men didn't do things like that. Goodbye Jez, Clive and Clive, Colin, Dave, Mick, Peter, Nigel, Mark, Terry, Robert and Roy, Don and Paul.

Big Bill was the first to leave education. The school were glad to see the back of him and get shot of all of us as they drew a line under some years of disciplinary drift. Two new heads were appointed who promised a new era. But it didn't all go to plan. A young PE teacher, emboldened by the new reforming regime at the school, decided it would be a good idea to face Bill down and show who was in charge now. Unfortunately for him Bill didn't back down, and when the teacher punched and grappled him Bill bashed him up. He walked out the school there and then and never returned.

Tony followed. We were already attending school less and less. Many of the boys were spending one day a week at technical college; some, like me and Derek, were going out doing gardening for old people; others were looking for jobs or working under the radar at places like Chessington Zoo. None of us had a last day as such, because when we attended for the last time we didn't know it. We just drifted away. There were no goodbyes with classmates or teachers, nobody wishing us luck in the big new world.

Bill became an apprentice bricklayer, Eddie got a job with the Greater London Council and Tony got in as a welder at Surrey Sheet Metal Works behind the estate. I just drifted. I knew what I didn't want to do but had little idea what I did want to do. I didn't feel physically equipped to work on a building site. I was not cut out for a trade apprenticeship and the thought of working in a factory terrified me – *Saturday Night And Sunday Morning* had conditioned me against that. I did not particularly want to work in an office either, so I had ruled out almost everything.

Mum and Dad were very patient as the weeks rolled by and there was no sign of me embarking on a career. One early evening Dad came in from work with a copy of the *Evening News*. In the small ads he had ringed in biro the following: MESSENGER BOY WANTED. FINANCIAL TIMES LONDON. 'Why don't you apply for that?

'What's a messenger boy?'

'A boy that delivers messages?'

I duly applied, and a few days later I received a letter from the manager of the *Financial Times* library, Mr Colin C. Abson, inviting me up to Bracken House, Cannon Street, London EC4 for an interview. The wages on offer were £17.96 per week. This seemed like a fortune to me. We calculated that were I to get the job I would pay my mum £3 a week housekeeping, my rail fares would cost the same. I would be left with over £11 to spend on sweets, clothes and going to the pub. Beer was less than 20p a pint. It was an enthralling prospect.

I do not know if it was then or at some other point in my early working life that Dad gave me some sage advice. 'Most people I've found either don't use their brains at work or they are fundamentally lazy. So, if you've got your head screwed on you will do well. If you just work hard you'll do well. If you're both – a grafter and you're a bit sharp – you will race ahead. You will do *very* well. So, Martin, you've got nothing to be apprehensive about.'

It was simple advice that I found to be generally true, and it has stood me in good stead all of my life. It gave me confidence when I was parachuted into an environment where university graduates were automatically assumed to be my superiors, regardless of who performed the best. Dad was aware of this and also how the class system still, then, prevailed. If he had given me a degree from Harvard or £50,000 in cash it would not have had the equivalent start-in-life boost that those few words did. Thanks, Dad.

Meanwhile, we had our annual family holiday in Hastings coming up. It would be the last I would go on with my parents, and I sort of knew it. Sally and Laurence had already dropped out. On the first evening in our usual accommodation on the top of the West Hill I wandered down to the rocks alone and shuffled along the little ledge and climbed into Cat's Cave. I sat there alone, my body now filling the cave more, and looked over to the East Hill to my left with the Victorian funicular railway stalled halfway up, and then down at the fishing huts and boating lake below me. The haunting melody and lyrics from 'Seasons In The Sun' by Terry Jacks floating up from a small funfair on the front. Me finding specific uplifting relevance in the lyrics despite the song being about a dying man: 'Goodbye to you my trusted friend / We've known each other since we were nine or ten.'

Perched in that cave up on the West Hill looking over my childhood holiday town I had a rush of excitement mixed with sadness. The prospect of going to work and meeting new people almost making me catch my breath. The thought that I would have my own money, my own car, my own girlfriend – hopefully – filling me with butterflies. The butterflies you get when you know it's going to happen: 'Pretty girls are everywhere / Think of me and I'll be there.'

Life so far had been a series of firsts. Most of them exhilarating: my first bike, my first day at school, my first film at the cinema, my first football match, my first girlfriend, my first rejection, my first proper hiding and so on. I knew the pattern was set to continue and accelerate. I could not wait. But that heady excitement was mixed with melancholy and apprehension, as I knew my wonderful happy and fun childhood had ended. Nothing was ever going to be the same.

EPILOGUE

Writing about my early childhood has been a joy, and it has reminded me of what a happy time I had. I was born at a fortunate juncture in history. Despite the cataclysmic predictions, there was no nuclear war, no dodging atomic bombs and no sheltering from acid rain. National Service had been abolished, so I was spared that too. Our family did not suffer the tragedy of very premature deaths, major ailments and disablement in the window of my young childhood. We lived in a time of increasing wealth. Our circumstances, in line with those of most of the country, improved year on year, and we were very lucky to reside at the more prosperous end of the country.

I *am* biased and may well be looking back with the biggest pair of Deirdre Barlow rose-tinted spectacles ever seen, but I believe society then was generally a lot happier and more at ease with itself than today. Furthermore, despite hindsight condemning the attitudes and beliefs prevalent in the 1960s and 1970s as dinosaurish and founded on a bedrock of prejudice and ignorance, I fervently believe that people generally were *more* tolerant and kinder to one another than today.

The 1970s, particularly, has been singled out as a debauched, seedy, superficial and politically incorrect decade by historical revisionists who weren't even there. Many people, products and personalities of the period have been judged by the alleged standards of today and duly condemned. A few genuine wrong 'uns have given licence to allow cultural snobs to malign them all – 'The past is a foreign country: they do things differently there' and all that – but these people have gone as far as trying to set up an extradition treaty with that decade. When I think of the 1970s I am joined in my mind by a delightful little man with corkscrew hair and glitter under his eyes, another with mutton-chop sideboards, a bawdy rasping voice bearing Christmas wishes, and behind them a slim, cosmic man in a latex suit with orange hair. I am filled with good vibes. Others, sadly, see only a middle-aged man with dyed-blond hair dressed in a mankini bouncing in on a space hopper, grotesquely clenching a large cigar between his manky teeth.

My early childhood spanned the entire 1960s and half of the 1970s although I had a fleeting glimpse of the 1950s. How blessed was I to share a planet with the Beatles, the Stones, the Kinks, Small Faces, Elvis Presley, Slade, David Bowie, George Best, Peter Osgood, Bobby Moore, Pele, Eusebio, mods, rockers, skinheads, Wimpy Bars, button-down collars, I'm Backing Britain, mini-skirts, beehive hairdos, rag-and-bone men, *The Man From Uncle*, Sooty and Sweep, *Batman, Carry Ons, Sunday Night At The London Palladium*, Lester Piggott, Eric Morecambe and Ernie Wise, *Budgie*, Carnaby Street, King's Road, Chopper bikes, Chopper Harris, Alan Hudson, Kathleen Harrison, *Jaws, Butch Cassidy And The Sundance Kid, The Godfather, Confessions Of A Window Cleaner* and so much more. How many musicians, footballers, actors, films and TV programmes of today will be remembered for so long, so fondly by so many? A century's worth of talent and charisma were packed into those two glorious decades.

I am sad to actually finish the book. I strained every cerebral sinew of my memory to recall events, people and places and was joyfully surprised at what came back. It was the little forgotten memories that were most rewarding. For example, the feeling of being 'tucked in' returned to this man in his sixties. The utter sense of love and security as a parent leaned over and cocooned the fresh sheets and blanket tight around me – like returning to the womb – for the night. Oh, what I would give now for my dear mum or dad to tuck me in one last time.

POSTSCRIPT

In 2014 I stumbled upon Bobby on social media. I had not seen or heard of him in forty-plus years, not since he was banished to approved school. We arranged to meet in the Windsor Castle in Battersea where he was now living. Tony and I had got there early, mildly apprehensive at seeing our old but relatively short-time friend after so long. Bobby walked in the door with his lop-sided grin intact and promptly emptied an array of penny sweets on the table – Black Jacks, Fruit Salads, shrimps and aniseed balls – 'Get stuck in, boys.'

The years melted away, and he told us his story. As I feared, it consisted of hard times and plenty of bird. He drank moderately, unlike us. It was lovely to meet up, and we all enjoyed it, but Bobby didn't remember nearly as much as we did. The truth was he'd made a much bigger impact on us than we had on him.

Nearly fifty years after the experience with a nasty man in the Gibraltar Recreation Ground an email dropped into my company inbox:

> I am trying to contact Martin Knight. Are you still diddy? I was wondering if you remember the unpleasant incident in Gibraltar Rec many years ago?

I was flabbergasted to hear from Denise, and those buried childhood emotions of unrequited love and the 'unpleasant incident' came flooding back. The Jimmy Savile revelations had triggered a febrile period of suppressed and unwelcome memories for many, including Denise.

We had lunch in a restaurant overlooking the grandstand on Epsom Downs. Considering that we had not had contact for forty-five years and had never formed an adult relationship we were pleasantly at ease with one another. She asked me to recount my memory of what happened. I relayed my memories. Her recall differed. She said that she thought I ran all the way home to tell my dad and left her at the mercy of the man. That felt like a smack in the face. I really don't think that was the case, as I have strong specific recollections of walking down the hill and her instructing me not to tell anyone. But who knows? Memory is pliable. What you thought happened and what you would have liked to have happened can merge and meld. She was considering going to the police and trying to find the file on the case. She said she'd had little support from her family at the time and that her mother almost acted as if she had invited the assault and the incident was never spoken about. She hinted that she was prevented from ever seeing me again. It was wonderful to reunite and hear about her life. Life has a habit of tying up the loose ends as it hurtles faster and faster towards the finish line.

The boy that pinched my bike and threatened my dad went on to become a murderer. Before that he burned down the squat Tony and I were living in on Lavender Hill in 1977. Thankfully, we didn't own much and were not in at the time.

Before my dad got the Alzheimer's and long before my mum suffered her debilitating stroke we were able to effect a reunion with our long-lost sister Fiona that was very satisfying. I wrote a letter to the Jamaican *Weekly Gleaner* for publication asking if anyone knew what happened to her and gave some details that we knew. Amazingly, I was contacted by the very lady who had chaperoned Fiona on to that big ship that sailed from Southampton all those years ago. Fiona was back in London, having left Tobago as soon as she was able. She was settled, had a career and a property and had grown into a mature, elegant, beautiful woman. She came down to the estate to visit. Her memories were vague, but as she climbed the stairs and looked out of the landing window she pointed over at the house over the road and said, 'That's where the ice cream man used to pull up. He was a nice man. He gave us broken wafers.'

*

POSTSCRIPT

One day my youngest daughter came home after being babysat at my mum and dad's. Something was troubling her. 'Daddy, somebody in the family has died.'

'What do you mean somebody in the family has died?'

'A man came around to Nanny and Granddad's last night, and he was very upset that somebody had died.'

I rang my mum's mobile and asked what all this was about. 'Stay there. I'm coming around now.'

That seemed ominous.

What then unravelled was the incredible (to us) story that my dad had been married before, and in the 1940s had had a son. Dad's ex-wife had just died, and it was that son who had gone to my parents' house to deliver the news. He was by this time almost sixty, and we knew nothing of him! He was the youth who used to help Frank West deliver the groceries and who stood and talked to me as I sat on my wall casing the estate for Red Indians in my full cowboy regalia. How terribly sad.

My dad by this time was well into the Alzheimer's that would rob him of his mind and, a little later, his life, so Mum had to answer the questions. Why on earth were we never told? Why was our brother not welcomed into the family? What happened between my dad and his first wife?

The marriage, it seems, was a casualty of the separation and dislocation that happened during the Second World War, and although the relationship soldiered on after Dad came home in 1946 it was damaged and faltering. Mum said that divorce carried a terrible stigma in the 1950s, and it was decided not to tell us children. How about when we reached our thirties, I asked? There were and are a lot of unanswered questions, not least of all why did Mum and Dad foster children yet reject the birth child of one of them, even into adulthood? I cannot imagine the impact the rejection and upheaval of his father leaving his life had on my brother, but, for me, I know that the realisation that my family wasn't really what I thought was a big and unexpected shock, even in my middle life. Nothing is as it seems, it seems.

The story with little brother Viv is arguably as sad. As Viv grew up he found attitudes towards him changed. As a cherubic little black boy he was

219

accepted and cherished by his peers and the people around him, even if he was sometimes a novelty, but as a youth and an adult he noticed that many people's attitudes hardened, and some people were rude and nasty to him. It was as if he had outstayed his welcome. As a gentle, warm, and sensitive person he found this hard. He was routinely called a wog, a coon, a nigger and a jungle bunny. Viv was forced to toughen up fast. Not only, I now know, was he coping with hurtful everyday racism he was also struggling with his sexuality.

He trained as a chef and moved out of home to south London where he embraced his Jamaican heritage and appeared to find his feet and grow in confidence. I can remember him turning up at the house with his hair in Afro style topped with a multi-coloured woollen hat.

'What's that tea cosy on your head?' I asked. Not very funny, but he took it all in good part.

Sadly, he fell out with Mum and Dad over some money he borrowed and did not repay, and a family tiff slipped into a chasm. A month went by and then a year and then a decade. We lost all contact from the mid-1980s onwards. My guess is that not only did Viv want to immerse himself in his own culture, but he wanted to come out, fully or partly, as gay, and the debt row was merely an excuse to secure space in which to find himself. He thought, rightly, that some of his Epsom circle might have found his coming out a difficult development to cope with. At school there were no outwardly gay children. Their lives would have been made a misery. At the time the rift with Viv happened I had barely knowingly met a gay person, let alone associated with one and I was typical.

Homophobic is the widely used term nowadays to describe people like me in the 1960s, 1970s and 1980s. But homophobia is a term that does not do justice to the condition. I did not have an irrational fear of homosexuality. I had a *rational dislike* of homosexuality and believed it was wrong. That's very different from an *irrational fear*. And those views were majority held. I believed it was wrong because for centuries my government and the establishment decreed it so. That's where the 'rational' comes in. Homosexual relations between consenting men over the age of twenty-one were only grudgingly permitted by law in 1967. The establishment's legal position on homosexuality was reinforced by the media. Way after 1967 on the television, homosexuals were painted as figures of fun by the likes of

Dick Emery and John Inman and in the newspapers were the subject of regular 'exposure' stings. The prevailing attitude remained that being homosexual was sordid and/or something to poke fun at.

In the 1990s a close friend of mine revealed to me he was gay and dying of AIDS. My attitudes, along with much of the world, were already shifting. Like millions I'd seen Tom Hanks in *Philadelphia*. My friend's bravery in telling me accelerated that shift in me dramatically. He laughed when he told me that he confided in another close friend's mother who had been like a mum to him in early life. 'Oh dear,' she said. 'When were you diagnosed?'

When the Friends Reunited database came out in the 1990s Viv eventually broke cover.

'My name is Viv. I went to this school and later worked at Bentalls in Kingston. Does anyone remember me?' he posted.

I couldn't resist. 'Hi Viv. My name is Martin. Yes, I remember you. I'm your brother.'

Viv did not reply. His offence was still running deep. Or so I thought.

In 2018 we received a message from Viv's lovely niece. She brought us the tragic news that my dear little brother was dying of lung cancer and his time left on earth was being measured in weeks. He would love to see us if we would like to see him. She put us in touch with Viv's husband.

The family, including Mum in a wheelchair, travelled down to a hospice near Brighton. There he was. Lovely Viv, looking frail but strong, sat straight-backed in a chair, and as we walked in the nerves we were all feeling dissipated as he broke into his infectious smile that crumbled all the years away and melted our hearts.

'I'm sorry,' he said. 'I'm so, so sorry.'

'No, we're sorry,' somebody said as we fell into a family scrum of flailing arms, kisses, cuddles and tears. We had not seen each other since 1984, and I probably hadn't held and kissed my little brother Viv since 1972. I recognised his smell even after thirty-four years. We talked and chatted and reminisced. I decided not to raise the Friends Reunited incident. It was lovely, and we did it all again once more before Viv finally died a couple of weeks later.

A month or so following Viv's brilliant funeral I sat at home cleaning up my computer, as I had been alerted that disk space was running out. I started to delete emails, and as I was cleaning off a junk folder I found two unopened emails from Viv. They were still emboldened in black as I had not seen them. They were in response to my chases on Friends Reunited. The first one said: 'Love to meet up and hear all the news. I am living in Streatham now and there is a nice pub at the bottom of the road we could meet in.' And then a few days later: 'Did you get my email, Martin? I can't wait to hear all the news.'

He must have thought I had blanked *him*. The revelation was like a knife twisting in my guts. Viv *had* tried to heal the rift and thought I had changed *my* mind. We could have enjoyed some precious years together following a family reconciliation. It upsets me now. Thank God he made that last dying attempt to reach out. Two things I have learned: do not let family or friend fall-outs drift *and* check your junk-mail folders.

Recently my sister Liz, who bravely and selflessly cares for my mum, was going through her things and organising them when she came across a diary Mum kept briefly. Mum reread it and gave permission for me to read it. In it she apologises for fostering black children in a white family. She says she believes now it was wrong and experimental and to force our culture on to them was damaging to their lives. She concluded, 'I believed all they needed was love, but I was wrong.'

Mum, it was not wrong! You did what you thought was right, and I believe it was right. They were tiny, defenceless children in the care system with low-to-nil chances of being placed in a stable, long-term foster home. With what we know now about what was going on in children's homes in and around London, who knows what sort of lives they would have endured?

Also, as we bore witness in the 1960s, the mixing of the races was practically non-existent. You and Dad blazed the trail for genuine integration. Action, not words! Your selfless 'experiment' in racial harmony was an example to others. You didn't make a big deal out of it, just got on with it. How it should be. You got the ball rolling. Well done, Mum and Dad.

My dear friend Tony left school and promptly embarked on the adventure of growing up in a mad, reckless way. It was like letting a bird out of a cage. Girls loved him and he loved them too. I could not keep up with the catalogue of very pretty females that attached themselves to him. He was one of those enviable blokes who never chased, and the more he didn't chase the more they came. Bastard. At fifteen he got a Yamaha FS1-E moped, a 'Fizzy' as we called them, and his world opened out further. But very quickly two wheels were not enough for Tony, and he took to driving cars, but, problematically, most of them did not belong to him.

We lived together in the flat in Battersea that suffered the arson attack in the Elvis-dying, Queen's-Jubilee summer of 1977. Tony was very happy here, donning an apron and vacuuming around my feet. He decided our domestic bliss could only be complete if we had a dog. I cautioned against it and said it would be his responsibility, but Tony was already out of the door walking down to Battersea Dogs' Home. He returned with a grateful, affectionate mongrel called Rindy.

Like everything else with Tony, the novelty of Rindy wore off within a week, and he was finding carting a devoted dog around with him a chore. He eventually decided to get rid of her by taking her into Epsom police station and pretending he had found her wandering aimlessly. They reluctantly took the dog from him and placed her in a pen at the back of the station.

Back in the Blenheim, with each pint Tony became more and more morose and was filling up with guilt. He was imagining Rindy pining for him, wondering what had happened. That night he decided to break into the police pound and rescue Rindy. Par for the course, he was caught in the act. By this time the Epsom police officers knew Tony well, and one commented, 'I'd fully expect to catch you breaking out the station, Tony, but not breaking *in*.'

In middle age Tony met and married a delightful younger lady, and they had a beautiful baby girl together. Tony had been waiting for a girl, having had three boys from a previous relationship. It was great to see him so happy and content.

Sadly, six years ago Tony's previous life in the fast lane caught up with him, and his body started to pack up. I was fortunate to be able to spend time with him in his last days in hospital. His illness caused him to have periods of restlessness where he would become physically distressed and attempt to climb out of the bed. With his brother Martin, we tried to restrain him gently one time, but Tony was still strong. I fiddled hurriedly with my phone and pressed play. The first chorus of 'Daydream Believer' floated across the hospital room: 'Cheer up, sleepy Jean.' Tony slumped back into his pillows, visibly relaxed, and that big, lovely smile spread across his face.

Uncle Terry died in 2017. He made it to ninety-two. His sister Betty, who he lived with, had died a few years earlier. That was a massive blow to him. However, he truly enjoyed his final years and formed a strong bond with all my family (and Tony). We went out for a drink most Sunday lunchtimes. Wonderful chats. He had a great old London dignity. He always said that when he stopped enjoying life and/or he couldn't get up the stairs to his council flat on the Winstanley estate in Battersea he'd bow out. He also had a letter from the council informing him that the estate was to be redeveloped. The coming upheaval was too much for him. So he made the decision to bow out. He stopped eating and died. It's a family thing: my Battersea gran did the same when she hit her century thirty years earlier.

I wrote this book for my grandchildren in the hope that one day they become interested in what went before. How we lived. How we loved. How we thought. So far four little boys have arrived – Harry, Alfie, Reggie and Henry – and a baby girl, Nyla Blue, and there will be several more, and it's for them too. There will probably be a Minnie, a Terry and a Tony. It makes me warm inside to think there are bits of my mum and dad and their mums and dads and many of the people in this book in them. Hearing and watching them play I wish them a good life and hope they have as much fun as I did. I am sure they will. One day, eighty or more years from now, they too will be sitting watching their grandchildren thinking the same thoughts. Life is like that roundabout at the park. We climb aboard for a few heady rides and then, dizzy with life, jump off. Then somebody else alights, and later they step off too. But the roundabout keeps spinning.

Mum died, aged ninety, on 22 November 2021.